Digital Imaging in Popular Cinema

T0386761

To my parents, the great encouragers

Digital Imaging in Popular Cinema

Lisa Purse

EDINBURGH
University Press

© Lisa Purse, 2013

Edinburgh University Press Ltd
22 George Square, Edinburgh EH8 9LF

www.euppublishing.com

Typeset in 11/13 Ehrhardt
by Servis Filmsetting Ltd, Stockport, Cheshire, and
printed and bound in Great Britain by
CPI Group (UK) Ltd, Croydon CR0 4YY

A CIP record for this book is available from the British Library

ISBN 978 0 7486 4690 6 (hardback)
ISBN 978 0 7486 4689 0 (paperback)
ISBN 978 0 7486 4691 3 (webready PDF)
ISBN 978 0 7486 7562 3 (epub)
ISBN 978 0 7486 7561 6 (Amazon ebook)

The right of Lisa Purse
to be identified as author of this work
has been asserted in accordance with
the Copyright, Designs and Patents Act 1988.

Contents

Illustrations

Acknowledgements

I would like to thank the colleagues and friends who generously gave their time to read chapter drafts and offer valuable suggestions and insights, including John Gibbs, Doug Pye, Jonathan Bignell, Iris Luppa, Ian Banks, and Tamzin Morphy. Thanks also to those who shared both direct and tangential insights as the project progressed, including Alison Butler, Tom Brown, Faye Woods and Lucy Fife Donaldson. I thank Vicki Donald and the readers who reviewed the proposal for seeing the potential in the project, and for their astute and very useful comments at the outset. I also thank Gillian Leslie and the rest of the editorial team at Edinburgh University Press for their assistance and expertise in bringing the book to completion. The development and completion of the study was supported by research leave awarded under the University of Reading's Research Endowment Trust Fund, and benefited greatly from the support of colleagues both within and beyond the Department of Film, Theatre & Television, to whom I am very grateful. The Sewing Circle, the close reading group based at the department, has over the years consistently provided a welcoming but keenly stimulating forum in which to develop one's ideas, and my thanks extend to current and previous members of the Circle. I am also grateful to staff and graduate students at the University of Warwick to whom I presented initial thoughts on *King Kong*, and to the delegates of the 2008 *Continuity and Innovation* conference and the 2008 *Point of Feminism* conference at the University of Reading for their responses to my work on *300*. More generally I would like to thank my students, who over the years have been both a pleasure to teach and an inspiration in my own encounters with popular cinema.

A number of particular pleasures brightened the writing process, including the generous friendship of Iris Luppa, a series of extremely satisfying cinephiliac conversations with Ian Banks, the discovery of new ways of getting away from the computer, and the arrival of the excellent Isla. I am grateful to my family for their ongoing unconditional support, encouragement and good humour, and to Hendrix and Rafiki for being the Joan Collins and Linda Evans of the cat world. Finally, and with love, I thank Tamzin for her patience and her splendid life-enhancing powers.

Introduction

CINEMA IN THE ERA OF DIGITAL IMAGING

In the early part of Paul Greengrass's 2007 film *United 93*, a moment-by-moment dramatisation of one of the plane hijackings on 11 September 2001, the passengers settle themselves into their seats and wait for their plane to take off while the cabin staff close lockers and check that seat belts are fastened. In brief, mobile takes, a hand-held camera picks out different passengers in close-up, working with the available light in the cabin (occasioning the odd lens flare and over-exposed image) on what is a sunny day. The shots feel intimate, observing the passengers' private moments as well as their public interactions, in shifting compositions that partially 'hide' the camera's gaze behind various seatbacks. A woman stretches and sighs, two men absorb themselves in their reading in different parts of the plane, another puts on his headphones and shifts in his seat. There are several such sequences in this pre-airborne phase of the flight, and their aesthetic characteristics recall the contingent framings and lighting of observational cinema, an important reference point in a film clearly invested in positioning itself as an attempt to in some way 'authentically' document the events of that day.[1] They also produce an impression of ordinariness that frames the familiar banalities of waiting for take-off. Here the passengers' evident disinterest in the cabin safety procedures generates pathos precisely because these ordinary, everyday moments are juxtaposed with our extra-textual knowledge of the extraordinary and tragic events of 9/11, and specifically that none of the passengers played by these actors survived the hijacking of United Airlines Flight 93.

In this interior sequence, as elsewhere in the film, the exterior views through windows are achieved using green screens and subsequent digital matte painting and compositing, to simulate the environs and prevailing weather conditions at Newark Airport on 11 September 2001. This enabled the production to circumvent the Newark authorities' refusal to permit filming at the airport, and also allowed shooting to take place in the controlled conditions of a reconstructed Boeing 757 fuselage that could be mounted on motion gimbals to replicate the plane's final erratic movements.[2] Here, then, the digital visual effects function as a solution to a number of practical challenges in order to help maintain the sense of cameras capturing events 'as they happen' in a naturalistic, realistic-looking environment. That is, digital imaging interventions allow the sequence to produce the illusion of photographic indexicality, the idea that the scene we are witnessing has to have happened in the real world in front of the camera because it has been imprinted by the action of light onto a strip of celluloid.

That this relatively low budget film includes digital visual effects at all is an indicator of the increasing affordability and resulting prevalence of digital imaging solutions to filmmaking challenges in mainstream film production.[3] Of this prevalence Stephen Prince has wryly commented, 'film is no longer a necessary condition for cinema' (2004: 30), his apparently paradoxical declaration accurately speaking of a contemporary cinema that no longer requires celluloid to produce or display its feature films. Against the backdrop of the wider proliferation of digital technologies, media and communication networks, digital or digitised practices have found their way into almost every aspect of filmmaking, including sequence pre-visualisation, blue and green screen shooting, face and body motion capture, compositing of image elements and digital rotoscoping, non-linear editing and sound mixing. Digital video formats are now a real alternative to celluloid film stock for capturing live action, subject to the aesthetic requirements and budgetary constraints under which the director and cinematographer are working. The majority of current mainstream US cinema releases go through a 'digital intermediate' process, whereby the film is converted to a digital format to enable an electronic version of traditional processes such as editing and colour timing, and to make possible a huge range of post-production alterations, including painting out unwanted image elements (such as surface reflections or safety wires) and adding new ones. The finished movie is then printed back onto celluloid to create a negative that can be used for striking distribution prints. The electronic distribution and projection of feature films in digital format is on its way to becoming standard practice, removing the need for the digital intermediate to be transferred 'back' to celluloid (Bordwell 2011).

As in other areas of human endeavour, in cinema digital technologies not only replace earlier technologies, they also replace the rituals and processes that clustered around those earlier technologies. Thus, the recent history of digital 'progress' is often experienced as a history of loss. The most materially felt loss in cinema is celluloid, its 'ever rapid slide into obsolescence' (Krauss 2011: 86) marked in various ways: by the comprehensive substitution of 35 mm projectors for digital projectors in movie theatres across the world in the last decade; by the recent reduction of 16mm and 35 mm print services by Deluxe and Technicolor, the bankruptcy of Kodak Eastman and the withdrawal of rental services for celluloid-format camera equipment by long established equipment houses (Giardina 2011; Caranicas 2011); by artists' and cinephiles' public eulogies for a passing medium and the loss of the expertise that goes with it, such as Tacita Dean's *Film* installation at the Tate Modern in London (Unilever series, 2011–12) and connected essays (Dean 2011a and 2011b; Spielberg et al. 2011). In celluloid's place is a digital medium that facilitates the manipulation of every pixel that makes up its moving image, and every aspect of its spatialised soundtrack, a level of control frequently championed by film directors like George Lucas and James Cameron, and by studios wishing to promote their products as the latest iteration of state of the art digital visual effects sequences or digital delivery formats. The 'rhetoric of the new' is persistent in these contexts, evident not least in the ubiquitous deployment of the descriptive term 'game-changer' in relation to this or that advance in digital cinema technology. It is tempting to conclude that cinema is being irrevocably transformed by the advent of the digital, but we should be as wary of what Anne Friedberg calls the 'the agonistic claims of a technologically determined digital break' (2006: 3) as of Lucas and Cameron's evangelism. As John Belton noted relatively early in the transition to digital, the 'potential for a totally digital cinema – digital production, post-production, distribution, and exhibition – caught the attention and imagination of the media', but changed very little of the majority audience's moviegoing experience (Belton 2002: 103). In the light of these observations, we need to develop a rather more nuanced, and perhaps less sensationalist, set of conclusions about the manner and impact of the incorporation of digital imaging into mainstream narrative film. The remainder of this introduction will explore the extent to which the advent of digital imaging represents less a radical break than a continuation of many characteristics of celluloid cinema, while also pointing up the necessity of an awareness of digital imaging's specificity in the act of film analysis.

DIGITAL IMAGING, CELLULOID NOSTALGIA AND INDEXICALITY

The prospect of end-to-end digital film production has prompted a nostalgic return to cinema's celluloid history, most explicitly through homage. Digital imaging technologies have been used to simulate earlier pre-digital cinema technologies and practices in various homages, for example to 1930s and 1940s cinematography, lighting and colour design in films such as *The Aviator* (Martin Scorsese, 2004), *Sky Captain and the World of Tomorrow* (Kerry

Conran, 2004), *King Kong* (Peter Jackson, 2005), *Sin City* (Frank Miller and Robert Rodriguez, 2005), and *The Good German* (Steven Soderbergh, 2006), or to the era of early cinema in *The Artist* (Michel Hazanavicius, 2011) and *Hugo* (Martin Scorsese, 2011). Nostalgic consumption has also grown, facilitated not just by the digital availability of celluloid films on DVD, Blu-ray, iTunes and video on demand, but by platforms like YouTube and Vimeo which curate a vast, proliferating database of rediscovered and favourite moments from cinema's past. Nick Rombes has suggested that this nostalgia for the celluloid format and its imperfections is a response to the cultural conception of the digital image as pristine and seamless (2009: 2), but he draws on Raymond Williams to eloquently frame it as a nostalgia for celluloid as a cultural experience:

> In the digital age, there is nostalgia for what Raymond Williams termed 'residual culture', which he defined as 'experiences, meanings and values . . . [which are] lived and practiced on the basis of the residue – cultural as well as social – of some previous social formation' (2001: 170). In cinema, this involves not only movies whose content hearkens back to the 1970s (such as *American Gangster*), but movies whose very texture is nostalgic for the golden era of analogue warmth and super saturated colours. *Planet Terror* and *Death Proof* reflect upon the physical *experience* of going to movies and the humanising elements of the 'mistakes' that characterised that experience. (2009: 9)

As Belton's point quoted earlier reveals, not much has *literally* changed in the moviegoing experience, but despite this a notion of a *previous* moviegoing history that the digital 'replaces' holds sway (the grindhouse experience celebrated by *Planet Terror* (Robert Rodriguez, 2007) and *Death Proof* (Quentin Tarantino, 2007) in fact disappeared for a number of reasons, none of which are related to the arrival of the digital era). In this way we can see that many of the ideas that circulate around digital filmmaking are culturally produced, a point relevant to the task of analysis precisely because cultural ideas can influence meaning at the level of the text, a point we will return to a number of times in this study.

We need to frame digital imaging's simulation of photochemical photography in broader terms than simply nostalgia, however. Many established processes of photochemical compositing such as optical static and travelling mattes, back projection, and rotoscoping now have digital equivalents, and digital imaging is also put to use simulating 'those very photochemical idiosyncrasies which gave the photographic image its claim to verity' (North 2008: 22). But in both cases, the aim remains to create the illusion that events are unfolding in a spatiotemporally continuous environment. Digital imaging technologies become another tool in narrative cinema's longstanding illusionist project, joining continuity editing, set facades, trick photography and physical special effects (among others) in the creation of fictional spaces and events. For example, the digital matte paintings of exterior views out of the cabin windows in *United 93* are not obviously digital in appearance, and skilful digital compositing means that they do not interrupt the impression the film has been working to create, that the cabin environment and its location on an airport runway (and later airborne) is real. Real, that is, in terms of 'what is *accepted* as real' (Buscombe 1985: 88) within the parameters of the film's fiction: we understand that this is not, cannot be, the actual United Airlines Flight 93, but accept it as a fictional representation of the plane's environs and its passengers. The practical realities and connotative import of a film moment such as this locates this type of digital imaging practice in a tradition of illusionism that characterises much of narrative cinema's celluloid history. The strategies used in these sequences from *United 93* might remind us, for example, of the creation of virtual set extensions to increase the verisimilitude (the appearance of being real) of some of the interior scenes in *The Great Train Robbery* (Edwin S. Porter, 1903). In the first shot of this film, an interior scene in a railroad office is 'authenticated' by the view out of the office window of a train arriving. The shot was achieved by masking off different areas of the frame using mattes, and filming the action on the set in one exposure and the view out of the window in another. The type of use of digital imaging we see in the example from *United 93* might be a 'considered impersonation of indexicality' (North 2008: 22), but it is the *same* impersonation of indexicality that photochemically-based cinema also performed in its composited, optical or practical effects-based sequences.

This throws into a different light the commonplace assertion that digital imaging has ruptured the indexical connection to the real-world, profilmic referent, the object in front of the camera inscribed by light and lens onto celluloid, that André Bazin, Roland Barthes, and Siegfried Kracauer, in their different ways, felt was the foundational characteristic of cinema as an art form.[4] As the *United 93* example implies, the indexical connection between what we see on the screen and what was placed in front of the camera has been problematised since the dawn of cinema by practical effects, trick photography, and mainstream cinema's various other tools of illusion. Hollywood has always sought not to reproduce reality itself, but to present its fictionalised representation, to create the illusion – temporary of course – that what we are watching 'really happened'. Thus to characterise the advent of digital imaging in cinema as a break – a move *from* indexicality *to* the digital – is too simplistic. If the opposition between the digital and the indexical disavows the frequently hybrid nature of indexicality in the celluloid era, it simultaneously disavows the *equally* hybrid nature of cinema in an era of digital imaging. As the case studies in this book attest, most films in the digital era are inherently hybrid, combining computer generated or digitally composited elements with profilmic material – that is, a figure, object or scene that actually was in front of a camera in the real world; indeed the presence of digital imaging 'does not absolutely rule out a profilmic origin' (Rosen 2001: 309). The much-touted digital versus indexical binary thus seems less a technically robust distinction than a polemical one founded on the idealisation of its two opposing terms (302). In the rush to provide the grand narrative of cinema's digital 'turn', a binary is invoked which points outwards to cultural ideas about digitality and pre-digitality, rather than inwards to the detail of the films themselves.

What is clear from the films being made in the digital era is that digital effects and compositing most often work to generate verisimilitude in strictly photographic terms, a 'performance of "photographicness"' (North 2008: 12) which scholars in this field refer to as 'photorealism'. Photorealism invokes the idea of photochemical photography as 'document', which is based on its indexical connection to the object or event photographed. But as we have already begun to discover, photorealism in its performance of indexicality also bears traces of narrative cinema's traditional attempts to simulate photochemical photography's 'reality effect': to create, through a range of filmmaking strategies (including continuity editing), the impression that life is playing out before our eyes, rather than a complex fiction. What is notable is the extent to which the photorealist principle is adhered to even in the depiction of the most fantastical subject matter, and even within sequences which function as explicit 'showcases' for – and thus explicit acknowledgments of – computer-generated imagery (CGI).

The 2007 summer blockbuster *Transformers*, directed by Michael Bay, uses digital imaging heavily in its action sequences and in its set-piece shots of motor vehicles transforming into fully computer generated robots. In a key scene, human protagonists Sam (Shia LaBeouf) and Mikaela (Megan Fox) meet the Autobots and their leader Optimus Prime (voiced by Peter Cullen) for the first time. It is night, and the large lorry cab that is Optimus's disguised form approaches Sam and Mikaela in a rain-strewn alleyway. In a close-up framed by the humans, the lorry's engine grille moves into the foreground. This low angle shot shows the beginning of the cab's transformation into the giant robot, tilting upwards as the cab starts to ratchet, whir and rearrange its mass of mechanical components into the rising figure of the robot. The shot is notable (and optically uncomfortable) because of the brilliant glare from the cab's headlights, which bleaches the entire lower half of the frame for several moments. As the sequence continues, alternating tilting low angle shots with rising, high angle crane shots, we notice that the vehicular robots gathering around Optimus display, like their surroundings, a plethora of reflective surfaces; rain-slick asphalt becomes a stage for the steely sheen of transformed automobile body parts, while the robots' headlights produce a significant amount of lens flare in a number of the shots.

The sequence is an exhibitionist display of digital imaging, the intricate structural rearrangements that characterise the Autobots' transformations from vehicles into giant bipeds presented at a speed and a level of complexity that is testament to digital imaging's generative capacity. But despite *Transformers* occupying a fantasy mode that does not have to depend on maintaining verisimilitude, and thus which offers a potential space for alternatives to a photorealist aesthetic, the sequence displays a persistent photorealism. It works hard to anchor the computer generated Autobots perceptually 'in front' of the camera and in relation to other elements of the *mise-en-scène*: their bodywork 'reflects' diegetic light sources convincingly, achieved by digitally painting reflections onto their computer generated surfaces, and digital effects carefully simulate the in-camera effects that would have been produced by the robots' headlights if they had existed in the real world, such as lens flare and lens distortion. These strategies create the impression that the digital elements of the frame are profilmic events occurring in the space in front of the camera. As in a variety of other digitally assisted mainstream films, complex software and computer generated imaging processes are employed to simulate the effects of light on celluloid as mediated by a mechanical moving image camera (film stock, grain, flare, overexposure, focus, superfluous lens artifacts, motion blur, and so on), as well as the kinds of responses a mechanical camera might give to profilmic phenomena (including accidental loss of focus and unintentional movements), regardless of whether a digital video camera, a mechanical celluloid camera or what we might call a 'virtual camera' has been used.[5] 'Photorealism' is thus here not simply the quality of appearing to be a seamless photographic image: to guarantee (as far as possible) the verisimilitude of sequences that include digital elements, those elements also need to be convincingly located in the three-dimensional spatial coordinates of the film world.

Despite the hybrid indexicality of celluloid cinema and the equally hybrid indexicality of digital cinema, then, where digital imaging is present a common impulse is to produce a convincing photorealism that is characterised by the simulation of what we would see onscreen if a real, mechanical camera was photographing an actual profilmic event (Spielmann 1999a: 135), including the compositional tendencies familiar to us from mainstream cinema in the period of its photochemical production (Rosen 2001: 309). If celluloid *is* 'no longer a necessary condition for cinema', as Prince claims, then the illusion of indexicality and the performance of photographicness clearly remain necessary. This is a necessity not dictated by the nature of digital imaging technologies themselves, but by filmmakers, and as I have already begun to suggest, by the ways in which digitality and what it replaces have been conceptualised in the wider culture. If these observations demonstrate clear ways in which the advent of digital imaging should not be seen as a rupturing of mainstream cinema's basic forms, the most emphatic proof is the persistence of narrative:

> As 'film' disappears in the successive substitutions of the digital for the analog [*sic*], what persists is *cinema* as a narrative form and a psychological experience – a certain modality of articulating visuality, signification, and desire through space, movement, and time. (Rodowick 2007: 184–5, emphasis in original)

Despite the proliferation of delivery platforms, despite the power of digital imaging to alter any pixel of the frame, despite the encroachment of digital image capture in a traditionally celluloid-based medium, a profoundly familiar mode of narrative cinema persists.

READING THE DIGITAL

This is not an argument, however, to disregard the specificity of the digital order of images completely. In the process of analysis and interpretation the digital demands attention in the way it mimics earlier cinematic technologies, because of its malleable and generative nature, and because of the ideas about the digital and the pre-digital it evokes. Digital technologies are defined by their basis in machine-readable binary codes, which can then be manipulated in various ways. Analogue information is converted to a numerical format, and by the same principle such codes can also simulate analogue information. The specificity of digital imaging can be defined as this basis in binary code and its resulting flexibility, but describing the onscreen results of these characteristics is more complicated. Digital imaging can mimic but can also transform, shape, metamorphose, and generate fantastical or mundane objects and phenomena from scratch, while cultural ideas about digital imaging or the digital more generally can also influence meaning within a film, a scene or a shot. As a consequence, assessing the impact of the digital on aesthetics, and by extension on meaning, is a slippery business, as Elsaesser's description of digital imaging technologies eloquently implies:

> [D]igitization is not altogether a neutral tool . . . it could be argued that digitization has replaced the camera by the pen. Yet instead of handling like a pen, it works like a brush, but instead of using paint, the digital signal is more like electronic putty. (2000: 191)

In *Transformers* the digital images intersect with the staging to attempt to convey the commanding presence of the towering robots, their forms silhouetted by lamplight and marked out by their reflective bodywork, in mobile shots that emphasise their stature in relation to the human protagonists. The lens flare, the audible whirring, grinding and clicking of mechanical parts, and the shuddering of the camera as each robot jumps and hits the ground affirm a sense of the robots' weighty presence within the film world. However, some smaller aspects of the scene trouble this sense: to convey mechanical transformations that are too quick to track with the naked eye, the visual effects team blur the detail of the process, but to a somewhat alienating extent; the hue of the red panels on Optimus Prime's bodywork does not unfailingly correlate with the diegetic light sources shown; and the interactions between machine parts do not always reflect real-world physics when they come into contact with each other. One might suggest that these small deviations in the photorealism of the sequence problematise our ability to be convinced by the illusion of the robots' material presence. But one could alternatively conclude from these small signals that the Autobots are constructed using a different order of images which produces the Autobots as sites of exciting possibility, the unreadability of their metamorphoses signalling the extent of their potential, the digital's ability to alter and originate offered as a metaphor for the Autobots' own powers of transformation. This reading depends on the spectator's extra-textual awareness of the digital's presence and of its generative capacities, a 'digital literacy' (Everett 2003: 9) that I will discuss further in Chapter 1.

How do we negotiate this shifting terrain of possible image interventions and understand their consequences for meaning? Visual effects artists' published accounts of their work would seem to offer a foothold from which to begin this negotiation, and they are accessible not just in the trade press but in DVD featurettes and other publicity materials. The ready availability of sound bites and edited interviews is not always as useful as it might appear, however, a point illustrated by a return to our initial example, *United 93*. Double Negative, the visual effects house coordinating the digital imaging work on *United 93*, emphasised that their aim was 'to make our visual effects contribution to the film completely invisible to the audience' (Seymour 2006: para. 11). However, such an assertion focuses on the digital achievement of naturalistic-looking photorealism to the exclusion of other artistic aims. The digital matte paintings of the airport surroundings through the cabin windows anchor the verisimilitude of the cabin, but they also display characteristics that seem to have been actively selected by the filmmakers to mobilise certain connotations and effects. The paintings are not sharply defined, detailed, direct representations of the airport, but rather are indistinct 'impressions', blocks of pale delicate colour that glow and shimmer. In the same shots, the profilmic lighting (from the studio rig) sends shafts of iridescent white 'sunlight' into the cabin, at times haloing the profiles and faces of the passengers. The combination of the digital matte paintings and the on-set lighting design produce an ethereal effect, commemorative of these now-dead passengers, but also the calm before the events that will soon envelop them. Cinematographer Barry Ackroyd also used the enhanced grading opportunities made available by the digital intermediate to modulate the lighting state in the cabin as the film progressed, in keeping with the narrative's darkening tone. '[With the digital intermediate], it's a great advantage to be able to integrate all the visual-effects shots, put shadows in where they didn't exist, and enhance and strengthen the contrast', Ackroyd explained. 'Over the next hour and half, I darken the whole scenario as the events unfold' (quoted in Pavlus, 2006: para. 16). By the time the hijacking is in its final stages, the contrast between lighter and darker areas of the frame in the cabin sequences is much more pronounced, the passengers often in the shadows as they crouch down between the seats to urgently discuss their next move against the hijackers. Digital imaging technologies here work with non-digital filmmaking technologies in the service not simply of practicality or verisimilitude (as implied by the visual effects team's comments), but of artistic expression.

This point may seem an obvious one, but it benefits from being restated, especially in the light of the ways in which digital visual effects artists themselves articulate the purpose of their work in the press. Speaking in *American Cinematographer* or one of the industry magazines on visual effects such as *Cinefex*, *VFXWorld* or *Post*, digital visual effects artists consistently focus on technological achievements and the goal of seamless photorealism, rather than the ways in which their work is part of a larger artistic effort to generate particular kinds of meaning. In our own interpretive engagement with digital elements of the film frame, it is essential not to follow this lead in allowing the technological aspects of digital imaging to take our attention away from other questions. Digital imaging technologies may solve a range of practical filmmaking challenges and simulate earlier cinematic technologies, but in the same way as those earlier technologies, they can be used expressively in the service of the filmmakers' goals, and thus are equally deserving of attention in the process of interpretation. The critical writing on earlier technological developments (like the advent of colour film stock, of sound, CinemaScope, and so on) and their aesthetic and epistemic consequences indicates that it is not simply the deployment of the tool itself which is at issue in the process of interpretation, but how it intersects with the narrative, thematic and representational structures of a film, and, importantly, how it registers with the spectator. As the observable properties, uses and outputs of the tool are themselves not fixed and stable this is a task that must be undertaken on a film-by-film basis, and with a close attention to textual detail. In this way we can begin to assess how the presence of digital imaging affects the way a moment, a scene, or a whole film is experienced; how it affects what meanings are mobilised and how they develop across a narrative; and in what ways we should take account of digital imaging when we are engaged in the task of interpreting a film.

This study has emerged from my conviction that to ignore the digital completely – to pretend it isn't 'there', or that its digital nature isn't relevant to the task of interpretation – is to ignore the reality that digital imaging is now one of the tools for artistic expression at filmmakers' disposal, and that as such it has the potential to produce meaning alongside and in concert with the other cinematic tools deployed. The chapters comprising the study ask a cluster of related questions about the relationship of digital imaging to the films in which it is used, and the relationship of digital imaging to questions of meaning and interpretation in those film texts. For example, how do we respond to digital elements of the frame, or to the knowledge that they might be present, even if we cannot definitively see them? How might the alterations, large or small, that digital imaging permits, affect our reception of a character, an action, or a narrative development? Indeed, how might contemporary cinema's desire to mimic or reference its celluloid past itself contribute to the play of theme and connotation? Such questions cannot be answered by general statements about the state of the cinematic medium in a digital era, although these kinds of accounts have their place. Instead, such questions can be answered most fully through attention to the detail of the films themselves, their narrative operations, the terms on which they choose to dramatise action, the stylistic choices evident in their audio-visual presentation. In this way the digital is considered *in situ*, as it were, assessed as a part of the whole. This is appropriate, given that meaning in any film is generated through the interaction of textual elements, as well as the influence of extra- and intra-textual factors. From another direction, then, my contention that we need to be alert to the presence of the digital within the film frame is also an argument *not* to look at digital elements in isolation from the wider film, or in an interpretive vacuum, and in Chapter 1 I begin to set out how this process of interpretation can work in practice. In all of this it is crucial to keep in mind that the deployment of digital imaging technologies on the screen is the result of a series of decisions by the filmmakers. Expressing the idea in this way helps us to think about the alternatives that were refused in constructing the image as it appears in the final film. What choices have been made about what can and cannot be shown, about what is appropriate, about what seems most effective? And what are the consequences of these choices? Such questions remind us to think about how deployments of digital imaging are 'mediated by filmmakers' (North 2008: 12), and the artistic, pragmatic but also ideological drivers that might lie behind how that mediation manifests itself.

In the chapters that follow I will move between shorter analyses of film moments and extended case studies to explore what the wide-ranging digital developments in film production and post-production mean for those of us interested in the interpretation of film. As the preceding discussion implies, what follows is not intended to provide monolithic answers to questions about the impact of digital imaging technologies on cinema. Instead the study is driven by a desire to understand the ways in which digital elements interact with other areas of decision making to produce meaning, and to point to the variety and texture of digital images' connotative powers. Focussing on digital imaging processes (that is, computer generated image elements) *in relation to* the wider aesthetic and epistemic systems of mainstream narrative cinema is a necessity that shapes the study in particular and perhaps slightly surprising ways. That is, sometimes I will speak about digital elements directly, and at other times I will not talk about the digital, in order to address the other elements with which the digital intersects.

Across the study, I ask how the presence and 'nature' of digitally generated images within film's visual, aural, spatial and temporal coordinates contribute to the production of meaning, and how this 'digital turn' has affected the epistemic and ideological dynamics of mainstream narrative cinema,[6] and I do so through a series of case studies in order to illustrate the approaches others might also take when faced with the digital's presence in other film texts. Chapter 1 will develop some of these initial ideas and questions further, illustrating how and why we must be 'alert' to the digital presence within the film frame, and locating this discussion in the context of existing debates pertinent to, or often invoked by, critical approaches to the digital in film: debates about visual spectacle and narrative, cinema and technology. Chapter 2 uses Steven Spielberg's *Minority Report* (2000) as an extended case study to illustrate the complex ways in which the inherent characteristics of digital imagery – its malleability, its illusory 'presence', its ability to manipulate other orders of image – can resonate connotatively in ways that enhance and intensify the meanings in play across a film. Drawing on a number of examples, Chapter 3 turns its attention to the construction and reception of the computer-generated body as central protagonist. Investigating the relationship between digital imaging processes, principles of photorealism and characterisation, the chapter reveals the terms under which a digital body is integrated into a film's visual and narrative structures. Chapter 4 explores the relationship of digital imaging to earlier special effects traditions, through a comparative analysis of the 1933 and 2005 versions of *King Kong*. Investigating how the 2005 film remediates moments from the 1933 original, the chapter argues for the importance of historicising the digital's manipulations of the image, and their consequences for meaning and representation. Chapter 5 returns to the issue of how digital effects stage and shape the body, considered initially in Chapter 3, but this time looking at the profilmic body. Using *300* as an extended case study, Chapter 5 interrogates the digital manipulation of the live action body and its framing by digital environments, and continues Chapter 4's scrutiny of the relationship between digital imaging and the politics of cinematic representation. The final chapter considers digital imaging from a different perspective, turning its interpretive eye on the narrative operations and visual aesthetics of an emerging digital format, Digital 3-D. Taken as a whole, the study aims to demystify the relationship between digital imaging and processes of watching and reading the growing number of films within which the digital has made its home.

NOTES

1. Performances were filmed in real-time single takes that matched the duration of the events portrayed; some characters on the ground were played by their real-life counterparts or by non-actors sharing the same profession. When interviewed, Greengrass repeatedly described the production's respectful drive to depict the events and the victims as authentically as possible. 'Collectively, we gathered together to try to make sense of this event, to try to reconstruct it, to relive it, to dramatize it... [to] recreate a believable truth that reflects the record.' In Smith 2006: 28.
2. See *United 93* production notes 2006: 10.
3. A budget of $15 million compared with the same director's *Bourne Ultimatum* (2007, $110 million), or the budget of a blockbuster digital effects vehicle like *Iron Man* (Jon Favreau, 2008, $140 million).
4. See Bazin (2005a), Barthes (2000), Kracauer (1997).
5. 'Virtual' here designates that the images have been constructed inside a computer without using an actual camera. The visual aspects listed above are designed in, even – indeed especially – where the camera is virtual. A common strategy is to simulate the effects of the physics of the fictional environment on the virtual camera – sometimes subtly, at other times more explicitly. In *I, Robot* (Alex Proyas, 2004) the virtual camera judders as it is passed by large vehicles and shakes violently during an explosion, while Thompson and Bordwell note that in *The Lord of the Rings: The Two Towers* (Peter Jackson, 2002) the virtual camera bangs into a flagpole during a CG tracking shot of thousands of Saruman's soldiers, causing the flagpole to move (Thompson and Bordwell 2007: para 32).
6. Live action cinema will be the focus of the study rather than, say, digitally produced animated films like *WALL-E* (Andrew Stanton, 2008) or *Waltz with Bashir* (Ari Folman, 2008).

CHAPTER I

Interpretation and the Digital

In this chapter we will look at some of the ways that digital images are integrated into mainstream cinema, so that we can begin to address why (and how) our interpretations should take into account the digital's presence in that cinema. In service of this aim, the chapter opens with a comparison of two brief sequences where the digital intervention impacts differently on processes of interpretation. In a sense this chapter continues the Introduction's contextualising project, by locating the book and its claims for the digital in relation to a number of pertinent contexts, including existing writing on digital imaging in film. The chapter develops a case for the narrative communicativeness of digital image elements, but not simply in their mimicry of, or interaction with, other filmic systems. I argue that the 'digital-ness' of the digital image has the potential to produce connotations of its own, not least because of the audience's growing awareness of the digital's capacities and its presence within the film frame, even where that presence is not directly visible.

David Fincher's film *Zodiac* (2007) is the account of the search to apprehend the self-titled 'Zodiac' serial killer who was at large in the San Francisco Bay area in the late 1960s and early 1970s. In the late evening, at the scene of a taxi driver's murder on a dark suburban street, investigating detectives Toschi (Mark Ruffalo) and Armstrong (Anthony Edwards) and lab technician Dagitz (Jason Wiles) try to act out the killer's strategy. The residences on either side of the road are visible in the shadows, and the street stretches out into the distance towards the Bay, streetlamps marking the route at intervals. Behind the darkly clothed men, the taxicab in which the killing took place is brightly lit by the nearest streetlamp, lending the focus of their discussion a forceful presence within the frame. This shot, the investigation sequence as a whole and the preceding murder sequence were filmed on a blue screen outdoor stage, and the street, some of the buildings and other details were subsequently painted in digitally by visual effects house Digital Domain.[1] As

in the *United 93* example I considered in the Introduction, here digital effects
are used for practical reasons; the residents of the real-world location did not
want the production to shoot there, necessitating its recreation on a stage,
while the digital matte paintings were able to generate a historically accurate
view of the street in question as it would have looked in 1969. But equally the
digital imaging in these shots also works for the aesthetic systems of the film,
its browns and yellows in keeping with *Zodiac*'s palette of yellows, greens and
browns, evocative of the historical period and inspired by the 1970s photography of William Egglestone and Stephen Shore (see Williams 2007a: para. 17).
This latter point would have been equally true had the visual effect provided
by the digital matte paintings been supplied by physical set extensions or a
location shoot instead. As a result this moment from *Zodiac* points to the significant fact that the presence of digital elements in the frame is not *necessarily*
relevant to the conclusions an interpretation will reach. However, I will argue
that there are many occasions on which the use of digital imaging in place of
an established traditional optical or physical effects process (a large proportion
of digital effects work in mainstream cinema) is directly relevant to the task of
interpretation. While we may discount the relevance of the digital's presence
in a particular instance, maintaining an alertness to the digital will allow us to
be open to, and to identify, those moments when it is relevant.

Alfonso Cuarón's *Children of Men* (2006) is a dystopic vision of 2027 in
which the world's population is infertile, and Britain has become a violent
totalitarian state. In the narrative's final stages Theo (Clive Owen) must
transport new mother Kee (Clare-Hope Ashitey) in secret through a volatile
immigrant detention camp to attempt a rendezvous with the fabled sea-based
'Human Project' where she and her baby might find sanctuary. Theo is mor-
tally wounded in a gun battle with activists who want to take the baby, but the
pair manage to escape in a small rowboat through the Bexhill drainage system
onto the open sea. They float beside a buoy awaiting collection by the Project's
ship, though Theo dies before it arrives.

Throughout, the film has presented the human race's infertility as emblematic of a world in social and political decay. Correspondingly, the hope the new
birth generates, and Theo and Kee's successful escape from those who would
use the baby as a political bargaining chip, are the optimistic notes the film
strikes at its end. In this context Theo's death registers as a heroic sacrifice
that makes possible Kee's escape. And yet this optimistic ending – and the certainty of that escape – is qualified by the final shots showing the arrival of the
ship. The sequence has already mobilised the possibility that the ship will not
come, through uncertainty around the project's existence expressed in the dialogue (echoing an uncertainty voiced in previous exchanges), and by means of
a shot of Kee desperately scanning the horizon for the ship, the camera pulling
back to leave the tiny rowboat isolated in a dense, oppressive grey fog. As Kee

Figure 1.1 Frame grab from *Children of Men* (Universal / UIP): An apparent point of view shot shows the Tomorrow Ship close by.

spots the ship's lights in the distance there is a cut to her optical point of view. The ship is barely visible in the fog, while Theo's slumped body in the bottom corner of the frame functions as a bitter comment on the timing of the ship's arrival. A reverse angle shot shows Kee's relief at being found. A low angle shot that seems to be, once again, from Kee's optical point of view inside the rowboat (we hear her close by, singing to her baby) shows the 'Tomorrow' ship up close, as if it is drawing alongside her (see Fig. 1.1). Yet this is impossible: the ship could not have moved to the rowboat's position so quickly – and sure enough the crew are pointing into the distance, presumably at Kee (although we cannot be certain of this), as if she is still some way up ahead. The next and final shot of the film is a wide shot that confirms the ship is still in the distance, beyond the buoy and the rowboat which are both visible in the foreground (see Fig. 1.2). The ship draws closer very slowly, but before it is anywhere near the rowboat the film cuts to a black screen and the end credits begin.

The strange view of the ship close by and the longer shots that frame it thus imply that the ship is both 'here' and 'not here': already at the side of the rowboat, and still at a distance, an ambiguity that refers us back to the Human Project's intangibility in the film as a whole (various characters assert but cannot prove its existence). The final digital composite shot redoubles this sense of its intangibility: the moving image plate of the distant ship is combined with the rowboat and the computer generated buoy in the foreground, while the fog is further enhanced by 2-D and 3-D digital elements.[2] As the ship moves from the background to the middle ground of the shot, it shifts slightly in relation to the assumed sea level, the wave formations and the frame

Figure 1.2 Frame grab from *Children of Men* (Universal / UIP): But a wider shot shows the ship still in the distance.

itself. The shot's staging in thick banks of fog gave the visual effects team the option to hide any compositing issues with additional digital fog elements, but instead the seamlessness that contemporary digital imaging can achieve (and audiences would be familiar with) is noticeably refused. Here the digital composite subtly resists anchoring the ship fully in the three-dimensional coordinates of the film's world, momentarily investing it with the mark of a mirage, in order to present a final image of ambiguity. The digital compositing of the ship in the final shot thus works with other aspects of the sequence to produce a cluster of competing meanings that leave the narrative open-ended. Whereas in the *Zodiac* example the digital-ness of the digital set extensions was not relevant to the analysis of the scene, in this example from *Children of Men* we need to take account of the digital nature of the image in order to acquire a fuller sense of the sequence's epistemic operations. The digital composite's construction of uncertain spatial relations between the rescue ship, the rowboat, sea and buoy suggests not a genuine happy ending but a moment of subjective wish-fulfilment, Kee's desperation to be saved with her baby – an aim that has structured the narrative but seems increasingly impossible – calling up a reassuring mirage of salvation.

Setting these examples alongside each other illustrates a central point of this study: that in our analysis of contemporary mainstream film we need to remain always 'alert to the digital'; that is, alert to the possibility that a digital element or elements will need to be explicitly discussed as part of the interpretive process. The study as a whole works through a number of examples of this approach in depth, but in this first chapter I want to make some general observations about how the digital can operate connotatively within the frame of live action cinema, alongside some points about how the digital has thus far been discussed. The above analyses demonstrate that digital elements within the film frame intersect with – and often mimic – other elements of *mise-en-scène*, but also function narratively and semantically. In the *Children of Men* example it does not make sense to analyse the digital elements at work in the final scene in isolation from the film's wider thematic and aesthetic structures, nor in isolation from the final scene's other compositional and editorial decisions. As a result, this book makes the case for a critical engagement with the digital that is productive precisely because it locates digital elements in the context of a film as a whole, an approach that the extended case studies illustrate in some detail. It is worth contextualising this aim a little further by briefly surveying one of the most common ways in which digital imaging in popular cinema has been discussed.

THE DIGITAL SPECIAL EFFECTS SEQUENCE

Digital imaging's original incarnation was as a 'special effect', the 'digital effects' first showcased in specific shots and later specific sequences of particular films, such as the compositing of the digital morph effect with live action footage in *The Abyss* (James Cameron, 1989).[3] At one level what was evident in such moments was an exhibitionist dynamic familiar from very early cinema (see Gunning 1986, 1993), encouraging intense contemplation by temporally or spatially bracketing the effect off from the rest of the film or shot. At another level this was a way for early digital effects movies to trial visual effects artists' capacity to integrate the digital with the profilmic in a convincing way, and to test out the spectator's tolerance of the digital elements and the composited image within safe limits (Pierson 2002: 124–5). This 'bracketing off' of digital effects placed the technology firmly in the special effects tradition, and therefore within a critical debate about special effects and their relationship to narrative that was already significantly underway. Writing on digital imaging technologies in mainstream cinema first emerged in critical engagements with the traditionally special effects-heavy science fiction genre (for instance, Sobchack 1987, Kuhn 1990, Cubitt 1999a, Bukatman 1999). This writing focused on a particular kind of special effects moment: large-scale special effects sequences such as the panoramic views of outer space, huge galactic ships and other phenomena that stretch beyond the image frame in films like *2001: A Space Odyssey* (Stanley Kubrick, 1968), *Star Wars* (George Lucas, 1977) and *Close Encounters of the Third Kind* (Steven Spielberg, 1977). The affective impact of such sequences was characterised as generating a kind of spectatorial absorption that paused the forward flow of the narrative. For example, adapting Laura Mulvey's account of visual pleasure (Mulvey 1975) Annette Kuhn suggested that such moments invite a particular response, constituting 'an appeal to scopophilia' whose 'only function must be to invite the spectator's awed gaze' at the world-building spectacle being offered (Kuhn 1990: 148). In relation to specific shots in a cerebral, spectacular mode of 1970s and 1980s science fiction cinema (and its related cultural contexts), such claims are persuasive. However, as the critical project of analysis has moved to take account of emergent digital imaging technologies, these ideas have been applied to a much broader set of films that feature digital visual effects. Andrew Darley, for example, extrapolates from Kuhn's formulation to conclude that the contemporary digital special effects spectacle is 'the antithesis of narrative' and 'effectively halts motivated movement' (2000: 104).

This assertion bears the traces of Gunning's correlation of the original cinema of attractions (in the early cinema period) with what he characterised as a more recent 'Spielberg-Lucas-Coppola cinema of effects' that 'has reaffirmed its roots in stimulus and carnival rides' (1990: 61). Gunning's words have been used by a number of writers to delineate a mode of special effects cinema in which visual spectacle does not simply interrupt the narrative but suppresses its 'proper' function. Justin Wyatt, for example, suggests that the emphasis on visual stylistic excess he observed in the high concept movie caused 'a weakening of identification with character and narrative' (1994: 60).[4] This anxiety that visual spectacle is somehow devaluing narrative (even among those, like Darley, who have a direct and positive interest in digital visual culture) finds its contemporary 'proof' in films that deploy digital effects overtly and extensively. Such a position is evident not only in some quarters of academic debate but also in press discussion that focuses on whether CGI has lost its capacity to engage the audience. For example, David Mamet has lamented in the popular press that the 'day of the dramatic script is ending' and that stunts and explosions, 'once but ornaments in an actual story, are now fairly exclusively, the film's reason for being' (2007: xi). Articles like Mamet's recur frequently (for example Child 2007; Somalya 2008). Looking at one of these sequences in some detail provides an opportunity to put these anxious criticisms to the test, and to argue for a rather different position on these kinds of explicit digital effects deployments.

The opening digital effects-heavy action sequence of *Charlie's Angels: Full Throttle* (McG, 2003) operates in a fantasy-action mode that is often accused of providing action spectacle hung on a perfunctory narrative framework. The heroic detective agency operatives (Cameron Diaz, Lucy Liu and Drew Barrymore) have managed to extract a US Marshal (Robert Patrick) being held hostage in a Mongolian military stronghold. They make their escape in a large truck that holds a camouflaged load, but become trapped on a high bridge between a tank with its gun barrel aimed in their direction, and a soldier armed with a rocket launcher. To avoid capture they drive the truck off the bridge, an action that separates the humans from the truck cab, and the truck from a load that is now revealed as an Apache helicopter. A low angle shot frames the humans as they free fall towards the camera, miraculously avoiding the helicopter as it spirals past them. Subsequent shots show the Angels manoeuvring themselves and the rescued Marshall into the helicopter cockpit in mid-air, all the while dodging helicopter blades, debris and the falling truck. One of the Angels (Lucy Liu) has difficulty managing her free fall to take up position aboard the helicopter, but handily the battered truck explodes and the force of the explosion pushes her onto the wing of the Apache. The helicopter's engine fires and it becomes safely airborne just in time to avoid plunging all of its occupants into the river below.

That the sequence's excess is intended to be humorous should already be evident from this outline of the hectic sequence of events. In part it seems to function as an ironic comment on the way that digital imaging technologies have pushed the traditional action sequence's dynamics further into the physically impossible, becoming, then, an elaborate genre joke. But on closer inspection the sequence also serves to establish the mode the film will be operating in, and several narratively significant points. It might have been possible to put together a sequence like this without the aid of digital imaging and digital compositing technologies, but they are crucial to its significance, not only enabling an excessive articulation, but reflexively underlining it. The over-saturated digital colour grading of the blue sky in the low angle free fall shot emphasises the edge 'bleed' around the falling figures, perceptually separating out the different image elements so that the digital composite feels more like a gesture towards photorealism than its achievement, an approach I will consider further in Chapter 3. In subsequent shots a similar effect is created by plotting wildly unrealistic trajectories for the falling bodies, which move in wide curves that disregard the physics of real-world air currents and human physiology, and which sometimes seem to move 'through' falling debris or helicopter rotor blades without harm. This is not careless compositing but the clear declaration of the rules of this hyper-real fantasy film and its diegesis: those 'rules' being its generic status as comedy, its penchant for knowing and often self-reflexive parody, and its depiction of its three Angels as almost superhuman action heroines. The opening sequence thus establishes the visual and tonal register within which the subsequent action/rescue sequences of the film will operate, as well as the super-abilities of its heroines. But there is more narrative import to the sequence than this. As the helicopter banks back up into the sky, disaster averted, the US Marshal says 'I'm afraid I underestimated you guys' and an Angel (Cameron Diaz) replies, 'Yeah, that happens a lot.' This seems like a straightforward declaration of the principle, present in both movies, that the Angels' success often depends on the fact that men underestimate them because they are women. But the Angels' almost parental concern for the people they help – here conveyed visually in the protective handling of the Marshall into the helicopter – is their weakness, making them blind to potential deception. The pattern of males underestimating females established in this opening sequence in fact actively misdirects the spectator away from two later plot revelations. Despite their super-abilities, it will be the Angels themselves that are revealed to have underestimated *others*; first, the US Marshal, whose rescue is an elaborate double-cross, and second, an ex-Angel (played by Demi Moore) who emerges as the architect of several attempts on the Angels' life and the destruction of their headquarters. While the aesthetic decisions in the digital compositing establish the generic framework and the fantastical register of the film's action, the sequence also sets up the pattern of underestimation that will characterise the subsequent developments.

The above account does not claim profundity or complexity for *Charlie's Angels: Full Throttle*, but it does demonstrate that a significant amount of information (narrative, thematic, aesthetic, and generic) is available in even the most absurdly excessive digital special effects sequence. Disdainful positions in the press and in academic discourse on digital imaging technologies (and corollary allegations of their detrimental impact on narrative cinema) seem to map a dissatisfaction with the perceptual 'flatness' of some electronic images onto fears about what are described as increasingly 'shallow' narratives. Such positions usually cite the proliferation of spectacular digital special effects in Hollywood films that lack narrative complexity or thematic depth, but in doing so take weaknesses in narrative design to be in some way a consequence of using digital imaging, rather than of the failure of script writers, directors or producers. Observations (often taking the form of accusations) that current popular cinema's spectacular mode of address undermines narrative seem rooted in a nostalgic recollection of a 'golden age' of classical Hollywood filmmaking, when narrative managed to hold sway over the distractions of spectacle.[5] This is an amnesiac position that ignores the fact that popular cinema 'has long been a spectacular, indeed sensational tradition' (Tasker 2004: 2), and which erroneously characterises narrative and spectacle as mutually exclusive. Sean Cubitt proposes a more dialectical relationship between these frequently opposed terms. He suggests that digital special effects sequences do interrupt narrative with their 'sublime' temporality, but they do so in the service of legitimating what remains a predominantly narrative medium:

> Laying on a second temporal axis across the narrative time of the film brings on marvel at the capabilities of the medium itself, throwing before the audience the specificity of the medium as well as a terminal form of illusion that succeeds by exceeding the *apparent* limits of the medium. (1999a: 130, emphasis added)

In this way digitally achieved spectacles may well represent a difference in degree – rather than kind – from earlier spectacles. Any assertion that narrative is devalued by special effects spectacles also overvalues *overt* narrative elements (dialogue, characterisation, character action, structures of causality), without acknowledging that special effects sequences can supply *all* of these, albeit sometimes in altered form.[6] For example, Aylish Wood has noted how the screen duration of a spectacle or spectacular element can contribute narrative meaning. Using the example of *Twister* (Jan de Bont, 1996), Wood suggests that the longer the digitally generated twister tornadoes stay on the screen, the more they communicate the power of nature that the human characters are up against (2002: 374), and thus gain their own narrative agency:

> The tornadoes do not appear briefly as a plot device to allow something else to happen; instead, they form an additional narrative dimension that competes with that of the human figures. (2002: 377)

The contention that spectacular digital effects sequences – with their inherent invitation to contemplate the image – always halt the narrative is unconvincing, then, since it rests on a refusal to allow that such sequences might also generate narratively significant meaning. It is uncontroversial, today, to suggest that a film's *mise-en-scène* can be as communicative as its dialogue, so it seems reasonable to observe that digital special effects sequences' presentation of carefully designed spaces and actions – their *mise-en-scène* – can be similarly communicative.

Implicit in Wood's account is the centrality of the human body to such sequences' connotative purchase, either as a structuring presence (the hero in action, the family in peril) or as a structuring absence (natural events or forces that threaten to overwhelm human protagonists). Digital special effects sequences, particularly those that play out on a large canvas – that is, across an extended diegetic space – can dramatise power relations forcefully, articulating fantasies of empowerment in which the mastery of the visible offered by the sequence metaphorically correlates to the physical mastery or dramatic disempowerment of the protagonist. The manner of the body's staging within the spaces and actions of such sequences is thus as communicative as the depicted events themselves. Well before the advent of the digital, sequences of dramatic physical action or large-scale events already offered a sensory identification with the cinematic body's trials and transformations that communicated character development and action corporeally, as well as intellectually pushing the narrative forward, in Westerns, historical epics, and other action genres.[7] The difference in the contemporary, digitally assisted examples lies not in their underlying impulse, but in the expanded scale and dynamism of the imagery that the imaging technologies make possible. We might suggest that digital imaging allows films to find more expressive and expansive ways to 'body forth' fantasies of physical achievement and mastery. Consider for example the *Matrix* bullet-time sequences, which deploy digitally constructed slow motion and digital special effects to foreground bodily gestures and postures that map the shifts in power relations between characters across the trilogy of films (Wachowskis, 1999, 2003) (see Purse 2008). The presence of digital imaging within the film frame can have complex effects on how the human body, placed in front of the camera, registers on screen – in digital special effects blockbusters, but also in a range of movies that do not fit that category. Digital imaging can help locate that 'profilmic' body in a particular world or space – such as the digital compositing of background and foreground elements in war films such as *Saving Private Ryan* (Steven Spielberg, 1998) and *Flags of Our Fathers* (Clint Eastwood, 2006), and the provision of digital set extensions in *Zodiac* that I described earlier – and Chapters 2, 3 and 4 will further explore how the staging of bodies in relation to digital as well as practical objects in the film world can significantly shape meaning. Digital imaging can also manipulate the body in subtle ways, such as the reversed ageing process in *The Curious Case of Benjamin Button* (David Fincher, 2008) or changes to the tone or pallor of an actor's face such as the digital whitening of Sweeney Todd (Johnny Depp)'s visage in certain shots of *Sweeney Todd: The Demon Barber of Fleet Street* (Tim Burton, 2007). The analyses in subsequent chapters indicate ways in which we can be alert to these digital manipulations – both large and small, exhibitionist and barely perceptible – and investigate their potential consequences for meaning.

Before we finish our consideration of the digital special effects sequence, it is important to also acknowledge such sequences' thematic communicativeness. Cubitt admits this epistemic dimension in his description of what the sublime moment 'points towards' in such movies: for him, it is 'a time beyond the mundane, a post-mortem time, or a time of the gods' (1999a: 128–9). Much of the time the thematic dimension of a film will speak in some way to the cultural moment in which it was made, and this is equally true of the digital effects spectacle. Various scholars have speculated on the thematic resonance of these sequences: Scott Bukatman suggests that the call to scopophilia Kuhn found in such moments was a compensatory fantasy of mastery over the visual that helped audiences rehearse and contain fears about being overwhelmed by an increasingly technologised Western socio-cultural context (1999: 265), while Vivian Sobchack finds that the increasing popularity of digital slow motion in more recent digital special effects sequences (from the bullet-time sequences in *The Matrix* to *300*'s 'speed-ramped' battle scenes which I discuss further in Chapter 5) delights because it allows us 'to take time out of' and simultaneously visually interrogate 'the increasing accelerations of cinematic and social life' (2006: 342). Since any cultural context is inherently fluid and changeable, this aspect of digital special effects sequences can only be accurately analysed on a film by film basis: by asking how the thematic potential registers in *this* or *that* particular set of narrative, visual and cultural circumstances. Kristen Whissel's account of the tendency towards vertical staging of action in effects sequences illustrates this well. Having asserted a general tendency 'to map the violent collision of opposed forces onto a vertical axis marked by extreme highs and lows' in order to effectively express the dynamic relationship between power and powerlessness in a range of post-1996 blockbusters (2006: 23), Whissel then makes clear that the 'new verticality' mobilises different meanings in each film. In *Titanic* (James Cameron, 1997) for example, Whissel proposes that this verticality dramatises an imbalanced and polarised social hierarchy, and Rose's battle to achieve a middle ground; in *Hero* (Yimou Zhang, 2002) it communicates opposed characters' desires, shifting power relations and conflicting political ideals, and in *Crouching Tiger, Hidden Dragon* (Ang Lee, 2000) it expresses 'the complicated relations between the past and the future, the desire for change and the insistent pull of tradition, and the struggle of emergent power against the dominant' (2006: 30). Thus in digital effects sequences, the way in which digital imaging elements contribute to the dramatisation of interactions between characters and objects onscreen can generate thematic resonance alongside the more direct, literal meanings conveyed.

In looking at some of the ways in which other writers have discussed the digital special effects sequence, this part of the chapter has begun to suggest that effects sequences can be much more complexly and comprehensively expressive than certain commentators have allowed. But while digital imaging technologies continue to produce special effects which each have their own individual arcs from novelty to familiarity – what Tom Gunning calls the 'cycle from wonder to habit' (2003: 47) – special effects do not comprise the entirety of digital cinematic practice; far from it. The spectrum of digital imaging uses evident in contemporary mainstream live action cinema render 'special effect' a rather outdated label (Wyatt 1999: 378) and a rather contested status. Michele Pierson rehearsed this possibility in 2002, speculating that digital special effects would effectively begin to 'disappear' as a visual category, as CGI became a more persistent and wide-ranging presence onscreen, and as the impulse towards photorealism in digital imaging eradicated the 'bracketing off' and stylistic foregrounding of special effects that Pierson had identified in earlier phases of the digital effects tradition. She asks, 'What counts as a special effect in a film in which nearly every shot is an effects shot?' (Pierson 2002: 152). The ten or so years that have followed Pierson's question provide a number of answers. From a marketing perspective it is clear that the 'special effect' remains central to promotional discourse and to the big budget studio offerings they advertise. A distinction is still drawn between movies that involve 'special effects' (read: digital) and those that do not – although, as the discussion in this chapter and the Introduction illustrates, this is not an accurate reflection of the proportion of effects shots in any particular film, but a categorisation for promotional purposes. Special effects sequences which function as explicit demonstrations/celebrations of digital effects technologies (featuring familiar fare: explosions, vehicular chases, impossible vistas and impossible bodies) continue to be heavily promoted as the initial 'draw' for moviegoers, excised from the surrounding film so that they can circulate in a dense paratextual realm of multi-platform trailers, web-sites, TV spots, social media, and smart phone apps.

THE DIGITALLY LITERATE SPECTATOR

Studios work hard to prime spectators to appreciate special effects, to become connoisseurs in assessing their technical realisation. As Dan North reminds us,

> The most engaged spectator (and therefore the one who will represent repeat business) is the one who is always aware that she is being tricked, perhaps has a partial knowledge of how that trick is being effected, but who wishes to see *how* that trick *looks* when performed. Special effects operate in the same way, requiring an engagement with the technique as well as the appearance of an illusion. (2008: 182, emphasis in original)

In the multiplying plethora of promotional texts circulating around contemporary releases, the digital is promoted *as* 'high' technology, as the detailed narrative of the visual effects work on many major digital special effects movies is told and re-told across a spectrum of ancillary websites, weekly pre-production, production and post-production video diaries, and multiple releases of DVD material. In such ancillary materials, digital elements are artificially isolated from the wider film in order to celebrate the achievements of a range of technologically sophisticated 'behind the scenes' personnel, and to underscore (and thus promote) the film itself as a novel and technologically advanced visual spectacle. Filmmakers' capacity to alter every pixel of the film image – offering a fantasy of omniscient control – is promoted, but significantly, only in a very generalised way; the spectator is dissuaded from considering the full range of digital interventions present in the film by promotional materials offering instead detailed engagement with isolated and explicit uses of digital imaging in specific 'special effects' sequences. This is a move designed to point away from any consideration of the impact these myriad smaller digital manipulations have at the level of meaning. Aylish Wood has rightly noted that 'if attention is drawn to the technology this is in order to display its possibilities and *not* to question its operations and manipulations' (2007a: 27, emphasis in original).[8] Caught up in the paratextual 'real story' of a movie's technological sophistication provided by promotional materials, which itself draws on a utopian cultural conception of digitally enabled technological empowerment, the spectator is much less likely to closely ponder the mechanics – and politics – of the film's representational dynamics and visual narration. One of the tasks of this book, therefore, is to resist the temptation to fetishise the digital technologies and digital special effects of mainstream cinema, while countering the arguments of those who would dismiss digital imaging technologies' significance as somehow outside of narrative, and not worthy of consideration in the 'serious' analysis of narrative cinema.

Nevertheless, the spectator's awareness of the potential presence of digital imaging, and of that imaging's digital nature, can contribute in complex ways to the play of meaning in a sequence or film. In *Live Free or Die Hard* (Len Wiseman, 2007; released under the alternative title *Die Hard 4.0* in European territories) both exhibitionist and unassuming uses of digital images intersect with action genre conventions and cultural notions of the digital. The most recent movie in the *Die Hard* franchise, the film features a group of terrorists who are bent on disrupting US communications, transport and security infrastructures, using the internet, and computer and satellite technologies. The terrorists are hackers and digital technology experts; the franchise hero, John McClane (Bruce Willis) is out of step with this kind of technology, preferring physical action to the sedentary (but highly effective) remote computerised interventions of the terrorists. In a sequence that persuasively communicates the reach of the terrorists' grip on national communications networks, they take control of broadcast television, replacing normal programming with blanket images of the Capitol building in Washington DC presented in the style of live rolling news coverage. Initially accompanied by a soundtrack of patriotic music, these images take on an unsettling aspect as a series of questions scroll across the screen: 'What if this is just the beginning? What if you're hurt and alone and you dial 911 and no one answers? What if help will never come?' Seconds later the Capitol building explodes and its structure collapses. It is only when McClane has rushed onto one of the main streets to verify the explosion that he and the spectator learn that this was only an illusion, a bogus moving image constructed by the terrorists using the same sophisticated digital imaging technologies that the movie itself calls upon; the actual Capitol building remains visibly intact on the skyline.

The sequence is energised by cultural anxieties concerning the ontological status of digital images, as well as fears about modern terrorism and the ways that national security systems and communications, reliant on digital technologies, might be infiltrated and co-opted. Digital imaging also contributes to the import of the sequence – and not just through the fake images of the Capitol explosion. The sequence starts with McClane in a Washington alley-

Figure 1.3 Frame grab from *Live Free or Die Hard* (20th Century Fox): McClane watches the Capitol building on a café television.

way placing a call to his contact in the FBI, the Deputy Director of the 'Cyber Division' Agent Miguel Bowman (Cliff Curtis), who is in a different part of the city. While he waits for Bowman to return to the phone, McClane's attention is caught by the large flat screen television in the adjacent art gallery café that is showing the Capitol building images. Framed by the window from the café's interior, McClane's growing interest in the television (and the dramatic significance of what it is broadcasting) is signalled both by the camera's zoom into a close-up of his face and a dissonant note in the film score. The subsequent reverse angle shows what McClane can see through the window: the café interior, customers turned toward the television, the television screen itself. But while a point of view shot would have achieved this perfectly well, the decision is made instead to adopt a camera position from behind McClane's shoulder, so that the reverse angle shot shares his perspective and frames his reflection in the café window. McClane's proximity to the camera causes him to be slightly out of focus, but his digitally inserted reflection is unusually sharp and bright (given the limited light in the alley), and conspicuously bisects the other area of brightness in the frame, the café's television screen (see Fig. 1.3). Thus the choice of shot, its composition and its mobilisation of its digital elements signals that there is a significant link between these two presences in the frame, a point confirmed when McClane is spurred into action by the images on the television screen.

As McClane updates Bowman by mobile phone, the sequence cuts between their different locations, and the vivid gold of the logo emblazoned on the art gallery café's window (which appears to have been digitally inserted) works with McClane's digital reflection to foreground the contrasting colour palettes of these different environments. The gold logo complements the natural golds, greens and browns of McClane and his reflection's sunlit skin and clothing. This warm, vibrant colour palette is used consistently in shots of McClane, locating him as the lively, 'red-blooded' man of action, and here (as elsewhere) it contrasts with the palette of metallic blues and greys in shots which define the deskbound and technologised nature of both the FBI computer security headquarters and the terrorists' hi-tech mobile control centre. The divergent colour palettes emphasised by this digital composite shot support the unfolding narrative opposition between the computer-savvy, rather sedentary terrorists and McClane's highly active, physical response: networked computers make possible the terrorist threat (and its significant reach) in the film world, but McClane's physical actions will be the disruptive force that brings the terror campaign to a close. While the contrasting colour palette and *mise-en-scène* have underlined the fact that Agent Bowman's FBI approach is distinct in general terms from McClane's, it is the two men's capacity for cooperation and their shared values that are cemented in the climax of the sequence. As everyone else stares in horror at television images of the Capitol building's destruction, McClane and Bowman are the only two characters who run to a different real-world geographical vantage point to test the truth of the image with their own eyes. This identical response to, and shared suspicion of, the digital image's apparent veracity demonstrates that both men favour the material over the digital, and thus have some chance of overcoming the digital terrorism that has been unleashed.

Live Free or Die Hard knowingly draws on spectators' extra-textual knowledge of digital technologies and the cultural discourses circulating around them, from the early play on McClane's clumsy ignorance of contemporary digital communications, via the self-reflexive images of the Capitol exploding, to the construction of the terrorists and their modus operandi. Part of the specificity of the presence of digital imaging in mainstream cinema that the film analyst has to be aware of is the increased digital literacy of cinema audiences, that is, their awareness of the presence and power of the digital in cinema. Spectators are more digitally literate than they were, not least because of a socio-cultural environment in which digital images are accessed, used, exchanged and manipulated in a range of everyday situations, and cinemagoers can pick sophisticated digital imaging software packages directly off the shelf for their personal use. In addition, a range of ancillary websites, media articles, DVD featurettes and special interest magazines proclaim popular cinema's flagship digital imaging achievements, replete with broad brush detail on 'how it was done'. Spectators know the digital's possibilities, its capacity for generating real-seeming events inside a computer, and for visible or invisible transformation and alteration. They know that digital imaging is present onscreen even when they can't tell what has been digitally generated, composited or manipulated and what has not, and they know something of the technological processes involved. The reason why this is significant to interpretation is not simply because digital literacy contributes to how meaning is produced in those films that *explicitly* address this digital context through their aesthetic and narrative design. What digital literacy also opens up is the possibility that the inherent qualities of the digital image can also function on a metaphorical level. Each of the digital image element's properties – its immateriality, its non-indexicality, its endless capacity for transformation – has the potential to function as a metaphor within a film's wider epistemic structures and operations; in Chapter 2 we will see examples of this kind of metaphorical function in practice. What these possibilities also imply is that the traditional account of the spectator's experience of a special effect – the oscillation between an awareness of the technical feat being witnessed and a narrative immersion in the fictional event being shown[9] – fails to capture the complex manner in which digital literacy of various kinds might intersect with narrative meaning.

There is a need, then, to consolidate a move away from thinking of digital imaging only in terms of 'special effects' practice, and towards a detailed attention to the range of ways digital imaging is used in contemporary mainstream cinema. The cognitive and perceptual distinctions between digital and profilmic elements of the film frame occupy a continuum between the exaggeratedly obvious and the utterly imperceptible, and if we consider the digital imaging deployments in *United 93* or *Zodiac*, the category of 'imperceptible' has a spectrum of its own.[10] Sean Cubitt's observation that in digitally assisted or fully computer generated sequences some or all of the 'accidents . . . that so enchanted Bazin' have to be designed in (2004: 251) is at once self-evident and thought provoking. Self-evident in that a simulation of a real-world object or space over time must necessitate the designing in of such 'accidents' in order to be perceptually convincing; thought provoking in that it implies an active and invisible manipulation of apparently straightforwardly profilmic events the imperceptibility of which should give us pause. George Lucas is one of those who have praised this capacity for imperceptible manipulation of the image. For Lucas, digital imaging technologies give filmmakers 'more to work with. It's a much more malleable medium than film, by far; you can make it do whatever you want it to do' (in Magid 2002: para. 6). What these technologies really promise is an absolute control over the image the extent of which – in any particular scene or film – is not fully discernible by the spectator. This presence of the digital intervention is also potentially an absence, then; we might think of innocuous absences like the removal of wirework wires and unsightly smudges from actors' faces, but the digital intervention also manifests as the absence of indicators of what has been changed or omitted and why. Each invisible or imperceptible manipulation, transformation and omission is a filmmaking decision that has consequences for the way in which an image, a dramatic action, a character or scene will be perceived and interpreted, a filmmaking decision that is, then, driven by both aesthetic and ideological factors. The spectres of revisionism and censorship haunt these digital removals and amendments; as a result the impulses behind them, and the alternative ways in which such moments could have been visualised, should be considered alongside what appears on the screen itself.

This chapter and the preceding Introduction have suggested that the epistemic dimensions of digital elements present within the audio-visual frame can only be fruitfully analysed and understood in relation to a film's wider narrative, representational and aesthetic structures, that is, as part of the larger interpretive exploration of a film. The remaining chapters purposefully select the types of films often denigrated as hollowly spectacular – blockbusters, science fiction, fantasy and action – as the subject of detailed textual analysis, a strategy that I hope will work against pat assumptions about popular forms of cinema, as well as providing highly suitable case studies for the study's analysis of the digital within the cinematic frame. Laura Mulvey has said that '[t]hinking about film within the framework of the digital is like watching a kaleidoscope pattern reconfigure very slowly. The same aesthetic attributes are there but the relations between them have shifted' (2006: 30). The same can be said for the epistemic dimensions of films that incorporate the digital in some way. While arguing against the interpretive 'isolation' of the digital, and for an approach that analyses digital elements in the context of all of a film's systems of signification, I have also suggested that the presence and the specificity of digital images themselves can generate meanings, and that the task of interpretation must take account of this. Close textual analysis provides the most appropriate tools with which to understand the relationships between systems of representation, narrative frameworks, dramatic construction, *mise-en-scène* and the digital, and between the ideological and the (digital-) technological, in mainstream cinema. The remaining chapters will chart a path through such issues and relationships, opening up specific texts to detailed consideration, and in doing so opening up to detailed examination the digital's role in the production of meaning.

NOTES

1. See 'The Making of *Zodiac*' at http://www.digitaldomain.com/#.
2. I am grateful to Melissa Taylor at Double Negative and Frazer Churchill, the visual effects supervisor on the film (also at Double Negative), for taking the time to clarify the circumstances of this shot for me.
3. Here and elsewhere in the study I will use 'digital effects' as a shorthand for 'digital special effects', where this phrase delineates those uses of digital imaging technologies which are explicit, declarative and spectacular. 'Digital imaging' will be used to refer to digital image interventions of any kind.
4. Wyatt also mentions other elements, like a self-conscious intertextuality, star casting, music, and ancillary promotional texts, which in combination 'distance the viewer from

the traditional task of reading the films' narrative. In place of this identification with narrative', Wyatt suggests, 'the viewer becomes sewn into the "surface" of the film, contemplating the style of the narrative and the production' (1994: 60).

5. One could draw a parallel here between the reductive dismissals of these aspects of contemporary popular cinema and the low critical standing of the popular cinema which preceded the intervention of *Cahiers du Cinéma* in the 1950s and *Movie* in the 1960s. See Gibbs (2002) for an insightful overview of this project.

6. Geoff King concurs that contemporary special effects-heavy spectacle 'is often just as much a core aspect of Hollywood cinema as coherent narrative and should not necessarily be seen as a disruptive intrusion from outside . . . Moments of spectacle [can] help to move the plot significantly forward' (2000: 4–5), while Scott McQuire offers a salutary corrective by pragmatically separating the quality of narration from the quantity of exhibitionist digital effects shots in any particular contemporary movie (2000: 53).

7. We might think of the sword fights in *The Black Pirate* (Albert Parker, 1926), the defence of the coach from attack in *Stagecoach* (John Ford, 1939), or the chariot race in *Ben-Hur* (William Wyler, 1959), for example.

8. Wood's assertion is made in the context of a discussion of contemporary computer generated animation films such as *Monsters, Inc.* (Pete Docter et al. 2001) and *The Incredibles* (Brad Bird, 2004), but is also highly applicable to live action cinema's promotional discourses around digital effects, and has echoes of Jean-Louis Comolli's still relevant warning to question technician's demands for '"a place apart" for cinematographic technique'. Comolli asks

> Why is the diffuse and insistent discourse of technicians (often backed up by filmmakers and critics now that the question is becoming important) so anxious to defend the field of technical and mechanical practices from any influence from or bearing on ideology; and to place it so firmly in the wings rather than on the stage where meanings are in play? For setting technique to one side and keeping it in reserve is also giving it a place – making it fill a slot in the ideological discourse. (1985 [1977]: 42)

9. This popular characterisation draws on Christian Metz's 1975 account of the 'cinema fetishist' (2000: 431).

10. In my view recent attempts to provide a taxonomy of levels or categories of digital visual effects practice produce classifications that are too generalising or rigid to be very useful. Instead I propose the more flexible notion of a continuum, which allows a more fluid approach to the shape that the intersection of the digital with other filmic elements takes in a specific film.

CHAPTER 2

Digital Imaging as Metaphor

T his is the first of the book's extended case studies which explore what it means in practice to be alert to the digital when undertaking the task of interpretation. In a close analysis of *Minority Report* that considers the relationship of the film's digital imaging strategies to issues of staging, genre, and narrative theme, this chapter demonstrates digital imaging's capacity to function at a metaphorical level.

FIGURES OF DIGITAL MEDIATION

From the very first moments of *Minority Report*, its central thematic concerns are rehearsed through uses of digital imaging that explicitly mediate the spectator's access to the spatial and epistemic coordinates of the fictional world. The film is preceded by the computer-animated logos of its two major production and distribution companies, Twentieth Century Fox and DreamWorks SKG. The Twentieth Century Fox logo sequence is familiar: three-dimensional and situated in a mock Los Angeles nightscape, it is revealed with the usual camera track up and over the logo, and accompanied by the traditional musical fanfare. Similarly the DreamWorks animated logo replays its familiar visual 'phrase' and musical theme: the reflection of moon and clouds in water is framed in close-up before a fishing line breaks the surface of the water and the camera, in a sweeping tilt, follows the fishing line's path into the sky, coming to rest on a little boy fishing from where he lies in the curve of the moon. The logo sequences have been digitally altered to correspond to – and introduce – the film that they precede: in both, the colour has been drained out, replaced with a blue-grey monochromatic tonal spectrum.[1] This digitally approximates the de-saturated, high contrast cinematography that will characterise the rest of the film, but also visually references the sharpened shadows and black and white film stock of 1940s film noir to which the film's visual and narrative design is indebted.[2] Notably, the glare from the Fox searchlights is much more pronounced than usual: the illumination from a searchlight positioned directly below the Twentieth Century Fox monolith spills across the entire screen for a moment as the camera passes above it, obscuring other details of the frame. Very bright light here becomes an obscuring 'surface' that threatens to interrupt the spectator's visual access. This duality of light, its ability to blind or interrupt sight as well as reveal information, will be an important thematic and visual motif in the film and is succinctly introduced here.

In both logo sequences a digital effect simulating crosshatched water ripples has been layered on top of the image, giving the impression that each logo is being seen through moving water. Water is narratively significant, and is also a recurrent visual presence in the film (Friedman 2006: 50–1): Anderton (Tom Cruise) is tormented by the kidnapping of his young son from a public swimming pool six years previously; while on the run from police he must submerge himself in a bath of freezing water to evade detection, and images of a drowning prove to be key to his framing. The rather unsubtle manner in which the water ripple effect is uniformly overlaid over both logo sequences implies that it is simply a visual foreshadowing of the importance of water within the film that will follow, but I would suggest it also has a more sophisticated function. It is a layer, produced by digital effects, that mediates the spectator's perception and access to diegetic space, thus introducing a figure of 'digitally mediated perception' that will characterise the most obvious digital effects moments in the film, and which will also be prevalent within *Minority Report*'s future world, with its proliferating screens, digital-visual surveillance and identification systems. This layer, which 'sits on top of' the image, works to trouble the spectator's spatial positioning relative to the fictional world. To make sense of the ripple effect in relation to the other image elements, the spectator is presented with more than one possible perspectival position: we are either viewing the logo sequence through the water from above the water line, looking down, or we are viewing the logo sequence through the water from below the water line, looking up. The camera movement in each sequence adds to this perspectival confusion, contradicting whichever spatial position the spectator has adopted in relation to the water. So in the Fox sequence, if one decides one is looking down through water, the final camera position looking up at the logo monolith contradicts this spatial orientation, while if one decides instead one is looking up through water, the opening high angle shot of the monolith from above contradicts this. So too with the DreamWorks sequence, which intensifies this perspectival confusion through the coincidence within the frame of two ripple effects, one diegetic and the other extra-diegetic, a moment that allows contradictory spectator positions (looking 'up' *and* 'down' at different rippling water surfaces) to be held simultaneously.[3] The uniformly applied digital ripple effect, by introducing the visual trope of the mediating, ambiguous digital layer, thus embodies issues that will be explored in the film as a whole – access to space, questions of perspective and point of view in relation to knowledge, and digitally mediated perception.

PROCESSES OF DETECTION

Minority Report fuses the diegetic worlds, narrative tropes and visual iconography of science fiction, the detective and thriller genres with those of film noir.[4] This generic hybridity shows itself in the narrative situation established at the start of the film. It is 2054, and crime detection has been transformed in the District of Columbia, where a new form of murder prevention is being piloted. Based on a 1956 Philip K Dick short story, *Minority Report* literalises science fiction's basic generic impulse to see into the future with Dick's narrative conceit of a trio of beings, called 'pre-cognitives', who can literally *see* the future: specifically, future murders. In the film, these 'pre-cogs' are connected to a computer system that records and projects their predictive visualisations ('pre-visions') onto a screen so that they can be accessed and interpreted by the Police Department of 'PreCrime'; PreCrime officers then apprehend the future criminal before the murder can be committed. An investment in the process of detection, characteristic of detective fiction and film noir, is evident here, not least in the introduction of the central protagonist police chief John Anderton in the act of detection itself. Rather than using flashbacks to produce the oppressive sense of predetermination typical of much film noir (Schrader 1996: 58) and which often directly structures the central protagonist's predicament, *Minority Report* uses the device of pre-visualised murder to do so instead. In true 'noir' style, Anderton will soon be framed, and will seek desperately to clear his name before the murder takes place.

Minority Report draws on the structural differences as well as the similarities between the detective narrative and film noir.[5] Prior to the emergence of literary hardboiled detectives (in the work of writers such as Raymond Chandler, Dashiell Hammett, and Cornell Woolrich), the narrative trajectory of the 'classical detective' (epitomised by Conan Doyle's Sherlock Holmes), while predominantly concerned with the process of detection, moved towards the *rational* solution to the mystery, the restoration of order achieved 'through the detective's superior powers of deductive reasoning' (Porfirio 1996: 90). Roger Caillois emphasises this rationalist destination: 'At bottom, the unmasking of a criminal [was] less important than the reduction of the impossible to the possible, of the inexplicable to the explained, of the supernatural to the natural' (1983: 3); certainty arrives in the end (in Neale 2000: 74). Film noir and detective fiction share mystery plots in which certain information has been suppressed and must be discovered, resulting in a preoccupation with investigation as process. However film noir distinguishes itself in two ways: the investigation itself can be mysterious or lack clarity (Borde and Chaumeton 1996: 23–4), and the mystery's solution is rarely a successful resolution of the wider anxieties and problems the narrative has explored. The corrupt, morally bankrupt noir milieu persists unchanged after the story's end; '[t]here is nothing the protagonist can do; the city will outlast and negate even his best efforts' (Schrader 1996: 57). *Minority Report* draws intentionally on our awareness of the narrative tropes of both classical detective narrative and film noir, and the questions of knowledge and control over the discovery of knowledge, that are differently inflected across both forms.

SURFACES AND LAYERS

Knowledge and perspective are key elements in detective fiction and in film noir narratives, both of which usually concern the protagonist-detective's attempts to peel back layers of subterfuge to solve the mystery. In *Minority Report*, as in these literary and cinematic forebears, for much of the narrative the truth will remain hidden behind those surfaces (alibis, falsehoods, performances of innocence) that the guilty choose to project. Evidence already discovered may need only to be looked at from a different perspective for the mystery to be solved – a shift in point of view can obscure or reveal information. The film's logo sequences with their digital layers, obscuring surfaces, and foregrounding of shifting optical perspectives, foreshadow the film's interest in such concerns, and digital imaging plays a fundamental part in the visualisation of processes of detection and concealment in the film itself.

Minority Report's initial series of shots is pointedly opaque. Two moving black masses slowly resolve into focus and back out again, briefly revealing a kissing couple. There follow snatched shots of scissors, bloodied water rushing over the side of a bath, a man walking upstairs, a couple being discovered, a man stabbing ferociously. The sequence is characterised by expressionistic image distortions, temporal ellipses and repetitions that gradually and non-chronologically build up a picture of a double murder taking place. The detailed texture of the image distortions produces a strong sense of looking at the events through an alternating number of mediating layers. Some images stretch as if being viewed through a fisheye lens; image undulations both random and vertical produce the impression of an 'underwater' view, and in other shots lines of flickering distortion replicate vertical lens flare or scratch lines on celluloid.

The series of disordered images was achieved through extensive digital manipulation of the original footage by the visual effects studio, Imaginary Forces. While the distortion effects invoke non-digital viewing technologies (such as traditional lenses and celluloid film stock), the digital nature of the 'layer' that mediates visual access to the murder is readable because the speeding up and slowing down of certain images is reminiscent of the variable speed digital effects spectators would be familiar with from contemporaneous television advertising, music videos, and films like *The Matrix* and *Snatch* (Guy Ritchie, 2000).[6] The sequence is extremely restrictive: it not only withholds narrative information (not simply 'what is happening?' but 'where are these images being viewed from?') but refuses to present it in ways that would aid speedy assimilation. The digital layer masks, re-orders and distorts the images spatially and temporally; it operates as a metaphor – a pre-vision, even – for the way in which information will be hidden and manipulated throughout the narrative. As in the logo sequences, the spectator is forced to experience a problematic mode of digitally mediated perception, occupying an enforced perspective from which information about the film world – about the event itself, the characters, the milieu, the narrative context – is difficult to access. As a result, the film provokes an intense desire for this information to be appropriately organised and rationalised, its mysteries resolved, clarity of vision on the events to be achieved.[7]

The introduction of the central protagonist, police chief John Anderton, seems to promise this is possible, providing a detective figure who answers these desires with an emphatic demonstration of rational, ordered detection. Anderton stands in front of a wide, curved Perspex screen and, as classical music starts to swell on the soundtrack, the room darkens and the shifting, smudgy images and sounds from the opening sequence start to play across the screen, their status – as a pre-vision of a future murder being communicated from the pre-cogs' brains – now clarified. The 'detection wall', the screen on which the pre-cogs' image data is displayed, is transparent, so that the images being captured from the pre-cogs and outputted in the analytical room seem to occupy the space in front of Anderton of their own volition. The focus has thus moved from the extra-diegetically digitally mediated images of the logos and opening film sequence, which foregrounded questions of knowledge and perception in a generalised way, to a figure of digitally mediated perception that exists within the fictional world (see Fig. 2.1). Anderton uses specially-equipped gloves to manipulate, sort and prioritise the data from the pre-cogs, interacting with the images in a plastic, fluid way, bits of information becoming pliable and mobile, his hands able to 'dip in', replaying and pulling out information, rearranging it. The data is displayed as two-dimensional shifting images, but multiply-layered over one another, hanging in space, so that Anderton can, for example, divide two 'moments' to grab a third which lies underneath. The classical music is diegetic, matching its swirling violins to Anderton's graceful hand movements. Reminiscent of a surgeon who listens to music while operating, Anderton's use of music reveals his sense of mastery, artistry, and control. He occupies the centre of the 'analytical room', and often

Figure 2.1 Frame grab from *Minority Report* (20th Century Fox / Dreamworks): Police chief John Anderton searches the pre-vision images for clues

the spectator is aligned with his perspective, as close framings from just behind him show both the screen that he sees and his gestures as he sorts the data.[8] Here layers can obscure the truth, then, but Anderton is able to sift them, to peel them back; while the pre-cogs have provided the name of the murderer (Howard Marks, played by Arye Gross) and his victims (Marks' wife (Ashley Crow) and her lover (Joel Gretsch)), by the end of the scene Anderton has discovered the murder location and can mobilise a police team in time to prevent the killing. Aylish Wood notes that once he 'steps up to the wall of images, controlling the flow of information, and contextualizing it through discussions with his colleagues, the ambiguity [of the pre-vision as it is presented in the opening sequence] is edited out' (2004: 4). Enacting the rational resolution of the traditional detective narrative, Anderton delivers the desired demystifying explanation for the initially confusing imagery. It is worth noting that the spectator is left in no doubt as to the fact that this murder would have happened if the PreCrime officers had not intervened: the would-be killer is pulled back as the stabbing arc of his murder weapon travels down towards the victim's chest.

The clear screen the pre-visions are displayed upon calls up notions of transparency that have their metaphorical relation in Anderton's apparent ability to get at the truth. Meanwhile the dialogue speaks of 'scrubbing the image', a phrase that neatly conveys the sense of layers being scrubbed away to reveal a stable interpretation underneath.[9] But as Wood indicates in her description of Anderton's detective work as 'editing out' the 'ambiguity' of the pre-cogs' pre-visions, the process of detection, of organising the images, is also a process of elision, and even of dissimulation; Anderton is constructing a narrative from the raw material, a seemingly coherent layer of action *in front of* the rather less certain basis of the PreCrime process, which is reliant on three pre-visions of the future that do not always correspond. Within the analytical room there are other clues to this underlying reality, clues that evoke associations with notions of ambiguity and chance. In addition to the fact that the pre-visions cover the transparent surface of the detection screen with obscure, ambiguous, confusing images, Anderton's mood music is Schubert's *Unfinished* Symphony (1822), while the machine linked to the pre-cogs, which delivers balls engraved with the names of victim and perpetrator, is reminiscent of a lottery ball dispenser. Such elements further support the connotations generated by the digital screen and its placement in these scenes of detection.

In a perceptive article on the film, Wood describes the connotative effects of the pre-visions' status as a mediating digital layer in the detection process. The pre-visions arrayed on the vitreous detection wall become a dynamic free-standing surface dividing the space of the analytical room, screening Anderton from the pre-cogs (who cannot filter or control the flow of their own pre-visions) and positioning him as the primary spectator and interpreter of the images, producing apparently stable divisions between objective (Anderton) and subjective (pre-cogs) subject positions. However, as Wood goes on to point out, this spatial configuration is also inherently reversible and thus unstable, demonstrated by circular camera movements and straight cuts that shift the spectator's position from one side of the screen to the other. The semi-transparency of the screen already indicates that Anderton *could* occupy either side of this digital divide between objective and subjective, criminal and innocent positions. Wood suggests:

> Like the slash apparently dividing an opposing pair of terms, the interface establishes distinct locations for objective and subjective ways of being. And just as the slash has come to be understood as holding apart mutually informing terms, rather than ones of absolute difference, the interface will eventually collapse to reveal the permeability of the locations. (2004: 6–7)

Indeed, in certain shots from behind the screen the camera frames Anderton 'through' the pre-visions, as if *he* were part of the image flow, and by implication a participant in the murder scene (see Fig. 2.1). To use Victor Perkins' term (1972: 113), this operates as a pre-echo of the moment at which his status as perpetrator will be visualised on the same screen; the pre-vision that will show Anderton's own act of future murder.

Anderton's expertise and certitude are soon revealed to be a projection, a 'screen' of their own, and the sequence's celebration of the traditional, rational resolution of the narrative trajectory of detection is exemplified at the beginning of the film precisely so that it can then be radically undercut. From this point of certainty and clarity, the spectator is tipped into a film noir world in which processes of detection and questions of perspective and knowledge will be much more unstable and contingent. The next scene relocates to the slums of the city (nicknamed the 'Sprawl') at street level, at night, in the rain. The grimy, dark surroundings provide a stark and ironic counterpoint to the luminescent electronic billboards in the district, across which an advertisement for the PreCrime technology's national implementation is playing. The bright endorsements of the PreCrime process from potential murder victims, politicians and children echo hollowly in the gloom. A solitary hooded jogger running unheeding past the images and through the voluminous shadows is exposed as Anderton himself: behind the façade of the confident, successful detective is an addict desperate enough to slip into the lawless parts of the city to obtain the drug he craves. The aesthetic markers of noir had already been hinted at in the sequences featuring Marks' attempted murder of his wife: references to 1940s style were evident in the cut of Marks' suit, his wife's gold embroidered dressing gown, and the rather old-fashioned décor of the home, while the light that streamed in through the large windows only served to plunge the Marks family and whole areas of particular rooms into pronounced, hard-edged shadow. Anderton had appeared separate from and uncontaminated by this milieu, its generic markers and the volatile emotions seething behind the reputable façade of the Georgetown brownstone. The circular PreCrime analytical room and its technology kept human emotions and actions at a distance, organising them, ordering them; Anderton was bounded with the protective layers of these structures, masterful in his control of the pre-vision imagery. But this scene, with its physical relocation of Anderton into the city's underbelly, initiates the revelation of the police officer as psychologically scarred, drug dependent and isolated, struggling to deal with the kidnapping of his child six years earlier. Even before the pre-cog Agatha (Samantha Morton) points him to an unsolved murder, and before the mystery of his own predicted act of future murder arrives, Anderton is not simply tipped into a darker incarnation of the noir universe, but is transformed into the noir protagonist – always a detective of sorts, but also the personification of existential crisis, 'a disoriented individual facing a confused world that he cannot accept' (Porfirio 1996: 81).

The analytical room's detection wall and the electronic billboards in the Sprawl are digital screen technologies within the fictional world of the film, elements of the *mise-en-scène* that convey in a generalised way the technologised character of this future city. In the specific nature of their deployment in their respective scenes they also develop ideas that were mobilised initially in the logo sequences and opening sequence – that of perception(s) mediated, thwarted, or manipulated.[10] However, these (diegetic) digital screen technologies are also overt, foregrounded uses of the film's (extra-diegetic) digital imaging technologies. Rather than being imperceptible digital interventions like set extensions, colour correction and so on, these deployments generate a fully digital object within the three-dimensional space of the fictional world, and often at the centre of the frame, so that the digital-ness of the object, as well as its status as an object within the film world, can be clearly registered. The explicit digital-ness of these screens' real world mode of production puts into play associations that enhance the connotations already operating within the sequence. The inherent malleability of the digital image, its capacity to hide its interventions into the image 'in plain sight', generates cultural connotations of information *manipulation* that connect to the film's themes. Our sense of the disingenuousness of the PreCrime advertisement's presentation of PreCrime as achieving only positive results is intensified not simply by the advertisement's incongruous placement in the lawless, dirty environment of the Sprawl, but by the cultural connotations of image manipulation associated with the very digital imaging technologies that have composited the advertisement into the film frame. In the analytical room, the coherent explanation Anderton produces by rearranging the disparate pre-vision fragments creates an image 'surface' of sequences that have been digitally altered, while obscuring the complex processes of their production. The film's deployment of digital compositing and the seamless digital image as metaphors for deceit is made explicit at the narrative's end, in the discovery that the pre-cogs have been manipulated into compositing images of two temporally discrete but visually similar acts of murder to produce a 'fake' pre-vision.

VISUALISING THE CITY

This ability of the digital to function as metaphor finds its elaboration in the filmic construction of the city itself, in which digital imaging plays a significant part. As he loses his place in the civil hierarchy and is threatened with incarceration, Anderton's predicament acquires its force from its relationship to the spaces of the city, spaces that can control, constrain and confine. The visual presentation of these urban spatial structures develops the figure of digitally mediated perception to reveal connections between the duplicitous environment within which Anderton has been framed, and the wider social and spatial urban networks that frame his fraught experiences.

Early in the film, prior to his criminalisation, Anderton's departure for work occasions an apparently celebratory spectacle of the futuristic Washington DC's networks and skyscapes, in a striking sunlit vista. We watch 'mag-lev' cars, attached magnetically to the curved roads, slide smoothly away from clean, white apartment blocks, their speed and distance regulated automatically along tracks that gracefully snake into the gleaming city in the distance. Yet the way this entirely digitally generated shot is staged, both spatially and in terms of specific digital effects, partly qualifies its celebratory aspect, and further, seems to foreground the artifice rather than the veracity of the shot. This should be an opportunity to deploy the 'omniscient and revelatory moving camera' of science fiction film (Bukatman 2003: 124), a mastering trajectory that moves forward over the city to better facilitate an all-encompassing perspective on its technologised spaces, exemplified by the 'fantastic topographies' (124) created by visual effects expert Douglas Trumbull in films like *Blade Runner* (Ridley Scott, 1982), *Silent Running* (Douglas Trumbull, 1972) and *2001: A Space Odyssey* (Kubrick, 1968). However, the camera movement in this sequence does not move into the fictional space in front of the (synthetic) camera; instead it tracks sideways with a rather untidy (and not very omnipotent) wobble, keeping its distance from the city, and refusing to provide the opportunity to 'authenticate' the city as photoreal that would have been available in a penetrative track into the city space.

Lens flare is also prominent. There is a recent trend for lens flare, either practically or digitally generated, to be included as an homage to particular eras of celluloid cinema, in films like *Star Trek* and *Super 8* (J. J. Abrams, 2009 and 2011). As we saw in the *Transformers* example in the Introduction, it also has the advantage of lending a photorealistic, illusory verisimilitude to digital effects shots. Nigel Morris argues for this purpose in the *Minority Report* cityscape, suggesting that including lens flare in what is 'clearly a computer generated shot . . . enhances realism, facilitating Imaginary involvement' (2007: 321–2). But Spielberg has a history of using lens flare (albeit practically achieved) for expressive purposes in films like *Close Encounters of the Third Kind* (1977) and *E.T.: The Extra-Terrestrial* (1982), so there may be other explanations. A closer look at the appearance and behaviour of this digital artifact here and elsewhere in the film points towards a different reading than the one Morris argues. In the logo sequences digitally generated lens flare momentarily prevented the spectator's access to diegetic space, while elsewhere in the film it occurs at moments when Anderton is feeling particularly uncertain, often seeming to threaten to erase him from the screen. For example, when he is trying to escape police capture in a mag-lev car, and despairingly trying to understand how a pre-vision could show him as a future murderer, light from outside the car floods the shot. Later, as he attempts desperately to put the pieces of the mystery together at his estranged wife's home, whispering 'I've got to figure this out', sunlight flares across the frame, obliterating his head and shoulders in a white glow. In the cityscape shot, the lens flare's persistent presence within what is a twelve second-long mobile take would seem to counter the idea that it is an attempt to contribute to the realism of the shot; the relatively large discs and arcs of digital flare bisect the entirety of the frame from two different angles, and in doing so noticeably obscure some of the frame's content. The lens flare operates as a layer in front of the fictional space, which combines with the camera's maintenance of a fixed distance from the digitally generated images to produce a distancing effect, a separation between the spectator and the city. The lens flare is what we might call a 'figure of separation' that isolates the spectator from these seemingly utopian city spaces, an estrangement and compartmentalisation that is then enacted by Anderton himself, as his body, already partially alienated by grief and addiction, is subsequently criminalised, and starts to lose its place in the city's official systems of human organisation. At the same time, the digitally generated artifice of the shot is foregrounded to emphasise the contingency of this celebratory perspective on the city, intensifying the sense – already in play as a result of the placement of this shot after our first discovery of the Sprawl and Anderton's drug addiction – that the smooth attractive surfaces of this city hide less attractive realities.[11]

These ideas are subsequently elaborated in sequences showing the city's detailed *mise-en-scène* up close. The movement from distanced views to proximity with the city's surfaces and the bodies of its citizens develops the notions of isolation, control and compartmentalisation that were hinted at in the analytical room's spatial arrangement. In the visual presentation of the modern zones of the city there is a prevalence of smooth surfaces and curved lines, a predominant softness of shape complemented by pale metallic hues that make surfaces and spaces appear light and airy. The city spaces of *Minority Report* where crowds move *look* attractive, an appearance of comfort and functionality created by technology and design, but as the subway, shopping mall and traffic network sequences attest, they channel people into designated spaces and predetermined routes – tunnels, walkways, motion controlled cars, uniform high-rise apartment blocks and cramped subways. The curves and soft edges of this technologised city point towards circularity and spatial enclosure; their very *seamlessness* (one of the often observed characteristics of digital photorealism) beginning to signify the impossibility of escape, physical entrapment and a denial of freedom of movement.

Henri Lefebvre's concept that social space is a social product, and is 'a means of control, and hence of domination, of power' (2007: 26) finds its illustration in these city structures. Within the film world, the city's spatial arrangement and its implicit control of the human flow enact a form of behavioural regulation that is further enhanced by digitally advanced surveillance technologies. Retinal scanners track individuals' movement everywhere through the city, in offices, shopping malls, streets, subway stations and even homes. The ubiquity of this technology is disturbingly conveyed in the sequences where mobile retinal scanners called 'spyders' penetrate the depths of the Sprawl's tenement blocks to interrupt a range of human activities (parenting, a marital argument, sex, defecation). People's behaviour in these scenes is notable: on the street they walk in a brisk, measured fashion, expressions blank as they pass without comment under retinal scanners that register their identity and location, and in private they submit their eyes to the scanners reluctantly but passively. Such body language suppresses more casual or carefree modes of movement and behaviour, implying that the very presence of the retinal scanners – and their ability to locate and track anyone identified as a trouble-maker or criminal – leads people to monitor their own actions, to 'police' themselves.[12] As Foucault found so fascinating in relation to Bentham's Panopticon, this mode of surveillance achieves conformity and regulation *in advance*. The function of the PreCrime Unit – to stop murders before they happen – becomes an analogy for how a range of other social and behavioural controls succeed. What becomes clear is that the apparent freedom of movement in the visually appealing spaces of this society is only made possible by adhering to invisible systems of control, and that these systems extend beyond the prevention of murders.

DIGITAL TECHNOLOGIES AND THE BODY

After being framed, Anderton tries to escape through the city, and his route takes him through a subway thoroughfare adorned with futuristic 'billboards'. Sumptuously coloured advertising holograms shimmer and curve around passers-by, marketing luxury purchases such as cars, holidays, and perfume. The holograms use retinal scanner technology to identify individuals in order to address personalised advertising messages to them. As Anderton passes, each hologram hails him loudly by name, thwarting his desire to remain discretely hidden in the crowd. The cheeriness of the advertising patter is in ironic contrast with Anderton's grave situation, while the alluring screens of the digital billboards mask not just advertising's own attempts to control future purchasing habits by selling 'too good to be true' fantasies, but the reality of the city's ubiquitous surveillance infrastructure, within which no citizen can hide.

The technologised city's surfaces and details may be visualised as stylish, expansive, efficient and visually seductive but like the digital 'plane' inserted into the spatial coordinates of the detection scenes, the film reveals that these are surfaces that register differently depending on one's position in relation to them. Anderton's body becomes the site at which this is most emphatically dramatised. Having been framed and 're-categorised' as a fugitive, but refusing to accede to his own arrest, Anderton interrupts the regulated flows and systems of Washington DC with his fugitive body, a process first visualised as a disruption of the digitally generated spectacle of the gleaming, attractive cityscape. As Anderton flees a police dragnet in his automobile, a 'security lockdown' forces his vehicle to automatically reverse its trajectory and return to the Department of PreCrime. The car is pulled away from the spectator into the distance in a wide angle composition that emphasises the inevitability of the enforced destination through a symmetrically arranged convergence of multiple perspective lines. Anderton kicks out the windscreen of the still-moving vehicle and clambers out onto its roof. For a moment, he is framed in a medium tracking shot, but suddenly the car slides downwards as the road becomes a vertical route down a skyscraper. The synthetic camera continues to film as the car disappears into the distance, producing a dramatic, canted aerial shot of the city road network, the regulated rhythms of the cars, and Anderton as he hangs onto his own car. Later a frontal shot depicts Anderton jumping from car to car across the vertical roadway; in both shots, the fully digitally generated backgrounds and rhythmic automated patterns of the car movements are contrasted with, and disrupted by, the writhing body of the actor. The human figure, inserted into this systematised digital vision, is a pronounced disturbance of the symmetry and 'digitality' of the image; Anderton's body functions as a striking visual indicator that he is 'out of synch' with the rest of the image's digital properties, as well as the fictional city systems they depict.

The opposition set up in the road escape sequence, between digital images and the body, is mapped onto the film's increasing concern with the impact of this society's systems on its inhabitants, extending the opposition into the fictional world as a contrast between the technologised city and its consequences for human beings.[13] A corresponding shift occurs in the film's visual presentation, as sequences of overt digital effects deployments are largely replaced by sequences focusing on the materiality and tactility of the body. The result is that the invasive impact of the city's technologies is repeatedly written across the body of the protagonist. Pursued by Danny Witwer (Colin Farrell)'s team of federal agents to a car factory's assembly line, Anderton finds himself trapped in the shell of a car that is being constructed by huge robotic assembly arms. A series of swinging, juddering camera movements into medium close-up from different directions makes clear the threat this automated machinery poses to Anderton's body, tracing each robotic movement as a cluster of metal arms thrust mechanical parts into the chassis: Anderton's head is almost smashed by the incoming engine block, his arm is nearly severed by the dashboard section, he is almost impaled as the steering column swings into place, and, as he tries to escape, the remaining car door pushes him back into the increasingly confined space of the car interior. As Anderton falls back, four spikes slam into the car floor around his head, ready to receive the seat unit that swoops down from above. The last thing we see is Anderton's horrified expression as the seat obliterates him from view. It is after a few long moments that we see him reappear, bloodied but intact, in the fully constructed Lexus automobile as it rolls off the production line.

Later, trying to circumvent the city's automated network of retinal scanners, Anderton undergoes a painful and risky black market eye transplant. In enforced convalescence, Anderton is told that taking off his eye bandages before twelve hours have passed will cause him to go blind. Before the allotted time has elapsed, PreCrime officers arrive to do a security sweep of the building, releasing small spider-shaped heat-seeking robots with built-in retinal scanners. The sequence cuts between views of Anderton, Steadicam shots tracking the bots' disconcertingly swift, smooth and unrelenting movements in extreme close-up, and an extended mobile aerial shot that probes each apartment in turn to reveal the speed and agility with which the 'spyders' insinuate themselves into all corners of the building. Anderton submerges himself for several minutes in freezing water, trying to lower his temperature to such a degree that the bots will not be able to detect his body's heat signature. Subtly shifting views frame the submerged fugitive in close-up, cutting in closer and closer on his still form. Anderton is not able to stop an air bubble escaping from his nose and breaking the surface of the bath water. The bots swarm to the bath's edge, sending electric shocks through the water to force him to the surface; when he emerges the camera frames Anderton in close-up as the spyders crowd round his head and continue to electrocute him. In an even closer framing, Anderton is forced to gingerly peel away the bandages around his head, and pulls back a swollen, scarred eyelid, gasping with discomfort, so that the bots can scan the retina of his new eye; a subsequent reverse field shot provides Anderton's point of view as a spyder's scanning mechanism fills the frame with piercing light. The extent of the reach of urban surveillance technologies into citizens' ostensibly private space is foregrounded through the aerial and Steadicam shots, culminating in the intrusive treatment of Anderton's body in the bathroom. His body becomes the site for a demonstration of the violent and painful consequences for those who seek to resist control. Physical action in the car factory has shifted to body horror here, but both sequences are strikingly overdetermined illustrations of the invasive potential of the city's technologisation.

Minority Report's generic hybridity is highly effective in helping to articulate both the social dystopia of the city and the predicament it constructs for the central protagonist. Dystopic conceptualisations of the future city are a familiar strand of science fiction cinema, but as Paul Schrader has argued, a similar 'fear of the future' (of urbanisation and its consequences) also drives film noir (1996: 58).[14] Just as the noir protagonist's body and mind are worked upon by paranoia-infused cityscapes in which acute physical violence can erupt without warning from any quarter, Anderton's contingent position in Washington DC's future cityscape becomes evident in his fugitive-on-the-run status and the resulting trials he must put his body through to survive and clear his name. If the 'mise-en-scène of *film noir* reinforced the vulnerability of its heroes' (Porfirio 1996: 85), here the machinery and structures of this technologised city are explicitly placed in an antagonistic relationship to Anderton's body. Even the kidnapping of his son, which renders Anderton psychologically unstable and vulnerable to being framed, takes place in a setting that speaks of the city's imposed urban planning and its negative effects. It is explicitly the over-crowding of this municipal swimming pool that allows the kidnapping to take place undetected, and prevents Anderton from being able to find his son, and anyone else there from being able to help him. In such ways the human cost of surveillance, condensed urban planning

Figure 2.2 Frame grab from *Minority Report* (20th Century Fox / Dreamworks): Anderton face to face with his memories in the home movies scene.

and the isolating effects of technology are brought to the surface, elaborated through diegetic and non-diegetic digital elements as well as non-digital elements. Such concerns are not simply expressed through Anderton's physical experiences but through his mental state, in particular his solitary existence and his grief for his lost son. A key scene in the film draws on figures of digitally mediated perception and spatial separation to elaborate the private ritual that characterises Anderton's grief.

HUMAN CONNECTIONS, DIGITAL SEPARATIONS

It is late at night and Anderton is in his apartment, reliving key home movies from his lost family life with son Sean (Dominic Scott Kay) and wife Lara (Kathryn Morris) while drugged up on 'Neuroin' (the fictional illegal narcotic he is addicted to). Judging by the Neuroin dispensers strewn around the projector controls, this is a regular occurrence. Close-ups show each of the projectors in the array that will holographically display the home movies, as they begin to cast coloured light into the room. The projection equipment throws a holographic projection of the home video footage into the space, directing light in order to construct a three-dimensional image that is viewable from Anderton's seated position in the room. The camera circles around Anderton to take up different positions in relation to the scene, and as it does so the holographic images acquire a hollowed out appearance, becoming a flattened, then a convex electronic surface, rather than the human presence that Anderton imagines and so desperately desires (see Fig. 2.2). Anderton physically flinches as the present absence of these absent presences is confirmed by the abrupt replacement of the moving images with a blank, mechanical 'end of file' notice, which protrudes forcefully into the space of the room to signal the end of the home video.

The scene clarifies the personal loss that Anderton has suffered, and his yearning for the family life that disappeared after his son's kidnapping. The film's established figure of digitally mediated perception here becomes a figure of separation, the holographic projection operating as the screen that marks out Anderton's temporal separation from his wife and son, despite the impression that they are sharing the same space. Notably the mobile camera divorces the spectator from optical alignment with Anderton's perspective on the image, and thus from his perceptual experience of the home videos. Through this mobile framing, the apparent solidity of the human figures is destroyed by a flattening out of the surfaces that initially constructed that illusion. The thematic emphasis on the way that shifts in position can change one's perspective on something intensifies the pathos of the scene's depiction of Anderton's psychological trauma at the disappearance of his son. But it is the inherent immateriality of digital images – the illusions they create and the celluloid technologies they seem to be replacing – that energise the scene's emotional centre. Morris (2007) sees *Minority Report* as brimming with self-reflexive metaphors for celluloid cinema, its cinematic apparatus, and projective spectatorial desire, and certainly the projection equipment (and by extension Anderton's projective desire) is marked for our notice in this scene. However, it is the relationship between digital images and celluloid cinema that is more pertinent here, celluloid cinema's apparatus nostalgically implied, but 'replaced' by the new technology of the digital image. The digital image's negative associations with flatness and unrealistic seamless perfection are also crucial.[15] Here the cinematic fallacy of depth perception and its material basis as a two-dimensional plane are laid bare, and the absence of the filmed body inherent in both the celluloid and digital moving image is made explicit. It is through the reflexive mode of the home movie scene's articulation that the filmmakers thus map celluloid cinema's lost moment of registration – what Walter Benjamin described as 'the immediacy of that long-past moment' (1972: 7) and Roland Barthes as 'the terrible thing which is there in every photograph, the return of the dead' (2000: 9) – onto Anderton's loss of his son and his desire to reanimate his relationship with him in the present. This figure of separation works across space and time as the brightly lit, smiling faces of Anderton's erstwhile family and Anderton's performances of reciprocal conversation take up a pathetic relation to the dark, silent emptiness of the apartment probed by the mobile camera.

Such figures of separation generate a sense of human isolation that pervades the film. Anderton's preference is for enclosed spaces and enclosing darkness (the circular analytical room that houses the detection wall, shrouded in semi-darkness when Anderton is in charge, but revealed as a well-lit space with transparent walls when Witwer uses it in Anderton's absence; Anderton's darkened apartment; his hooded jogs into the Sprawl). The urban *mise-en-scène* throws up other solitary spaces too: the Department of Containment, where future murderers are enclosed in claustrophobic tubes and forced to live with their own thoughts, and the pre-cogs' incarceration in the 'temple' pool which allows their pre-vision to be captured for police use. Even leaving the environs of the city seems less an escape but an exchange of one isolating location for another, as the voluntary seclusion of Anderton's wife Lara in what used to be their country summerhouse demonstrates. Each of these examples is a result of human loss, and so, while in part a warning of the potential for loneliness and separation in a compartmentalised, systematised, hi-tech future, at a deeper level this preponderance of disconnected persons dramatises a preoccupation with the secluding effects of human trauma and the need for human connection. In this context the nature of the film's persistent water imagery becomes resonant. Repeatedly re-enacting moments of submersion and drowning, the film invokes the suffocating effect of the enclosed, airless environment of water on the human body so that it can become a metaphor for the effect of psychological segregation on the human spirit.

Trauma and the necessity for connection energise the detective story that *Minority Report* tells, drawing from the opposition between genuine human contact and digitally mediated connection, and the concept of digitally mediated (and thus manipulable) perception, established by digital imaging deployments in the early part of the film. Anderton's inward-looking grief turns him away from the possibility that his mentor, and substitute father figure, Director Lamar Burgess might be corrupt, and blinds him to the PreCrime system's flaws. We learn at the end of the film that Agatha's mother Anne Lively (Jessica Harper) was drowned by Burgess so that her daughter could remain a pre-cog. It is Agatha's traumatic pre-vision of the murder – obsessively replaying on large and small digital screens throughout the film – that provides the key to revealing Lamar in his true light. The repeating image of the drowning woman functions as the unsolved mystery at the centre of the film, but is the catalyst for a human connection between Agatha and Anderton that will lead eventually to the revelation that the PreCrime system can never offer an objective view of the future, as well as identifying Lamar as the real killer of Lively and Witwer. Agatha and Anderton connect with each other as a result of their mirrored family losses, 'a powerful deep structure' in the film's narrative that consists of 'a four-way relationship between two parents (Anne Lively and John Anderton) and their lost children (Agatha and Sean)', as Buckland notes (2006: 207). A series of redemptive reconnections follows Agatha's initial reaching-out to Anderton: Anderton is reunited with his wife, and both are reconnected to the bright future their lost son would have had as Agatha, in a healing gesture, describes what his life would have been ('He's 23, he's at a university . . . he makes love to a pretty girl named Claire, he asks her to be his wife. He calls here and tells Lara who cries. He still runs across the university and in the stadium where John watches. . .'). As the film progresses, then, human emotional responses and interactions are privileged above the futuristic technologies that had seemed to offer the rationalist resolution to the detective narrative, and the characters' developing 'understanding of their mutual humanity' (Friedman 2006: 32) promises the capacity to overcome the figures of separation that have been imposed on society and the individual. Overt deployments of digital imaging technologies make way for scenes in which the proximate, feeling body becomes a reconnecting force without the need for digital intervention.

The film's ending seems to offer an unproblematically happy resolution of re-established human bonds. Anderton is shown in his apartment cupping the pregnant stomach of his reconciled wife, and his voice-over confirms the dismantlement of the PreCrime programme, its prisoners' release, and the relocation of the pre-cogs to an idyllic rural cottage. As Anderton explains that the pre-cogs have been 'transferred to an undisclosed location . . . a place where they could find relief from their gifts', each pre-cog is shown wrapped in warm, casual clothing that speaks of comfort and relaxation, sampling from piles of books which indicate their reinvigorated intellectual life. Here the pastoral setting, the absence of readable digital imaging or of instances of diegetic digital equipment appears to ground the film's implicit assertion that technology's dehumanising hold over its protagonists has been broken. Several reviewers criticised what they saw as a 'saccharine' ending 'typical of Spielberg' (McDonald 2003: para. 8), while others noted its incongruity: Leslie Felperin commented, for example, that the fact that 'the film's conclusion tries to smooth things over with the reconstitution of two triadic families . . . barely alleviates the latent traumas we've seen hitherto' (2002: 44). In my view it seems likely – as Felperin's review comes close to suggesting – that the film adopts the Sirkian strategy of mobilising 'a cloud of over-determined irreconcilables which put up a resistance to being neatly settled in the last five minutes' (Mulvey 1977/8: 54). Early in the film, the rationalist resolution of the traditional detective narrative was shown to be an illusion. In a similar fashion, the shots of Anderton and Lara and of the pre-cogs in their cottage qualify the voice-over's attempt to impose an ordered, positive ending. The Anderton couple are in their old apartment, and thus emphatically re-embedded in a compartmentalised urban regime. In stark contrast to the light, airy décor of the spacious summer house, the apartment is dark and sombre, and overrun with plants that recall the remote walled garden of Dr Hineman (Lois Smith) and the hostile, poisonous vines that almost kill Anderton on his visit there. Heavy rain is pouring down the apartment windows, and as the couple embrace in close-up, the shadows of rain channels mark both their faces, a reference back to the watery figure of digitally mediated perception present in the logo sequences. The *mise-en-scène* seems purposefully designed to invoke the visual tropes of film noir evident earlier in the film, rather than establishing more optimistic frames of reference.

The extended long take that cranes out from the pre-cogs' cottage initially appears to offer a much more positive perspective, the warm, natural hues of the décor a contrast to the dark interior of Anderton's city apartment. However, Agatha sits separately from Dashiell and Arthur, and as she reads she holds aloft a small disc on a string, within which swirl the digital images of her mother's drowning. The camera holds this talisman of Agatha's grief, a digital artifact, in the dead centre of the frame for a number of seconds. The inclusion of an explicit digital presence, a digital screen that in the rest of the film operates persistently as a figure of digitally mediated perception and spatial separation, interrupts the bucolic scene with renewed connotations of loss. These associations are strengthened as the final shot of the cottage develops. Keeping the digital screen at the centre of the frame, the camera tracks backwards out of the window and continues to retreat for a remarkable two minutes and eleven seconds, putting huge distance between the cottage's inhabitants and the spectator, and revealing that the cottage is highly remote, cut off from civilisation by both spatial distance and large stretches water that surround it.

The final image, then, is not so much one of peaceful seclusion but rather utter isolation, and a return to the motif of enclosure by water and the figure of separation that have haunted the film and dogged its characters. Buckland points out that the script 'leaves open the possibility that the two traumatised characters could overcome each other's loss, with Anderton acting as a substitute parent for Agatha, and Agatha acting as substitute child for Anderton', but the film does not complete this connective trajectory (2006: 207). Each time Agatha had previously thrown images of her mother's drowning onto a digital screen in the film (in the pre-cog chamber and in the Cyber-Parlor), it had drawn her together with John; literally, as she pulled him physically towards her, and metaphorically, as her question 'Can you see?' persuaded him to investigate the connections between their personal circumstances in order to solve the mystery of his framing. Such moments were an invitation to Anderton to shift his perspective, to dig into the circumstances of the construction of this pre-vision, and to join with Agatha in order to achieve this. This bore an analogous relationship to the film's own strategic presentation of figures of digitally mediated perception, which qualified the contexts within which they were embedded by drawing attention to the difference a shift in perspective (literal or figurative) could make. Agatha's pre-vision, one of the film's central figures of digitally mediated perception, reappears here in a new context, from a new perspective, as it were. Because the two mysteries, the drowning and the framing, have been solved, John is no longer present to witness the pre-vision, an absence that confirms Agatha's lack of human connection with the outside world. No longer a 'Jane Doe', the woman in the pre-vision has now been identified as Agatha's murdered mother, and yet this more 'accurate', informed perspective cannot resolve or bring to an end the loss Agatha has experienced. This is symbolised by the talisman's cyclical repetition of the drowning sequence, and also by Agatha's attention to it here, holding it aloft, looking at it and caressing it. In combining this emblem of bereavement with a backwards camera movement that soon dwarfs not just Agatha and the cottage but the island as well, the film literalises the withdrawal of human contact that the pre-cogs continue to suffer even as the PreCrime Unit is dismantled. The shot's first phase is preoccupied with its overt digital artifact, while its second phase is an emphatic spatial distancing from the artifact and its owner. Thus the final shot is a resonant visual articulation of a human alienation that cannot be fully eradicated, an expression of Anderton's failure to follow through on the human connection begun by Agatha, and a sombre conclusion indeed.[16]

Minority Report's most explicit digital deployments – its obscuring digital layers and diegetic digital screens – do not simply allow the film to explore the potential impacts of further technologisation on contemporary society. As this chapter's discussion has argued, they enable and elaborate its profound thematic concern with knowledge, perception, and alienation in complex and sophisticated ways. The next chapter demonstrates that the digital's contribution to meaning is no less complex when the central protagonist is digitally generated.

NOTES

1. This type of alteration is often the case with more recent mainstream releases such as *The Day After Tomorrow* (Roland Emmerich, 2004), *Live Free or Die Hard*, *Beowulf* (Robert Zemeckis, 2007) and so on, as well as being true of earlier films such as the sepia-toned Columbia Pictures logo at the beginning of *The Age of Innocence* (Martin Scorsese, 1993).
2. The film's look is achieved using Technicolor's laboratory bleach bypass process. See Holben 2002: 35.
3. In the DreamWorks sequence when the fishing line hits the water it produces a visual clash of extra-diegetic and diegetic ripple effects that awkwardly signals that the two notional stretches of water occupy separate space-times, a decision that increases the forcefulness with which the presence of the digital layer registers.
4. Film noir's visual and narrative tropes are highly significant to the generic shape *Minority Report* takes, as I will explain below. The reader is referred to Warren Buckland's skilful and insightful account of the film's generic hybridity; a rewarding essay despite the fact that film noir is not mentioned explicitly (2006: 193–7).
5. This is self-consciously acknowledged in the film itself through the naming of the pre-cogs as Arthur (as in Conan Doyle), Dash (as in Dashiell Hammett) and Agatha (as in Christie).
6. These so-called 'time remapping' techniques became very popular in movies, television advertising and music videos around the time of *Minority Report*'s release, so much so

that they are now available 'off the shelf' in Final Cut Pro, Adobe After Effects and Adobe Premier software releases. See Paar 2008: para. 1.

7. The film plays on this notion by calling the newest brand of 'Neuroin', drug of choice for addicts in this future city, 'Clarity'.

8. Such spectacles of technologised interfacing are common to science fiction cinema, but the interface is often valorised in highly qualified terms (the opaque interface in *The Matrix* (Andy and Larry Wachowski, 1999), the controlling interface in *2001: Space Odyssey* (Stanley Kubrick, 1968), the interface that absorbs the human in *Tron* (Steven Lisberger, 1982), or threatens to overwhelm the brain in *Johnny Mnemonic* (Robert Longo, 1995).

9. The phrase is used in the film to denote making the image clearer or more distinct by removing unwanted image elements.

10. Just like Anderton's use of the detection wall, the PreCrime advertisement elides the uncertain basis of the PreCrime process, instead presenting an overwhelmingly positive account of the process's accuracy and success (almost-victims declare 'They were waiting for me in the car,' 'I was going to be stabbed' and 'PreCrime – it works!').

11. The film's cityscapes invoke *Metropolis* (Fritz Lang, 1927); like *Minority Report*, the earlier film's city vistas are triumphs of special effects work, exhibitionist illusions deployed in a narrative similarly concerned with the future city's darker aspects and how they shape social hierarchies and citizens' experiences.

12. The city's systems of surveillance work on the citizen in a manner strikingly similar to Bentham's Panopticon, in which, Foucault observes, 'He who is subjected to a field of visibility, and who knows it, assumes responsibility for the constraints of power; he makes them play spontaneously upon himself; he inscribes in himself the power relation in which he simultaneously plays both roles; he becomes the principle of his own subjection' (1991: 203).

13. In this way the film displays anxieties about the processes of technologisation on contemporary society, particularly the advent of the notion of 'surveillance culture' that circulated in US and UK culture from the mid-1990s onwards.

14. Science fiction dystopias include *Metropolis*, *Fahrenheit 451* (François Truffaut, 1966), *Soylent Green* (Richard Fleischer, 1973), *Blade Runner*, *Brazil* (Terry Gilliam, 1985), *Total Recall* (Paul Verhoeven, 1990), and *Gattaca* (Andrew Niccol, 1997).

15. Such negative associations emerged in the early 1990s, before digital imaging technologies were able to replicate depth of field accurately and before the inherent seamlessness of the computer generated image was disrupted by the insertion of artifacts which mimicked the imperfections of photochemical photography, like motion- and distance-blur, lens distortion, and so on. This resulted in images that looked too 'flat' as well as too seamless, too 'clean'.

16. The shot itself is a feat of digital compositing, as the interior of the cottage is combined with separate footage of the exterior and its environs. However, this digital element lacks a metaphorical function due to the fact that its digital-ness is hidden. The shot's visual reference to the ending of Andrei Tarkovsky's *Solaris* (1972) underlines my conclusion here. Rather than a simple homage to Tarkovsky, the reference to the earlier film is an additional way in which positive readings of the long tracking shot are radically undercut. In *Solaris* the central protagonist, who has been plagued by a manifestation of his dead wife while living on a space station orbiting a mysterious planet, is shown in the final moments of the film reuniting with his father at their family home on Earth. But as the camera pulls back, the family home is revealed to be a 'copy' on an island in the middle of the Solaris planet's ocean. The reunion is an illusion; the protagonist remains separated from Earth and from human contact with his loved ones, a situation with a direct, rich correlation to the pre-cogs' new circumstances in *Minority Report*.

CHAPTER 3

Digital Imaging and the Body

A film's protagonist, the 'figure in a landscape' that commands our attention, is now more than ever likely to be shaped in some way by digital imaging. Analogue and digital processes co-exist across production and post-production phases to manipulate the profilmic body's appearance, through make-up, costume, or prosthetics of either practical (that is, profilmic) or digital origin, while the profilmic body can also be digitally substituted either temporarily or permanently with a virtual body. At the same time, as we saw in *Minority Report* and the other films we have already looked at, the presence of digital artifacts within the frame renders the protagonist's body as just one element of an often complexly digitally composited image, so that the body's relationship to the space of action is controlled by the vision and skill of digital compositors, visual effects supervisors and other digital imaging specialists as well as by the director, cinematographer and editor. I have argued that our encounter with the digital in popular cinema is inevitably coloured by our extra-textual digital literacy, and this is equally true of computer generated screen bodies, around which some of the most intense debate about technological realisation and artistic worth seems to cluster. This chapter speculates on how we might read bodies in cinema of the digital era, focusing primarily on the fully computer generated body, or 'digital body'. The chapter ends with some thoughts about how digital compositing stages the body, which lay the foundation for the consideration in Chapters 4 and 5 of how body-centred digital elements might press on the wider task of interpretation.

WATCHING THE DIGITAL BODY

In 2009, *Avatar* (James Cameron) included multiple scenes involving ensemble performances from computer generated beings called the 'Na'vi'; two years later *Rise of the Planet of the Apes* (Rupert Wyatt, 2011) featured not just one computer generated ape as a central character communicating with humans, but groups of digital apes communicating with each other, and scores running rough-shod through buildings, over parked cars and bridges. These films offer a succinct illustration of the fact that, in just over a decade, the digital body has become relatively ubiquitous in mainstream Hollywood cinema. Moreover, we have not arrived at the synthespian endgame that some commentators predicted, the quasi-mythical conception that emerged in the 1990s of a computer generated actor that could perform human-ness so convincingly and completely that real actors would no longer be needed. Instead the digital bodies on our screens still use profilmic human performances in their construction. They combine digital animation with the filming of profilmic face and/or body movements using cameras and bespoke software to track markers that the actor wears on his or her body, a process called performance capture. And they find their place alongside other digital or live action elements through digital compositing.

Despite their proliferation, these digital bodies are still emphatically promoted as *special* effects, and 'making of' featurettes and trade and popular press testimony from visual effects supervisors, actors and directors provide accounts of the construction of the digital body that work hard to appeal to moviegoers' curiosity and cinephilia. For example, a promotional video about the special effects in *Rise of the Planet of the Apes* shows detailed footage of the exterior motion capture shoots for the film that contributed to the finished digital apes, but also features celebratory interviews with the director and various people from visual effects house Weta Digital. The sound bites offered are revealing. Senior Visual Effects Supervisor Joe Letteri (Weta Digital) notes, 'It would have been impossible to do this movie a few years ago'; director Rupert Wyatt says, 'we were attempting to do something that had never been done before'; on location an actor tells us, 'This is the largest mo-cap volume in the world and the first time it's been done outside, so Weta is basically changing all the rules of motion capture'; and Wyatt returns at the end of the video to say 'We are breaking very new ground here.' Such testimony repeatedly reiterates the specialness, newness and advanced, cutting-edge nature of the technological solutions being used.[1] Posted on YouTube to coincide with the film's US theatrical release, the video promises that the film will deliver the fleeting novelty of the cinematic experience of these effects, and the corresponding sense of audience connoisseurship that comes from witnessing the state of the art from a position of partial insight.

If special effects retain their specialness for the purposes of marketing, the most intense attention is encouraged around the digital body, which is presented *as* a special effect. This seems partly due to the fact that, in its current manifestation, the digital body functions to curate, as it were, a demonstrative human contribution to a CGI-filled frame through the use of performance capture technology. Promotional discourse from studios, actors, directors and the media commentators that frame their contributions frequently present the human performer behind the performance capture as the not-so-secret ingredient which makes the difference between successful and unsuccessful digital protagonists. The *Rise of the Planet of the Apes* 'Making of' video is a good example of this, spending a large proportion of its time focusing on the motion capture and facial capture processes, and matching Andy Serkis's performance to that of the central digital character, Caesar, while concept art, creature/texture, modelling, shaders and shots departments get barely a few seconds of coverage in total. Sound bites underscore the importance of the human input: Letteri emphatically states 'This film is not possible without the work of Andy Serkis'; Wyatt describes Serkis's ability to '*push the technology to one side* and think about it in terms of just a real live action performance' (emphasis added); and Serkis himself says the onscreen apes will be 'infused with the heart and soul of an actor's performance'. Supporting such claims in this and other films are a plethora of studio-issued, side-by-side stills of the profilmic actor captured in the moment of performance for face or motion capture alongside a shot of the finished face or body in the same pose, stills which have circulated around the release of the *Lord of the Rings* franchise (Peter Jackson, 2001, 2002, 2003), *King Kong* (Peter Jackson, 2005), *Avatar*, and *Rise of the Planet of the Apes* among others.[2] There are also persistent calls from co-stars, directors and studio executives for these performance capture 'star turns' to be considered in the acting categories of the Academy Awards, requests commonly based on the argument that the digital imaging work involved represents little more than the digital equivalent of a practical prosthesis or make-up.[3]

The focus on finding the human in these digital bodies is not surprising when one considers that the synthespian had, by the 1990s and 2000s, become a contemporary 'Frankenstein myth' which embodied 'our own fear of replication and obsolescence, our replacement by digital constructs capable of outstripping our every capability and nuance' (North 2008: 155).[4] Motion capture offers a way to disavow such fears because it allows the technological process to be conceptually minimised in favour of a visible form of performance creation in which the human contribution is highly legible, via the paratextual footage of actors emoting and gesturing expressively in special suits and camera head rigs. Ironically this does not just elide the extensive role digital technologies play in constructing the final digital body's performance, but also another (much less visible) kind of human contribution: the large teams of visual effects artists that control and implement those processes of technological construction and transformation once the performance capture has taken place.[5] As Scott Balcerzak points out in his analysis of Serkis's contribution to Kong's characterisation in *King Kong*, the realities of how performance capture data is *actually* used by visual effects teams is rather different than its common portrayal. The information extracted from the performance capture process is a 'marker cloud', an abstraction of the actor's movements, and at each moment of the film is only ever used if it works with the other elements in the frame or scene (2009: 203, 201). Advances in the quantity and detail of data that can be seized in performance capture, and the more flexible conditions under which the process can be carried out (exterior locations, larger numbers of actors, and so on), do not change the fact that the alterations and additions made by the digital effects teams *post* performance capture are wide-ranging. Kristin Thompson offers a compelling illustration of this in a recent blog post, which compared the digital bodies and their 'performances' in the finished version of *Avatar* with the very side-by-side images of performers and digital bodies issued by the studios to promote the centrality of profilmic performance (2010). Thompson argues that the considerable alterations and additions she identifies are fundamental to the characterisation that ends up on the screen. Following his own analysis of performance capture, Balcerzak is moved to conclude, 'the technology is not about a digitisation of the human, but the humanisation of the digital through the addition of supposedly real movement. It is a process developed to make the special effect perform realistically as opposed to, as suggested by many, digitally enhance the actor' (2009: 196). It is more accurate, then, to reverse the prioritisation of human and technology proposed in the promotional discourse that swirls around performance capture.

There is no doubt that the paratextual materials I have described prime the spectator to 'view the film as a self-contained story and a technological performance simultaneously' (North 2008: 170). But with the digital body onscreen for as much time as any central protagonist played by a profilmic actor, duration puts a certain pressure on the term 'special effect'. If the desire to see the 'trick' performed gets us into the movie theatre, it is not really what keeps us there. To put it somewhat crudely, we may arrive wanting spectacle but we also want story, as the recurrent press refrain that CGI movies lack decent scripts attests. Murray Smith argues that 'human agency has a centrality to our comprehension of narratives', and this applies even in narratives about 'non-human agents (animals, inanimate objects, abstract concepts, social forces, natural forces, deities)' where our comprehension is 'modelled on our understanding of humans to a large degree' (Smith 1995: 20). In films like *Avatar*, *King Kong*, and *Rise of the Planet of the Apes*, the digital body takes the place of the human agent, and must therefore take its place within the film world, embedded in the narrative flow. I want to look at some relatively early digital bodies and their critical reception as a case study to illuminate aspects of the relationship between digital imaging workflows, narrative and meaning production, aspects which still hold true in the construction and reception of digital bodies today.

VISUAL ARTICULATION AND CHARACTERISATION

The early 2000s represented a period in which fully or partially digitally animated bodies became more common, as action-fantasy films and the returning superhero movie cycle, amongst other genres, took advantage of developments in computer generated imaging and digital compositing to manifest impossible bodies in fantastical situations, in productions like *Hulk* (Ang Lee, 2003), *Spider-Man* (Sam Raimi, 2002) and *Spider-Man 2* (Sam Raimi, 2004), the initial *X-Men* films (Bryan Singer, 2000, 2003), the *Matrix* sequels (Wachowskis, 2003), and the *Lord of the Rings* trilogy (Peter Jackson, 2001, 2002, 2003). Each of these digital bodies were realised using a combination of performance capture, digital key frame animation,[6] and digital compositing, but some were received more positively than others. Digital stunt doubles were used for extended periods in the action sequences of the first two *Spider-Man* films, composited with real and computer generated camera footage that emulated the virtual Spider-Man's airborne trajectory through the city. These web slinging and wall crawling sequences were singled out for criticism by reviewers such as Roger Ebert, who suggested that they 'zip along like perfunctory cartoons. Not even during Spidey's first experimental outings do we feel that flesh and blood are contending with gravity' (2002: para. 1). Despite *Spider-Man 2* showcasing a digital hero with a more advanced skeleton and musculature in comparison to the first film,[7] critics remained 'not entirely convinced by the CGI Spidey' (Kermode 2004: para. 15, see also Bernadelli 2004: para. 7). In *Hulk* the digital body was onscreen for longer periods, appearing whenever scientist Bruce Banner (Eric Bana) was transformed by rage into his unstable, giant green alter ego (see Fig. 3.1). This virtual Hulk had to interact emotionally and physically in complex ways with live actors and with real-world environments, and promotional materials emphasised the filmmakers' desire to create a computer-animated being you could 'invest your emotions into'.[8] However, critics panned the Hulk's technical realisation: A. O. Scott in *The New York Times* denigrated what he called 'clumsy, ugly special effects', suggesting that the Hulk was 'more like clay animation' than CGI (2003: para. 11), while Geoffrey O'Brien in *Film Comment* complained that the Hulk's bouncing movements in a desert chase sequence brought to mind the children's computer game *Donkey Kong* (2003: 30). No such qualms greeted the figure of Gollum, who appeared in fully realised form in *The Lord of the Rings: The Two Towers* (2002). Like in *Hulk*, the computer generation of the Gollum character in *Lord of the Rings* combined motion capture and key frame animation to render not just physical motion but a nuanced emotional 'performance' via complex gestures and facial expressions (see Fig. 3.2). *Variety*'s Todd McCarthy praised 'dextrous' CGI and described Gollum as 'a startling creation that constitutes one of the film's major talking points' (2002: para. 4),

Figure 3.1 Still from *Hulk* (Universal / Marvel Entertainment / The Kobal Collection): The digital Hulk rampages through the city.

while *Salon.com*'s Charles Taylor eulogised, 'We are both repelled by Gollum and moved to compassion. There wasn't a second he was on-screen when I felt I could take my eyes off him. He is the most amazing of this installment's wonders' (2002: para. 10). Why such different reactions to characters that had been generated using broadly the same processes?

Here I want to extend further the study's account of photorealism, begun in the Introduction and developed in Chapter 1, since in my view it is directly relevant to the reception of these digitally constructed bodies. The reviewers' comments assert a binary opposition in which 'bad' digitally produced bodies are those which replicate cartoons', children's video games' and the animation tradition's traditionally highly elastic relationship to our everyday visual experience of reality. What is at stake in how this opposition between 'good' and 'bad' digital bodies is expressed? What do these comments reveal about what constitutes an unsuccessful or an effective digital body, and how do we read the digital's impact on the body? Each of the alternative media mentioned

Figure 3.2 Still from *The Lord of the Rings: The Return of the King* (New Line Cinema / The Kobal Collection): Gollum with hobbits Frodo and Sam.

by reviewers – animation, cartoons, video games – have historically interrogated, challenged or set aside the indexical relationship between photographed image and profilmic object. As I suggested in the Introduction, even though the presence of the digital seems to overturn that claim to indexicality more incontrovertibly than ever, what persists is the principle of measuring verisimilitude (believability) in terms of the extent to which the image *looks* as if it has been photographed by a real camera. So could the issue with the digital Hulk and Spider-Man be a lack of photorealism? Photorealism can be generated by the in-camera or digital addition of celluloid image artifacts, such as film grain, reel changeover cues, or the lens flare I identified in *Minority Report* which finds its way into other films, like the *Transformers* franchise (Michael Bay, 2007, 2009, 2011), *Star Trek* and *Super 8*, artifacts which spatially situate bodies and objects in front of the (real or notional) camera lens. But photorealism does not *depend* on the inclusion of these artifacts: its 'performance of "photographicness"', to repeat North's suggestive phrase (2008: 12), is better seen as a *continuum* between an over-abundance of these explicit 'cues' of photographicness and an image whose qualities are only loosely based on the photographic. Stephen Prince gives the example of a shot in *True Lies* (James Cameron, 1994) which digitally composites 'a mansion from Newport, Rhode Island, water shot in Nevada and a digital matte painting of the Alps'. The shot seems believable, but is 'unnaturally luminant', the lighting states in the different sections of the shot failing to represent what a real landscape would look if it were photographed rather than digitally composited (2002: 119). We might also think of films like *Speed Racer* (Andy and Lana Wachowski, 2008) or *Alice in Wonderland* (Tim Burton, 2010) as examples where a highly stylised colour palette and an emphasis on certain kinds of textural detail is prioritised above a much more loosely defined photographicness.

If photorealism is, then, a continuum between looser and more strident performances of photographicness, why do reviewers baulk at what they imply is the lesser photorealism of the Hulk and Spider-Man bodies, particularly when both films exist within the same cluster of fantasy genres as *Speed Racer* and *Alice in Wonderland?* The answer is that this is not simply a question of how a film's genre might shape its chosen mode of photorealism, but how consistently that mode of photorealism is maintained. Within any image sequence, we expect different orders of images (digital, analogue) and different objects (bodies, props, setting) within the frame to share the same level of photorealism, to complete the illusion that all are part of a spatially and temporally continuous event playing out in front of the camera. This is not just a case of making sure that the 'joins' between different image elements do not show: they also need to be constructed or digitally painted so that they adequately 'perform' sharing the same space; the same lighting conditions, the same type and level of response to environmental forces like wind, water, impacts and so on. In *Alice in Wonderland* and *Speed Racer* the settings are a dream world (or some kind of parallel universe) and a future-distant fictional environment respectively; as such, their norms of photorealism are permitted to diverge somewhat from a precise simulation of photographed reality. But importantly once these norms are established, they are consistent across shots and sequences. *Hulk* and *Spider-Man* involve fantastical heroes transplanted into a contemporary urban environment readily recognisable to city-dwelling audiences. As a result the norms of photorealism must correspond much more closely to that of everyday reality, or our experience of it as mediated photographically through news coverage, film and television, city webcams and personal cameras. The digital bodies in question need to be appropriately manipulated (painted, animated, composited) in order to adequately complete the illusion that they are physically occupying the same quotidian environment as the citizens, buildings and vehicles that surround them, and the norms of photorealism need to be adhered to consistently within shots and image sequences. The language used by the reviewers quoted above indicate that this consistency between elements within shots was not always achieved in *Hulk* and *Spider-Man*; in fact that the digital body interrupted the level of photorealism that had been established by the scene that framed it. For example, the mention of 'clay animation' in relation to the Hulk suggests that his physical surfaces have the texture of inanimate clay rather than the real skin displayed by the human characters around him, while Spider-Man's appearance and movement is described in terms of two-dimensional cartoons, in the context of an urban setting that is strongly asserted as a photorealistic version of contemporary New York.[9]

The comments about the cartoon nature of Spider-Man's actions and the Hulk's bouncing trajectory across the desert also reveal a concern in the reviewers' responses with the veracity of physical *movement*. Motion helps anchor the fictional three-dimensionality of a film's diegesis, including the volume of objects and spaces within the frame, and demonstrates the mass and structural integrity of onscreen bodies and objects. When Ebert complains 'Not even during Spidey's first experimental outings do we feel that flesh and blood are contending with gravity', he is not just alleging a lack of consistent photorealism within the image, but is identifying a mismatch between his experience of how physical forces, physiology and surfaces (in motion) work in the real world, and how the film tries to replicate these through the digital Spider-Man's interactions. Stephen Prince's theory of correspondences helps account for what underlies Ebert's indignation. Prince argues that when the spectator looks at a cinematic representation, whether profilmic or digitally generated, she checks that the image 'structurally corresponds to the viewer's audio-visual experience of three-dimensional space'.[10] As a result, images striving for perceptual realism will 'display a nested hierarchy of cues which organize the display of light, color, texture, movement, and sound in ways that correspond with the viewer's own understanding of these phenomena in daily life' (2002: 121). By virtue of the fact that human interaction and human/ object interaction are central facets of that everyday audio-visual experience, the hierarchy of cues must also involve the onscreen body. Particular digital imaging challenges pertain to constructing the digital body so that it displays these correspondences that spectators are looking for. Visual effects artists are tasked not simply with designing a digital skeleton and muscular struc- tures of sufficient complexity, but with the animation of their parameters for movement so that they convey not only particular actions or gestures but a convincing sense of body mass as well. Ebert would likely argue that the appropriate levels and types of correspondence in this area were not achieved in *Spider-Man*; Barbara Flückiger notes that the Na'vi figures in *Avatar* are afflicted with similar difficulties, brought on by the decision to make them much taller than humans: since 'the pattern of movement changes in relation to age, height and, most significantly, mass' the Na'vi 'often seem too light, and it is immensely difficult to perceive their height correctly if no human characters are present for comparison' (2011: 19). It seems clear that the Hulk, with his inflated stature, suffers some of the same problems: the lack of refer- ence against which to measure his size was particularly damaging in the pil- loried desert scenes. Equally, the animation of the surfaces of a moving body need to correspond with our experience of how garments and skin respond to movement in the real world. Visual effects supervisor John Dykstra argues that 'there is a huge amount of artistry involved in making cloth work', with at least two or three different types of digital imaging software needed and, in the case of *Spider-Man 2*, multiple different simulations required, which were then blended together to create the finished look in each scene (in Wolff 2004: 2). Skin is even more challenging, because of its natural translucence. As Barbara Flückiger notes, 'Light rays penetrate the surface of the skin into its deeper layers, where they are scattered in a complex way and acquire the color values of the bodily tissue and blood vessels.' If the digital imaging strategy does not include simulating this subsurface scattering, 'the skin looks like plaster' (2011: 12). Here then the criticism that the Hulk's body looks like 'clay anima-tion' takes on an additional dimension: for A. O. Scott at least, the visual and physical texture of his skin simply does not correspond sufficiently effectively to our real-world experience.

There is an additional correspondence, to use Prince's term, that is crucial to our positive reception of the digital body as central protagonist, so crucial in fact that it has already been introduced in this chapter. Earlier I drew on Murray Smith's work to argue that the digital protagonist must simulate the possession of human or human-like agency, in order to engage the audi-ence in the narrative. What I want to do here is unpick a little further what this involves in terms of the construction of the digital body. What does this correspondence with our experience of human agency involve? The approxi-mation of the complexity of human communication is one part of the task. Since 'our perception of the body language of other people and our ability to model the minds of others have been all-important for our survival and social life' (Grodal 2009: 12), we are consequently highly skilled at decoding minute nuances in body language and facial expression. It is a necessary but also necessarily huge challenge for visual effects artists to attempt to replicate sufficient of this myriad detail to correlate comfortably to our daily experience of human interaction (Flückiger 2010: 18). One might imagine that this allows us to argue once again for the primacy of a real human's contribution to this challenge. But as our earlier discussion about the highly technologically medi-ated integration of performance capture footage suggested, the contribution of an actor, regardless of whether talented or highly experienced in performance capture, cannot guarantee whether the digital body's performance of emotion and nuanced human (or human-like) interaction corresponds sufficiently to our real-world experience. In fact, it would be erroneous to suggest it is any *specific* aspect of the construction of the digital body that is singularly responsi-ble. This is because of the way in which we assess the presence of personhood.

Murray Smith suggests that in order to perceive and relate to an onscreen body as a human agent, as a *person* (or, in the case of films like *King Kong* and *Hulk*, the anthropomorphised or humanoid equivalent), that body has to fulfil certain basic requirements, which include the demonstrable possession of per-ceptual activity, beliefs and desires, emotions, and the capacity for language (1995: 21). Smith calls this the 'person schema', and at the top of the list of requirements is 'a discrete human body, individuated and continuous through time and space' (ibid.). In the context of a film featuring a digital body, the achievement of this corporeal discrete-ness and spatiotemporal continuity is a matter of digital technology: the careful melding of profilmic and digital image data by digital animation and digital compositing. Flückiger gives some sense of the technical complexity of this process of constructing what she calls 'character consistency':

> To build such a consistent schema in CGI, a multitude of fragmented features must be integrated into a super-ordinate structure during modeling and animation . . . both appearance – involving shape and surface characteristics – and behavior are often created separately through divided processes. But if the characteristics of appearance and behavior disintegrate into their components with no plausible connections between them, no unified character possessing individual traits will result. It becomes difficult to attain the audience's emotional participation. (2010: 20–1)

For a digital body to 'correspond' as a credible, individualised agent within the diegesis and the narrative, all aspects of that body's realisation must achieve a consistent level of correspondence with real-world experience. To take a crude example, a convincing facial performance is worthless if the digital compositing fails to locate the rest of the body in the same space and time as the face. The segmented, compartmentalised nature of such films' visual effects, production and post-production workflows – to which we can add the myriad intuitive, subjective judgments from animators, painters and compositors to the director and producers that assess whether any aspect 'looks right' – problematises the straightforward achievement of that goal. The consequences of these highly compartmentalised and fragmented processes, of characterisation 'by committee', to use Balcerzak's phrase, are unpredictable, as are the nature and levels of character *in*consistency that can be tolerated by audiences. The conundrum with which this section began – why Gollum was celebrated as a compelling, credible character, and the Hulk dismissed as 'ugly, clumsy special effects' – offers an opportunity to explore a little further the intersection between these factors.

Hulk's flashbacks and initial dialogue scenes reveal a central protagonist, scientist Bruce Banner, who is fundamentally split: his calm, inexpressive exterior (registered as abnormal by both his mother and his ex-girlfriend) masks internalised childhood trauma and suppressed emotions that are constantly threatening to literally break out when he loses control. The film thus establishes early that its central concern is with the emotional dimensions of the Banner/Hulk narrative, rather than the super-powers of the Hulk alter ego. Most action scenes are in the service of Banner/Hulk's psychological journey: Hulk's trashing of buildings and smashing of tanks and helicopters are primarily expressive of his internal battles rather than those with external foes, and the film's final face-off is a confrontation between Banner/Hulk and the despotic father responsible for his traumatised condition, rather than the corporate villain who wants to steal Banner's research. Action sequences and the broader narrative flow are paused to provide sequences at which the Hulk face is presented in close-up and often in contemplation, allowing access to the detail of his facial expressions, and inviting us to reflect on his interiority as he struggles to understand his own emotions. Director Ang Lee was so concerned to ensure the emotional fidelity of such moments that he insisted on performing key scenes as the Hulk himself during the performance capture stage (body suit, markers and all).[11] The combination of performance capture data and key frame animation in the finished film generates gestures and countenances that clearly seek to reference norms of human communication (anger, fear, confusion and other familiar states are readable in the Hulk's features). But other elements of the Hulk's construction and staging as a digital body do not correlate as directly to everyday human experience. If the narrative set-up's patterns of displacement, internalisation, and hidden family-derived trauma reveal *Hulk*'s debt to classical Hollywood melodrama, that melodrama's externalisation of heightened emotional states[12] finds its corollary in the visual strategies Lee selects to express the Hulk's internal struggle between rationality and irrepressible rage. By design, the Hulk changes 'in size and color throughout the film as he reflects [alter-ego] Banner's disposition and internal chemistry' (Williams 2003: para. 5). As a result, the Hulk's expressions may be recognisable, but his lack of stable physical structure is not. Instability and exaggeration also infect the frame itself, as traditional scene and shot transitions are replaced with restless dissolves, wipes and various imaginative manifestations of split-screen, and as correlations to Newtonian physics are left behind in stylised action sequences that nod towards surrealism. Different elements of film design are thus in tension: the tasks of communicating emotional realism, a sense of physical instability, and a variably non-naturalistic aesthetic pull in opposing directions, occasionally directing unwelcome attention to a moment of unevenness in the Hulk's digital construction, but more frequently and importantly, failing to achieve often enough the material consistency and aesthetic coherence that the person schema demands. It seems likely that the decision to articulate the Hulk's internally conflicted state and his subsequent emotional trajectory through an expressionist mode of correspondences contributed directly to the reviewers' discontent that I reported earlier in this chapter.

Since Gollum did not suffer the same negative response as the Hulk, it would be logical to suggest that what might distinguish Gollum from the

Hulk is a more consistently maintained person schema, achieved through a model of coherent rather than competing correspondences. But let us test this out. Gollum appears as a fully formed digital figure in a pair of early scenes in *The Lord of the Rings: The Two Towers* (Peter Jackson, 2002). Under cover of darkness, he creeps up on sleeping Hobbits Frodo (Elijah Wood) and Sam (Sean Astin) in order to steal from them the One Ring which they are guarding. They wake just in time, and a fight ensues in which Gollum is overpowered. At dawn the following day, Gollum is leashed and begs wretchedly to be released. Sam wants to kill him for his treachery, but Frodo takes pity on Gollum and releases him in exchange for a promise that Gollum will lead them to their destination. In these scenes, Gollum's state of mind, shifting motivations and uncertainties are eloquently expressed through nuanced melding of performance capture data and key frame animation, to produce a sophisticated rendering of facial expressions and physical gestures. The level of detail in the rendering, the careful articulation of a skin texture which fits into the range of skin textures on show in the film as a whole, as well as the animation's accurate correspondence to human communication, contributes strongly to our sense of Gollum's personhood. However, the emotional and textural consistency achieved is not matched by consistency in other areas of his construction. If we subject Gollum's movements in this pair of scenes to closer scrutiny, we find that his physical integrity appears slightly unstable in the night scene. The density, structure and suppleness of his spindly limbs and back shift fluidly as he crawls around, giving the fleeting sense of an unworldly and unpredictable flexibility. There are also moments in both scenes where the weight and resistance of his body in its contact with the rocks seem momentarily out of step – a weightless slip where a heavier impact and corresponding physical recoil would have been more likely. More striking, in the light of our preceding discussion, is that the same shifts in size seen in the Hulk are also present here. Gollum's skull, body, and outstretched arms are all larger in the night scene than in the subsequent daylight scene. This is particularly noticeable in instances across the two scenes where Gollum is close to one or other of the Hobbits. For example, compare his lunge forward in the night scene, pulling Sam into his grasp to bite into his jugular vein (offering ample opportunity to compare the relative proportions of both characters' heads and torsos), with a moment the following morning when Frodo gently pulls the leash from around Gollum's neck. In daylight, and in a weaker position narratively speaking, Gollum appears literally diminished. As with *Hulk*, the variations in physical size seem likely to be an intentional strategy, a way to visually map Gollum's transition from a sinister, threatening figure who has the element of surprise to the next morning's weak, grovelling captive. The looseness of Gollum's skeletal structure under his skin at certain points may also be designed in as an additional method of dramatising his conflicted nature.

Here, then, inconsistencies are evident in the digital body's structures of correspondences, inconsistencies that in *Hulk* seemed to profoundly disrupt the attempt at a persuasive character consistency. As Martin Barker's recent analysis of Gollum as a cultural phenomenon helps to demonstrate, despite similar inconsistencies in correspondence with real-world physics and physiology, Gollum achieves character consistency so persuasively that his digitalness becomes almost moot. Barker says,

> Particularly striking to me is that, while clearly *everyone knows* that Gollum is a digital construct, this does not seem to be a basis for his cultural absorption. Contrary to the many theorisations that see special effects as driven by the split between spectacle and its technical achievement, Gollum clearly figures as a *unified creature*. Certainly, widespread admiration of the sheer technical achievement does contribute to Gollum's charge. But this does not shape the uses to which Gollum is then put. There are no signs at all, for instance, of Gollum being instanced as a symbol of ultra-modernity, or of the technologisation of society. He is a creature of basic malign and conflictual desires, before anything else. (2011: 29, emphasis in original)

Given Gollum's alter ego, Sméagol, it may not be quite true to say that Gollum is basically malign, but he is highly conflicted. While both Banner/ Hulk and Gollum/Sméagol are possessed by 'conflictual desires', the manner in which that internal conflict is framed by the narrative is quite different. Gollum/Sméagol and the internal struggle between them represents one of the most proximate and unpredictable threats to Frodo's guardianship of the ring, the creature's verbal and physical tics communicating effectively the unstably shifting nature of his allegiance and his mental state. As a result, the inconsistencies he displays do not ripple outwards as a character inconsistency. Instead they feed back into, and shore up the overall coherence of, Gollum's characterisation, locating him in a Judaeo-Christian tradition of metamorphosing monsters, shape-shifters and monstrous hybrids in which any unseemly mutability equates to villainy (see Warner 2002: 35). In contrast, the Hulk does not risk the hero's quest; rather, he embodies it with his attempts to resolve the traumas of his childhood and achieve emotional balance in the present. It is possible that the challenge the Hulk presents is that the predictability and familiarity of this heroic narrative trajectory is at odds with the unpredictable nature of his visual metamorphoses.

What this implies is that, perhaps flowing from the same Judaeo-Christian tradition, mutability or physical inconsistency is much less tolerable in a hero figure.[13] On reflection, the principle appears to be a commonplace in mainstream cinema: a heroic body's physical integrity can be compromised in the course of the narrative, by violence or illness for example, but it must possess a legible and understandable structural integrity in the first place, with the extent and nature of its correspondences with real-world physics and physiology clarified. Films set in fantastical universes or featuring comic book heroes who physically transform in some way might initially seem to problematise these distinctions. But actually they remain predominantly faithful to the underlying principle, by policing the distinction between metamorphosis and modulation in their visualisation of the body's transformative possibilities. As Steven Shaviro has pointed out, metamorphosis 'gives us the sense that anything can happen, because form is indefinitely malleable', an open-endedness that is inherently threatening to the model of classical narrative. Modulation, on the other hand, is 'schematic', requiring an 'underlying fixity' and operating within the bounds of 'a predetermined set of possibilities' (2010: 13). Digitally assisted or constructed heroic bodies (even those with the ability to transform) are predictable in this broad sense, even while they might behave unpredictably within the parameters of the fictional world, and villains correspondingly display volatile and unforeseen metamorphoses. For example, the mutant heroes of the *X-Men* franchise sometimes experience their literal mutations as unexpected or uncontrollable (the onset at puberty trope is invoked in relation to several characters' story arcs), but the visual presentation of their mutations stabilises expectation and foregrounds predictability. Each mutant hero displays a 'signature' transformation process which is established early on and then repeated: Wolverine (Hugh Jackman)'s claws shoot out of his knuckles in the same way each time; Nightcrawler (Alan Cummings)'s teleporting process always involves him disappearing into a cloud of particles which then resolve back into his original form in a different location. Villains in the franchise include an unpredictable shape-shifter Mystique (Rebecca Romijn-Stamos), and Phoenix (Famke Janssen), whose growing powers cause her body to unexpectedly glow and extend out into fiery tendrils (in *X2*), and the skin and bone structure of her face to contort (in *X-Men: The Last Stand* (Brett Ratner, 2006). Similarly, in *Ghost Rider* (Mark Steven Johnson, 2007), hero Johnny Blaze (Nicolas Cage) is shocked when he first transforms into the supernaturally empowered 'Ghost Rider', a transformation marked by his head being replaced by a flaming skull. Yet once the visual 'signature' has been established, its manifestation remains consistent through the rest of the film. Ghost Rider's demonic adversary Blackheart (Wes Bentley) is, contrastingly, prone to transformations that are unexpected in their detail, eventual scale, and ramifications (as well as being purposefully rather horrible to look at). His face is the main locus of distortion, eyes literally smouldering, sockets and jowls blackening and peeling away to reveal deformed, pointed teeth; later his skin turns blue and his mouth expands into a fang-filled maw; and in the final act, when Blackheart has absorbed all the souls in a cemetery in order to gain more power, his face becomes a palimpsestic mass of shifting surfaces to signal the 'legion' now occupying his body.

Narrative imperatives, therefore, also structure our reception of character inconsistencies. The heroic body will only display physical transformations that have legible parameters that can be 'justified' by the narrative (in *Hulk* the back story of irradiated cellular instability doesn't really help, because it is has gaps in its causal structure[14]). The Hulk, a divided figure but still the hero of the film in that he is working for good rather than ill, contravenes this principle. His body mutates, balloons, stretches and springs, but not according to any discernible rules.[15] This makes it almost impossible to 'close the loop', to find a way to integrate these visible inconsistencies back into a coherent characterisation within the film world. On the other hand, Gollum, struggling to control an evil impulse, can manifest visual instability because his 'inconsistencies' lead back to theme, story and characterisation. Rather than there being 'no stretch-and-squash in the CG animation world', as North puts it (2008: 151), there is no stretch-and-squash for the hero figures with whom we are expecting to fully sympathise or align.

In Chapter 2 I suggested, albeit in a slightly different context, that the co-presence of digital elements with human or profilmic elements can accrue meaning which feeds back into the narrative and thematic frameworks of a film. This is an operation that will be exemplified in a number of different instances and contexts across the book, and also here, in these movies that feature digital bodies. In the *Lord of the Rings* films and in *King Kong*, which I look at in detail in Chapter 4, co-presence generates meanings which frame and shape our interpretations, sometimes in complex ways, without problematising the perceived coherence of the digital protagonist or their anchoring within the world of the film. In the case of Gollum, co-presence, and the inconsistencies it has the capacity to generate, can be accommodated by the spectator: he manages, to use Flückiger's words, 'to develop his . . . own consistency within the representational and narrative aspects of fictional character conception' (2010: 20). In *Hulk*, similar inconsistencies mobilise unwanted connotations, pointing outwards too insistently towards issues of construction and artifice, rather than inwards to story and character. If digital bodies are marketed as one of the ultimate 'special effects' despite their relative ubiquity in recent digital effects movies, from an analytical viewpoint the designation risks denuding the digital body's effects on the production of meaning, and on audience reception. It is clear that we need to see digital bodies in the context of the narrative and aesthetic frames into which they are placed, to see them as characters attempting to assert personhood and a compelling narrative arc within a fictional world, as well as being digital-technological spectacles. It would be foolhardy to offer definitive rules, but what this main section of the chapter has attempted, and I hope has achieved, is to set out some of the key factors and considerations that we need to take account of when we analyse the communicative potential and epistemic consequences of the digital body.

We are currently in a period where movies involving digital bodies as *central* protagonists are, in terms of form and audiences' and critics' expectations, heavily invested in prioritising coherence: of characterisation, and of the diegesis and its audio-visual presentation. *Hulk*'s challenge to that coherence was roundly rejected by many critics, a rejection repeated in weak ticket sales.[16] The most recent iteration of the Hulk character, in Joss Whedon's *The Avengers* (2012), contrastingly garnered high praise in early reactions to the film, such as 'The Hulk we have been waiting for has arrived' and 'Hulk stole the show' (Lindelhof and Reid in Child 2012: para. 5), but the same factors are at work here that we have seen in the reception of the earlier digital bodies that this chapter considered. The human input (actor Mark Ruffalo) and its transformative effect on the characterisation of the digital Hulk is emphasised in press and studio paratexts (see Child 2012), while the Hulk's construction in the movie itself is consistent in terms of its photorealism, physical anchoring in the fictional environment, and the physical and emotional realism displayed in interactions with other characters.[17] If this is the Hulk people have been waiting for, it is because he displays more coherence and consistency than the other Hulk iterations managed or were willing to provide. Given this dominance of coherence in the reception of the digital body, is there any space in mainstream cinema for the expressionism Ang Lee's *Hulk* purposefully gestured towards, and which digital imaging technologies, by their very nature, enable?

COMPOSITING THE BODY

Earlier I characterised photorealism as a continuum, between highly specific and much looser performances of photographicness. Each performance of photorealism establishes conventions for how digital imaging processes like compositing, grading and so on will work. Across a film those conventions can be adhered to, but can also be resisted or played with. This description of photorealism's elasticity as a concept and as a practice reveals that seamlessness and coherence, often assumed to be the ultimate goal of any film which adopts a photorealist aesthetic, are not a necessary – or indeed a necessarily preferred – endpoint. At the same time, as we have seen, digital imaging technologies enable filmmakers 'to approach the painter's level of control over the elements of image creation' (Prince 2006: 33), and thus free filmmakers from the requirement to provide the illusion of indexicality and coherence. As we have seen, what Lev Manovich called 'the aesthetics of continuity' (2001: 142) still holds sway in much mainstream output, but some films are taking the opportunity to chart a subtly different route through digital imaging's possibilities for visual articulation. A key site for this is the digital compositing of the profilmic body, and it is this I want to offer some initial thoughts on to end the chapter.

Digital compositing is the practice most often associated with the simulation of spatiotemporal continuity in the film world, yet it speaks to the inherently fragmented nature of the film image in the digital era, because its task – to bring together multiple different image fragments into a single image – can as equally easily achieve the opposite. And, while photochemical compositing also involved bringing together image fragments, the spectator's awareness of digital imaging technologies' capabilities means that they are already watching with an awareness of the fact of digital compositing, its presence and conventional function, which also means being aware of the inherent discreteness of the elements that make up the composited image. Digital literacy thus prepares the spectator for the possibility of compositing experimentation. Rather than thinking of digital literacy as just a sense that everything is 'code', then, we might think of it as what it is: the awareness of the digital composite as a space for imaginative agency, a space for play.

In Chapter 1 I looked at a sequence from *Charlie's Angels: Full Throttle*, which establishes a hyper-real, self-reflexively parodic tone through the arch foregrounding of impossible combinations (human beings safely navigating falling trucks and helicopters whilst falling themselves), alongside compositing and colour grading strategies that worked to separate out the spatiotemporalities of the different elements of the shot. Notably the performances of the three Angels underscored this sense of proliferating disjunction; in the film world their falling bodies are being subjected to violent forces (wind, gravity), and risk violent impact against the large, heavy vehicles that are plummeting alongside them, but they counter-intuitively smile and laugh as if strolling in the proverbial park. Their performances imply an existence in a separate space-time to the one into which they have been composited, and thus underline that all the elements have different spatiotemporalities. This recalls Laura Mulvey's 'clumsy sublime', in which compositing does not complete the illusion of spatiotemporal coherence, but fascinates 'because of, not in spite of its clumsy visibility' (2007: 3). Such moments locate the profilmic body in an indeterminate spatiotemporality, creating a liminal space which can invite reflection on a character's state of mind or circumstances.[18] Mulvey's concept reveals how productive a visual tension between spatiotemporally distinct image elements can be, and helps us to reconceptualise digital compositing which refuses or disrupts spatiotemporal coherence as potentially equally productive.

A pronounced example of this type of digital compositing strategy is found in *Resident Evil: Afterlife* (Paul W. S. Anderson, 2010), the fourth film in a franchise based on the popular survival horror video game series *Resident Evil* (Capcom 1996–). The franchise is set in a world where a biological weapon genetically engineered by the evil Umbrella Corporation has been unleashed, infecting the human population with a 'T-virus' that turns them into flesh-eating zombies. Few human survivors remain. Alice (Milla Jovovich) is the recurring central protagonist, an agent who fights alongside other human survivors against the encroaching zombie hoards. Her narrative arc through the franchise is tortuous. She is captured by the Umbrella Corporation, who inject her with a modified form of the T-virus in order to turn her into a new kind of weapon: a super-powered human/zombie hybrid that retains its human form but is controlled by Umbrella. Managing to overcome Umbrella's mind control, Alice begins a battle against the Corporation and its genetic experimentation. Along the way she discovers she has also been cloned, but turns this technology to her advantage to create an army of Alice clones with which to attack Umbrella. In the scene I want to look at in *Afterlife*, Alice's clone army have attacked Umbrella's Tokyo headquarters, and manage to dismantle the corporate troops before being destroyed themselves in an explosion set by the escaping Umbrella chief Albert Wesker (Shawn Roberts). Wesker flies out of the detonating building in a helicopter, but soon discovers that the original Alice has stowed away onboard. During their confrontation Wesker injects Alice with a serum that strips her of her superpowers, and is about to kill her when a proximity alert warns of terrain ahead. Wesker runs to the controls, but it is too late: the aircraft crashes, and flames and shock waves rip through the aircraft. The moment of impact is realised by a sequence shot which begins facing the cockpit from the outside, the impact slowed almost to stillness then reverting to a faster slow motion speed for the rest of the shot. The camera tracks round the side of the aircraft, past a wall of flames, and (impossibly) into the interior. Tracking away from the impact point, the camera shows Wesker suspended mid-air as he reaches in vain for the cockpit controls, and then continues to track backwards to bring Alice into view, her body suspended further back in the cabin, along with various airborne aircraft paraphernalia: flares, medical kits, fire extinguishers, and so on. The camera reframes to bring the length of the cabin and both Alice and Wesker into view. The image shudders (more as if a celluloid print were being disturbed in its run through the projection gate, than as if from the explosion that begins to rumble on the soundtrack) and then all is obliterated in a flash of white fire.

As the above description indicates, at the point of impact time slows right down, allowing us to contemplate the image in detail. What we see are chunks of glass hurled at the camera from the cockpit, their surfaces reflecting red fire and the dusky sky; behind them are a wall of fire, aircraft bodywork, and Wesker glimpsed in the cockpit window. There are a number of ways that this first part of the sequence shot points to its composited nature. The elements of the image are organised clearly into layers, with no real sense of depth. The bodywork of the aircraft extends beyond the frame, but in a way that is perspectivally inaccurate, making it appear that the helicopter is very wide with a preternaturally flat nose section. The fire also similarly lacks discernible volume, and counter-intuitively it emanates from frame left rather than from below the frame's bottom edge where the aircraft nose would have hit ground first. The segments of shattered glass are oddly precise in their geometric design, and look too neatly shaped to be the type of glass fragment that would be produced by the shattering of a cockpit windshield. Edge 'bleed' between these different elements is not digitally painted out, and the shading of Wesker's face does not reflect the luminescence of the fire or the surroundings in any way that corresponds with the behaviour of real light waves on skin. Once inside the cabin, we notionally catch the bodies of Wesker and Alice at the point that they (and items of aircraft equipment) are thrown into the air by the force of the explosion. The movement of the camera now lends volume to the image and the cabin interior more successfully, with a slightly swooping track that shoots each body from shifting angles to give it dimensionality. However, the postures the two bodies display in the shot look *adopted* rather than reactive. In a real explosion, the body would be thrown, limbs and head, hair and skin pressed into unusual configurations by the force of the blast, clothing and skin ripped by shrapnel, the face displaying the results of physiological stresses even if the mind has had no time to process what is happening. In contrast, Wesker and Alice are artificially posed and poised, expressions blank, sleek costumes and hairstyles and Alice's make-up all intact. Meanwhile airborne objects in the cabin that might, in a different movie, have helped to anchor the three-dimensionality of the scene here look flat and two-dimensional, as if dropped onto a particular image plane at random.

This is resoundingly non-naturalistic digital compositing, which uses the means described above to break apart any sense that we have witnessed a spatiotemporally cohesive event. The shot insistently draws our attention to the co-presence of two-dimensional and three-dimensional image elements, a co-presence of different orders of images which is also invoked by the shot's deployment of extreme slow motion and the inclusion of posed bodies that seem to be *performing* stillness, image elements that refer us simultaneously both to the photographic still image and the cinematic freeze frame. In this way, this mode of digital compositing mimics the declarative approach and ironic play with impossible but instructive juxtapositions that are the hallmarks of avant-garde photomontage. There are several similar shots and sequences in *Afterlife*, which seem to take pleasure in (almost) pulling apart different layers or elements of the image, including the homage to rear projection when Alice and compatriot Claire (Ali Larter) share a plane journey; the highly stylised appearance of the prison facility's grey exteriors and its gleaming white basement; and the photomontage-like aspects of the presentation of Wesker's final showdown with Alice later in the film.

If this is a form of 'clumsy sublime', then, to what end is it being deployed? As a hybridised action-sci-fi-horror 'B' movie with a rather oppositional relationship to more extensively budgeted and more highly produced blockbuster fare, *Afterlife* inherits a generic frame and an audience that are able tolerate visual articulations of impossible events that may fail or falter, just as they tolerate looseness of narrative design and characterisation. This provides a space within which the digital compositing strategies I have described are permitted to exist: a space that does not demand but nonetheless permits some limited experimentation. As a result, it is not surprising to find that the other films that display similar or related forms of experimental digital compositing, such as *Surrogates* (Jonathan Mostow, 2009), *Gamer* (Mark Neveldine, Brian Taylor, 2009), and *G.I. Joe: The Rise of Cobra* (Stephen Sommers, 2009), broadly occupy the same generic parameters. Additionally, the shift into an expressionist mode in *Afterlife* and films like it is perhaps made more tolerable because of the spectacles that digital imaging has created in more mainstream blockbusters. Nick Rombes finds an avant-garde quality in contemporary digital effects sequences, the digital's ability to show anything resulting in unexpected and unexpectedly surreal juxtapositions (2009: 142, 143), and this trend may well have prepared the ground for the fragmenting mode of compositing under discussion here. Yet in my view Rombes significantly overstates the narrative and visual incoherence of the mainstream blockbuster sequences he references: it is in the lower-budget margins, in films like *Afterlife*, where a form of visual anti-coherence is permitted. Is this, then, play for play's sake, an emphatic acknowledgment of the outlandishness and digitally assisted constructedness of these films' B-movie universes – a visual inflection of their limited self-reflexivity and generically playful humour?

I want to suggest that one of the purposes of this fragmenting mode of digital compositing – or at least, one of its possibilities – is to make analogical relationships to a film's narrative concerns. To demonstrate this, let's return to the *Afterlife* example. The sequence shot's direct and indirect invocations of different orders of images being brought together, separated out and recombined in different amalgamations, and the malleability of the digital composite that these imply, correlates to the recombinant possibilities of genetic experimentation, cloning and identity transformation which are at the heart of the narrative. This is the general thematic import of the visual style of all such sequences in *Afterlife*, but the digital compositing also generates connotations which are specific to each sequence. The cabin section of the sequence shot in the helicopter, with its camera gravitating slowly around the characters, and the unsettling mixture of three-dimensional and two-dimensional elements, feels like some kind of holographic toy or Chinese puzzle box that you need to tilt in your hand in order to discover its secret. This is a fitting analogy for the moment of questioning uncertainty at which we find ourselves at this viewing juncture. At this point in the film, the things that defined Alice's power at the outset of the narrative have been swiftly and unceremoniously stripped away. Powerless and without her clone army, Alice's fate is back in the balance, and the direction of her narrative trajectory is wide open. Her suspension in mid-air, behind an encroaching explosion and a man with a gun, literalises her predicament and invites us to ask, 'What's next?' And yet the compositing strategy has also offered a clue as to her immediate fate: the shot depicts her as not in contact with anything, despite the many free-flying objects (and presumably crash debris) loose in the cabin space. The compositing explicitly separates her out from this debris that surrounds her, leaving her literally untouched, and in doing so operates as a metaphor for the possibility that she might emerge physically untouched after the crash has played out to its conclusion. The shot thus demonstrates the way in which the connotative and thematic operations of this fragmenting mode of digital compositing can be nuanced and communicative. In these films, visual strategies that stress spatiotemporal dissonance and fragmentation can work *for* the narrative, rather than against it.

The body at the centre of this fragmenting mode of digital compositing focuses the strategy's potential for narrative connotation, but it may also focus such sequences' more oblique pleasures, as well as suggesting why this experimental mode of compositing has emerged recently. In the face of the total control that digital imaging technologies have over the film image and over the profilmic elements within it, and in the face of the digital body's easy absorption of human performance 'data', digital compositing strategies that in some way pull apart the image have the power to place the profilmic human body in a new relation to the digital, and to other elements of the frame. Unmooring the profilmic body from its conventional embedment in the unified frame, such strategies gift the human body the potential to *disorder* the seamless surface of the digital image, to re-pose age-old questions of presence and absence in a disruptive manner (a potential fleetingly realised in a different way in the mag-lev sequence in *Minority Report* that I discussed in the last chapter). These strategies re-invest the profilmic human body with a playful agency in the face of digital imaging's totalising control, and in so doing provide a spectacle that offers viewers a fleeting, pleasurable fantasy of escape from the digitally mediated world that is our reality in the new millennium. It is notable that the same impulse to reinvest the profilmic body with renewed potential also finds expression in the popularity of *parkour* or 'free-running' sequences which showcase an emphatically profilmic physical virtuosity, in films like *The Bourne Supremacy* (Paul Greengrass, 2004) and *Casino Royale* (Martin Campbell, 2006).

In the construction and 'performance' of the digital body, and in the digital compositing of the profilmic body, the relationship of digital imaging deployments to narrative is complex. As we have seen, the mainstream presentation of the digital body-as-character insists on coherence and consistency, but elsewhere a space for experimentation with anti-coherent visual modes has opened up, and these modes utilise digital imaging's inherent capacities in a different direction, for different but equally narratively and thematically productive ends. We will return to the digital staging of the profilmic body in Chapter 5, but Chapter 4 will build on this chapter's mapping of the factors that contribute to the digital body's effectiveness and its connotative purchase in an extended analysis of the digital Kong in Peter Jackson's *King Kong*.

NOTES

1. See 'HD Weta Featurette Making Of Behind the Scenes', 20th Century Fox Film Corporation 2011, last accessed 1 April 2012 at http://www.youtube.com/watch?v=XM9Pvfq1KhE.
2. Some good examples include this *Rise of the Planet of the Apes* photo gallery image presented in *The Hollywood Reporter* (Giardina et al. 2011), at www.hollywoodreporter.com/gallery/rise-planet-apes-first-look-218818#5, and the *Lord of the Rings* and *Avatar* images which illustrate Kristin Thompson's insightful article on the subject (2010), at www.davidbordwell.net/blog/2010/02/23/motion-capturing-an-oscar.
3. See examples of the Oscar call and the make-up argument in Huffstutter and Pham 2002 and Abramowitz 2010.
4. In fact the possibility of a completely convincing CG human is some way off, and even if it is achieved its convincingness will be transient because of the cycle from wonder to habit, to use Gunning's phrase, and the shift in our sensibility to CG developments over time. Bob Rehak ponders this point in a recent blog post (2012), while North points out that fears about synthespians get confused with fears about artificial intelligence (expressed in modern science fiction, in films like the *Terminator* and *Matrix* franchises) (2008: 155).
5. I am pleased to say that the erasure of visual effects labour from studio and marketing discourses, and the serious ramifications this has for workers' rights, pay and benefits, both first mooted by Pierson (2002: 149), have recently begun to receive renewed press and scholarly attention. Press scrutiny has increased following Lee Stranahan's 'Open Letter to James Cameron: Fairness For Visual Effects Artists' (Stranahan 2010), the campaigning of Executive Director of the Visual Effects Society Eric Roth (Roth 2011a and 2011b), and the Visual Effects Society's 'Visual Effects Industry Bill of Rights', at http://www.visualeffectssociety.com/visual-effects-industry-bill-of-rights. Examples of scholarly work in this area include Mary Desjardin's emphasis on structures of labour in her ongoing research on synthespians, presented at the 2010 Screen Studies Conference, Glasgow UK, and Kevin McDonald's work on 'Rendering VFX: Below-the-Line Labor in the Age of High-Tech Entertainment,' presented at the 2012 Society for Cinema and Media Studies conference in Boston, MA.
6. Key frame animation in computer animation is a process whereby the animator sets the position of objects within the frame at intervals of several frames. The computer then interpolates between the key frames to create a smooth transition. The principle and the term were originally used in traditional 2-D cell animation, where the lead animator would

draw the key frames and more junior animators would draw the transitions between the key frames.

7. See *Spider-Man* and *Spider-Man 2* visual effects supervisor John Dykstra in Wolff 2004: 3.

8. Ang Lee, in 'The Making of the Hulk' Documentary, *Hulk* DVD (2 Disc Special Edition), Universal Studios, 2003.

9. Some of the strength of this assertion might lie beyond the diegesis, in the extra-textual discussion that certain scenes of the film had to be excised because they featured the World Trade Center towers which had recently been the subject of a horrific terrorist attack.

10. Torben Grodal more recently argued the same point from an evolutionary bioculturalist position, which draws on anthropology, neuroscience, and other biological sciences: 'The mental mechanisms through which we check that the world is behaving according to laws and expectations, and which are supported by the brain's innate architecture, are triggered when – as is the case with magic and supernatural events – something violates the assumptions developed by everyday experience' (Grodal 2009: 12).

11. See 'The Making of the Hulk' Documentary, *Hulk* DVD (2 Disc Special Edition), Universal Studios, 2003.

12. See Thomas Elsaesser's seminal 1972 essay 'Tales of Sound and Fury: Observations on the Family Melodrama', *Monogram* 4, reprinted in Bill Nichols (1985: 165–89).

13. As Warner notes, 'in the Christian heaven, nothing is mutable, whereas in hell, everything combines and recombines in terrible amalgams' (2002: 35–6).

14. Why, for example, do the metamorphosising effects manifest so differently in Banner/Hulk as compared to his father (and his father's dogs)?

15. The single rule that the filmmakers were working to – that these metamorphoses reflect Banner/Hulk's emotional state – does not fully explain the various kinds of metamorphosis we see the Hulk manifest, and in addition was clearly not a legible rule for some viewers, as the reviews quoted earlier demonstrate.

16. Rob White in *Sight and Sound* supplied the only positive mainstream review, claiming that it was 'richly mythopoeic and sophisticated' and pointing out the film's references to fairy-tale and surrealist practice (White 2003: 34–5).

17. My thanks to Faye Woods for discussions on the construction of the new Hulk.

18. Mulvey describes a moment in *Marnie* (Alfred Hitchcock, 1963), worth quoting at length, where the heroine loses herself riding her horse. Because of the rear projection staging, the 'intensity of movement is reduced to static studio gesturing. As the star appears in this strange, disorienting space, her emotion trumps her parody of movement. In fact, Marnie herself loses all sense of time and place just when the discordance of time and place characteristic of rear projection is most evident. This paradoxical, impossible space, detached from either an approximation to reality or the verisimilitude of fiction, allows the audience to see the dream space of the cinema. But rear projection renders the dream uncertain: the image of a cinematic sublime depends on a mechanism that is fascinating because of, not in spite of its clumsy visibility' (Mulvey 2007: 3). The 'clumsy visibility' of the rear projection, pointed up by the gestural detail of the actor's asynchronous performance, qualifies our reception of Marnie's moment of ecstatic equestrianism: her abandonment seems artificial, not the 'letting go' it first appears to be. This fits with the wider film's subject-matter: Marnie is psychologically blocked, trapped by childhood trauma into a cycle of compulsive behaviour and irrational fear, so the freedom she seems to be experiencing at this point is a severely qualified freedom, soon to fracture.

CHAPTER 4

Historicising the Digital

The previous chapter set out the diverse intersection of factors – around style and characterisation, but also production processes and promotional discourses – that need to be taken into account in any analysis of a digital body's perceived effectiveness and its capacity for meaning. Building on that foundation, this chapter will explore the construction of the digital body in an extended case study – of Peter Jackson's *King Kong* – which has two further aims. In the pages that follow I will suggest that the digital-ness of the digital body and the cultural ideas that cluster around it can have ramifications that reach beyond narrative or thematic meanings to affect a film's wider representational hierarchy. Kong is a fitting subject for such an enquiry, because in each of his movie iterations his figuration as a giant ape who falls in love with a white actress, is captured, displayed, and then killed, has been seen as a controversially racialised spectacle. This chapter will argue that we need to be alert not only to the politics of the computer generated Kong's visual articulation and characterisation, but to the negotiations around the representations of other characters that ripple out from those decisions. The second aim of the chapter, which dovetails with the first in ways that will become clear, is to assess the type of relationship that the 2005 *King Kong* film and its digital effects sequences have to their historical counterpart, the stop-motion animation and celluloid compositing sequences of the original *King Kong* (Merian C. Cooper and Ernest B. Schoedsack, 1933). Indeed, some of the issues that we encountered in Chapter 3, around the special effect as central protagonist, and around the expressive potential of the act of compositing, return in this chapter. What is at issue here is how some digital effects films choose to historicise themselves: that is, how they position their digital effects work in relation to a history of special effects and celluloid filmmaking practice.[1] North has noted the tendency in some digital effects sequences towards visual strategies that represent a 'boastful divergence' from whatever source text a film is based on (2008: 168). In the extensive paratexts around the 2005 *King Kong* film, Peter Jackson's love for the 1933 original and Willis O'Brien's stop-motion animation is clear,[2] but the manner of Jackson's homage reveals a desire to position the newer film 'as a source of *comparative* wonder' (North 2008: 180–1, emphasis in original), as a technologically superior special effects spectacle, as well as a more politically 'advanced' text. In order to fully investigate this claim and its textual implications, this chapter will take a slightly different form than preceding chapters, using developed comparative analysis of *both* texts to assess precisely how Peter Jackson's film positions itself in relation to its ancestor. In this way the chapter will offer the opportunity to map the manner in which the dialectical relationship between digital effects sequences and earlier forms of special effects spectacle can manifest itself, and in so doing aims to broaden and historicise our understanding of the way special effects sequences can shape both aesthetic choices and decisions around the politics of representation.

In both films, the narrative is broadly similar. A maker of jungle adventure movies, Carl Denham, sets off by ship in search of a mysterious island with an inexperienced actress Ann Darrow in tow, hoping to capture footage that will make his career. Once on the island, Denham and his team meet the indigenous people, who are fascinated by Darrow. They capture her, and offer her as a human sacrifice to a 'monster' who lives behind an ancient giant wall. The monster, a giant ape, snatches Darrow and becomes fascinated by her. Denham's crew embark on a rescue mission through the jungle, eventually managing to capture the creature. Denham sees his opportunity for money and glory: he names the giant ape 'Kong' and takes him back to New York, where he displays the creature to amazed theatre crowds. But Kong breaks out of his restraints, and wreaks havoc as he makes his way through the unfamiliar urban environment. Kong is finally cornered at the top of the Empire State Building, where fighter planes fatally shoot him, and he falls to his death in the street below. As remake and homage, Peter Jackson's *King Kong* re-stages many iconic shots or sequences from the original, including Kong's battle with a Tyrannosaurus Rex (T-Rex), Kong throwing men off a giant tree trunk into a crevasse below, Kong being attacked by a Pterodactyl and Kong at the top of the Empire State Building. This chapter's project, to understand how the newer film and the digital Kong are trying to position themselves in relation to the original, will be underpinned by a series of comparative analyses of some of these equivalent scenes. These will become extremely useful foci for establishing the continuities and distinctions in the construction of space and action in the two films, which themselves turn on important differences in the technology of what in each era were state of the art animated effects. The first pair of scenes I want to look at is the moment in each film when Denham and his men encounter the prehistoric dinosaurs of the island for the first time.

FIRST CONTACT, AND SPATIALISED METAPHORS

In the original film, Denham (Robert Armstrong) and his group of men first spot one of the island's dinosaurs feeding in the distance (see Fig. 4.1). The dinosaur wanders out of frame, but seconds later it returns, this time much closer to the humans (see Fig. 4.2). Spotting the group, the dinosaur charges them, but Denham is ready with a gas bomb and the men fire off volleys of shots. Initially only temporarily subdued, the dinosaur is stilled after a further burst of gunfire and the men creep forward to investigate its body close to. Standing at the dinosaur's head, Denham notices it is still alive, and fires a further shot to kill it.

The majority of this sequence unfolds in a single extended and relatively static take, broken only by a very brief reverse angle shot that serves to show Driscoll and Denham's expressions at the moment they mistakenly think they have felled the dinosaur. The single take is a long shot that simultaneously pictures the dinosaur in the background and the men cowering behind foliage in the extreme foreground, eloquently dramatising the danger Denham's men are in by forcing them to share the frame with the prehistoric beast. This 1933 scene exemplifies both the stop-motion animation used to create Kong and

Figure 4.1 Frame grab from *King Kong* (1933) (RKO): Denham and crew spot a dinosaur in the distance.

Figure 4.2 Frame grab from *King Kong* (1933) (RKO): The dinosaur charges the men, risking a fatal form of contact.

the other prehistoric monsters, and the staging and compositing techniques that animate them alongside live actors. In each shot a mostly static set-up was required that divided the frame into different spatial zones – usually foreground and background – which were then matched to the planes of the animation table and projection mattes that made up the image. Kong and the prehistoric dinosaurs that inhabit the mysterious island were in most cases miniatures animated along particular planes of action (dictated partly by ridges on the animation table), presented in composite images that combined the miniatures with live action footage and glass plates displaying rear projection or front projection onto mattes (see Goldner and Turner 1975). In the shot under discussion, the more distant elements of the composition are depicted using stop-motion footage of miniature flora, the animated dinosaur, and a painted backdrop, projected onto a matte. The space nearest the camera, roughly half of the space as we perceive it, is a film stage dressed in jungle foliage. In the stop-motion footage the dinosaur is at first animated along the furthest ridge of the animation table: when it returns, having wandered out of frame, it is animated along a different ridge, 'closer' to the actors, increasing the sense of danger. In a sudden unsettling shift from movement along the horizontal axis to movement along the depth or 'z' axis, the dinosaur charges into the extreme foreground of the stop-motion footage, its forbidding size and heft now dramatically revealed.

The dinosaur's movement from background to middle plane, and the men's – and the camera's – subsequent movement from foreground toward the middle, ingeniously lends the sequence's composite of stop-motion with live action footage an illusion of spatial continuity. But our awareness of the presence of the act of compositing, brought about in part by the impossible presence of prehistoric monsters, extends the connotative import of the scene. The performance of composition in depth at such moments may approximate spatial continuity, but the arrangement of figures on different, distinct planes fails to complete the illusion: as Noël Carroll has noted, dinosaurs in the film 'inhabit tangibly different spatial zones than the humans' (1998: 135). The staging thus operates as a spatialised metaphor for the temporal distance between the modern men and the prehistoric animal, while also always keeping in view the danger (within the film world) that they will be brought into destructive contact with each other.

The equivalent moment in the 2005 film is a longer scene combining a more mobile camera with digital effects that bring the actors into much closer proximity to the dinosaurs. Denham (Jack Black) and crew have been traversing the jungle in their search for Darrow (Naomi Watts), and stop for a rest in a ravine. Denham steals away from the main group to get some footage of the valley beyond, reluctantly accompanied by his preening male star Bruce Baxter (Kyle Chandler). The pair discovers that the valley is populated with scores of feeding brontosaurs, and Denham quickly sets up his camera and instructs Bruce to 'get into character and walk towards the animals'. Bruce's fearful disinclination is comically at odds with his adventurer star persona (earlier glimpsed on posters in his cabin), while Denham's stubborn instructions are a humorous disavowal of the brontosaurs' nearness and number. Bruce is the first to spot the small velociraptors that are beginning to unsettle the larger dinosaurs, and in a few short moments filmmaker, star and the rest of the ship's crew find themselves running through the ravine, attempting to escape the stampeding brontosaurs as they themselves take flight from the attentions of the smaller carnivorous predators. The result is an extended sequence in which the humans are repeatedly shown in imminent danger of being crushed to death as they dodge between the brontosaurs and the velociraptors.

The 2005 scene begins with a direct reference to the 1933 staging, compositing the two actors and some foliage in the foreground with a digital set extension which depicts a scene of dinosaurs feeding in the background of the shot. Unlike the original, however, the brontosaurs are positioned on multiple planes, some in the distance, but one or two already much closer to Denham and his male star (see Fig. 4.3). This initial set-up dramatises the threat of destructive contact with the prehistoric creatures in terms of distance and

Figure 4.3 Frame grab from *King Kong* (2005) (Universal / Wing Nut Films): Jackson's film echoes and extends the earlier film's composition in depth . . .

proximity, mapped onto the spatial distinction between background and foreground planes, in a manner strikingly similar to the original. But the 2005 film then pushes this logic much further. As Denham and the rest of the expedition attempt to run away from the brontosaurs only to be quickly overtaken and swept along within the mass of tumbling animals, juddering, fast-moving tracking shots pull back along the trajectory of the action. The original's fairly static framings are radically transformed by a jittery and emphatically mobile camera here. The intensification of movement and action also represents a transformation of the resourcefully simple compositing techniques in the original. As the sprinting, stumbling live action bodies are jostled by the digitally generated stampeding dinosaurs, different orders of images are forced into repeated 'contact' with each other, becoming a much more intense 'spectacle of comparison', to borrow North's phrase (2008: 2), than the corresponding 1933 scene (see Fig. 4.4). As digital and profilmic image elements literally jostle with each other, the risk increases that the complex digital compositing might fail to maintain a photorealistic illusion of spatiotemporal continuity in the cycle of apparent contacts. This extra-diegetic 'danger' parallels the risk for the characters of being crushed and trampled to death, as their 'edges' brush violently against the 'edges' of the dinosaurs.

Meanings attaching to the digital nature of the sequence's special effects expand the existing epistemic dimensions of the sequence, but as we have seen, this also happens in the original film in its deployment of celluloid compositing and stop-motion. Part of the task of historicising the digital for ourselves, then, is to understand that the special effects of previous eras can operate in equally complex ways in relation to questions of meaning. But what the comparison of these paired scenes also reveals is an important aspect of the 2005 film's relationship to the original. Both films enthusiastically engage with the special

Figure 4.4 Frame grab from *King Kong* (2005) (Universal / Wing Nut Films): . . . before providing a spectacle of repeated contact.

effects technologies at their disposal, but the Jackson film's deployment of state of the art digital technologies functions partly as an assertion of its technological distance from its 1933 forbear. In Jackson's reworking of the scene under discussion, the older film's composited and predominately static framing is carefully invoked through the initial visual composition, only to be purposefully 'transcended' by the introduction of an emphatically mobile staging impossible in 1933. The fear of contact with the prehistoric world, which the dramatic and technical staging of such moments in the original film evokes, is replaced in the 2005 remake by instances of potential impact or actual touch. Despite the director's evident love for the original's technical accomplishments, the remake's insistent return to complexly proximate compositing and dynamically mobile camera movements reveals an implicit attempt to upstage the original's special effects. The significant duration of the remake's re-staging of these moments, beyond any narrative causality, signals that the film is less interested in narrative momentum than in other things. The brontosaur stampede scene depends upon a laborious digital rotoscoping process in which the telltale markers (such as edge 'bleed') that might perceptually separate a composite image's different components are carefully removed pixel by pixel. In its prolongation of the stampede sequence, the 2005 film makes a spectacle of its deployment of such digital imaging expertise, the risk of contact that haunts the 1933 staging returning as a celebratory performance of the verisimilitude achieved in depicting actual, visible contact between two orders of images, the profilmic and the digital, the material and the 'immaterial'.

The same process of an initial direct re-staging of a moment from the 1933 film functioning as a precursor to a digitally-assisted 'transcendence' of the original occurs at a number of points in Jackson's remake, most famously in the scenes involving the interaction of Kong with Darrow, which I will turn to shortly. What I want to briefly address first is what is at stake in the specific means used to enact the transcendence I have described. The occasion of the ship leaving port to start the voyage to the island where Kong will be discovered is depicted in both films with a long shot that frames the ship against the backdrop of the New York skyline. However, where in the 1933 film the shot is static (save for the slight movement of the boat from which the camera is shooting), in the 2005 film it is a longer shot which is also an emphatically mobile shot. The original static framing is replaced by a large-scale circular camera movement, made possible by digital imaging technologies that construct a three-dimensional environment within which a virtual camera can take any route dictated by the filmmakers. The glittering night-time skyline shifts in the background as the camera traces a large curved path around the ship in an extended fifteen-second take. This fully digitally-generated shot reveals the ship's diminutive size in contrast to the vast expanse of water, and in this way registers narrative import: the ship's vulnerability in the uncharted seas that lie ahead. But lack of literal motivation for the expansive mobile framing also lends this shot of the ship leaving port a showy exhibitionism; it is a moment at which the film seems to delight in the possibilities of the digital. The shot appears symptomatic of a neo-baroque aesthetic that Angela Ndalianis (1999, 2004) and Sean Cubitt suggest has emerged in recent digital effects movies, in which 'awe at the majestic power of spectacle' is still 'of 'central importance' (Cubitt 2004: 264). Cubitt's description of the distinction between classical and neo-baroque modes is particularly resonant in the light of our comparative analysis of the 1933 and 2005 *King Kong* scenes:

> The classical (. . .) depends on a planar construction, in which each layer of depth is distinct from the others, as in the famous sequence of [*Citizen*] *Kane* in which the boy Kane and his sled, his father, and his mother and Thatcher occupy three meticulously separated zones of the image. In a typical neobaroque shot, mobile camerawork (and digital compositing) eliminates the cut between layers to promote a vectoral movement totalized in the bounded world inside the spatial image. (2004: 228)

But I think there are additional factors in play than simply spectacularisation. The recourse to, and foregrounding of, the excessively mobile camera in these scenes has implications for the way in which *Kong*, and his actions, are presented, and the meanings that presentation generates. Before we even meet Kong, the 2005 film makes a clear correlation between mastery and certain kinds of spatial reach, orientation and motion, through the expansive motion of the camera. At two key points on the island, large-scale circular camera movement with no literal diegetic motivation reveals a perspective on the action that the human protagonists *desire*, but cannot achieve. For example, when the newly arrived ship's crew try to penetrate the outer edge of the island village to discover the extent of its reach, medium shots of the uncertain explorers are abandoned in favour of a far-reaching crane shot that curves over the entirety of the settlement, giving privileged access for the spectator to its layout and features. Later, back on ship, the crew discover Darrow has been kidnapped by the indigenous people, and set off in dinghies towards the shore. Shots of Darrow being manhandled into place at the sacrifice ritual, protesting and terrified, are intercut with shots of the crew rowing frantically to shore. Driscoll (Adrien Brody), a writer who has formed a tentative romantic bond with Darrow over the voyage, leans forward in close-up, his desire to get ashore palpable. At precisely this moment there is a cut to a digitally composited crane shot which sweeps up from the pitching boats, rises over the cliffs, curves over the giant fortified wall and, finally, rotates to frame Darrow in medium close-up, struggling against her restraints on the other side. Thus the camera acts out the crew's, and Driscoll's, desperate desire to reach Darrow, by moving across the island terrain in a way that is impossible for them, lifting clear of the dangers and obstacles, and circling round to achieve the most pertinent viewpoint (interestingly, such movement *is* possible for the indigenous people, who use an ingenious pole-vaulting strategy to traverse the rocky outcrops between shore and ship when kidnapping Darrow). The camera's ability to make these sweeping arcs high above ground level is, as in the shot of the ship leaving port, made possible by digital imaging technologies, enacting what we might call a 'mastery of the visual' that is not just celebrated for itself, but is connected in the service of the narrative to privileged knowledge (what is happening to Darrow), and a striking ease of motion through the spaces of the fictional world.

These modes of digitally empowered camera movement find their correlative in Kong's own movements across the island and his elevated position within the landscape, traversing the treetops or ensconced in the rocky peaks of the island. Kong's intervention into the T-Rex's attack on Darrow embodies a style of movement and of mastery of space that mirrors that displayed by the digitally constructed mobile camera in the sequences I have just described. After being snatched by Kong from the sacrificial altar prepared on the ancient wall by the indigenous people, Darrow spends a period of time in Kong's possession as he traverses the jungle. Darrow manages to slip away from Kong, but begins to run into trouble in the unfamiliar and hostile environment. Having hidden from one dinosaur in the grooved crevice of a large overhanging tree bough, she is discovered by another, a T-Rex that proceeds to attempt to knock her free. Dislodged from the crevice, she hangs helplessly from the tree limb, about to be eaten, when Kong leaps from a high promontory. He grabs an outlying branch, pivots his body into a swinging motion and propels his feet into the side of the T-Rex's head, knocking away the fatal snap of the dinosaur's jaws. Kong's body movements here broadly resemble the camera's crane from the dinghy, over the giant wall to the sacrificial altar;[3] but where the men had no way to overcome the obstacles that prevented them from getting to Darrow quickly enough, Kong has the athletic capacities to reach her in time, and to save her. The camera's empowered movement has become Kong's.

This comparison also reveals that Kong has displaced the men in the film as the hero who will repeatedly save the imperilled woman from harm, a role conventionally conferred on the (human) male protagonist.[4] This becomes another way that the 2005 film attempts to mirror and then extend a strategy evident in the original version: this time, a strategy concerning representation. In both films the T-Rex sequence becomes one of several that allow Kong to demonstrate his protector role in terms of physical action; in both films, in contrast to Denham's explorers, Kong is shown to be impressively comfortable in this oversized tropical environment, and a physical match for the carnivorous dinosaurs. But in Jackson's remake the correlation of the gorilla's movements with the empowered motions of the digital camera takes Kong's representation to conclusions the original's animation could only gesture towards. Chivalrous in his protection and repeated rescue of Darrow, the 2005 Kong becomes a more emphatic manifestation of the traditional male action hero than the 1933 film manages, his heroism forged in the physical work of action and showcased in extended action sequences. He goes through the familiar series of 'tests', fight sequences that prove and display his heroic physical mastery in the arena of confrontation:[5] in the T-Rex sequence, for example, he fluidly demonstrates an extensive series of human and animal fighting styles, as opposed to the lumbering, rather limited moves of the dinosaurs. Like the action hero, Kong's physical prowess must persist through pain. Against multiple T-Rex attackers Kong fights on despite being hit, bodily dragged and bitten, displaying persistence and determination alongside his physical stamina and adaptability. Male action heroes traditionally 'demonstrate their wounds in public' (Schubart 2001: 196), and so does Kong, his healed and open wounds testament to his long history as a heroic fighter, the camera investigating this scarred corporeal terrain in repeated close-ups and medium shots. At the same time Driscoll, the human aspiring to the role of hero and Darrow's ostensible love interest prior to her arrival on the island, is diminished in comparison with his 1933 counterpart. In the earlier film, when Driscoll (Bruce Cabot) – a tough, straight-talking, sea-faring man – finally manages to reach Darrow, she falls into his arms and follows him willingly, and at the New York stage show Denham reveals that the pair are 'going to be married tomorrow', so that Kong's snatching of Darrow is but a temporary forestalling of this union. In Jackson's film, when Driscoll – rewritten as a shy, bookish playwright – reaches the promontory and gives Darrow the opportunity to steal away from the sleeping Kong, her hesitant reaction betrays a deep ambivalence about which 'protector companion' she wants to place herself with. This ambivalence turns into an allegiance to Kong and a refusal of Driscoll's overtures when all three are in New York. After Kong dies, the reunion of Driscoll with the devastated Darrow speaks more of convenience than reconciliation.

Kong's mastery of space, the landscape and his own body, and the camera's mobile command of the visual field, are both made possible by digital imaging that has its own connotations of mastery, in terms of its capacity to construct film worlds unfettered by physical realities. Kong's physical pre-eminence is expressed in a manner that is underpinned by metaphorical associations with the level of control this means of production allows. The camera's insistent preoccupation with the minutiae of Kong's expressions and physical actions, strongly evident in the scenes between him and Darrow, indicates a self-reflexive fascination with the film's own technical achievements. But Kong's status as digital spectacle also has consequences for the manner in which he, and those around him, function in terms of representation. To explore this further I want to turn to the staging of key moments in the interaction between Kong and Darrow across the two films. This once again offers the opportunity to throw light on the connotative complexity of the 1933 film's stop-motion and compositing practices, as well as to investigate the nature of the digital Kong's construction and its consequences for the 2005 film's representational framework.

DRAMAS OF TOUCH

After snatching Darrow from the giant wall, and carrying her through the jungle to a high promontory safely out of the way of predators, each film shows Kong enjoying a moment in which he curiously and carefully interacts with his captive. In the 1933 original Darrow is unconscious, having fainted after a harrowing journey through the jungle. In a long shot that takes in the rocky ledge and the horizon behind it, Kong appears concerned for Darrow, scooping her up to take a closer look. A relatively extended medium close-up follows in which Kong cradles Darrow in his hand. He starts to pull curiously at the prone woman's clothing, peeling off a piece of skirt fabric and contemplating it for a moment before it is discarded. He tugs at another swatch, this time from Darrow's blouse, and sniffs it. In a close-up, Darrow regains consciousness and begins to struggle. The medium close-up of the pair resumes; Kong looks around, as if surprised at the woman's sudden movement, and then begins to playfully prod and tickle her, sniffing his fingers afterwards, just as he had sniffed the fabric of her clothes earlier. Kong's removal of large strips from Darrow's clothing is an exposure which, alongside the phallic symbolism of Kong's giant fingers and Darrow's naked, writhing legs, evokes connotations of sexual display and sexualised looking. The earlier interactions between

Kong and Darrow have been characterised by a shot-reverse shot presentation that foregrounds looking relations, in particular Kong's persistent gaze at Darrow. Yet in this scene a static two-shot is used instead, enabling scrutiny of the pair's spatial relationship to each other, and their physical behaviours and movements. The framing reveals Kong's lack of certainty when confronted with a conscious Darrow. His clumsy prodding and experimental sniffing bring to mind a pre-sexual 'awkward child' (Carroll 1998: 137) or an animal (Bellin 2005: 21), rather than a sexual predator. The tension between sexual investigation and more innocent forms of curiosity is underpinned by a score that forgoes its thriller theme for subdued mystery followed by playful elements.

Joshua David Bellin suggests that the scene – 'remarkable as much for what it suppresses as for what it insinuates' (2005: 21) – allows the racist fantasy of the black sexual predator preying on the white woman to be staged as spectacle, while at the same time the hints of pre-sexual play work to disavow that this is what is at stake in the image. Bellin argues that the scene is part of the wider film's project to produce a Kong that functions as a substitute for a stereotype of the African American male as sexual predator. In the context of the fact that lynchings of African Americans were still prevalent in the 1930s, and frequently 'justified' by false stories about sexual attacks on white women by black men, Bellin's claims certainly resonate.[6] The racial politics of US society at the time of the original film's release also find expression in contemporaneous film cycles that influenced *King Kong*. The 1933 film draws its key narrative components – the exploration of an 'exotic' island with unknown flora and fauna, mysterious indigenous peoples, and the capture of animals for further study and display – from the jungle horrors, jungle adventure movies, and ethnographic films that were popular in the 1920s and 1930s. In each of these genres the indigenous tribe (or its stand-in, the ape) is identified as 'primitive' in relation to the white male explorer, hero, or ethnographer. In this representational economy, the white man's fears of contamination are projected onto the white woman, who represents an idealised figure of racial purity who is vulnerable to sexual attack as the alleged object of the Primitive Other's desire (Dyer 1997: 26, 127). This is a formulation sensationally dramatised in the jungle adventure and jungle horror films, which are, in this way, shaped by the late nineteenth century intersection of colonialism, Eurocentrism, biological determinism and Social Darwinism. Such discourses denied the historical simultaneity of indigenous peoples with the 'civilised' explorers who had discovered them in favour of a mythic conception of indigenous peoples as 'Primitive', temporally distant, and unable to progress to a Western mode of civilisation (Fabian 1983: 31). In taking on those genres' characteristics and narrative premises, *King Kong* also seems to adopt some of their primitivist and colonialist assumptions,[7] and the trope of the white woman as a site of threatened contamination by the primitive other seems very evident in the scene under discussion.

However, by deploying a close attentiveness to the staging of the scene and the mechanics of its special effects work, I think we can develop a more nuanced sense of the 1933 *King Kong*'s characterisation of its monster, and thus the film's relationship to the racist and primitivist discourses current at the time of its release,[8] an endeavour that will then allow us to more accurately assess the corresponding aesthetics and politics of the digital Kong's construction. The 1933 scene is achieved by combining a miniature animated Kong in the foreground with rear-projected footage of Fay Wray being held in a giant mechanical Kong hand, the animation synchronised with pieces of Wray's actual costume being pulled from her body with wires.[9] It is a remarkably achieved composite image but not completely seamless; the medium close-up in the scene is close enough to allow the paler hue of the rear-projected footage compared to its surroundings, and the contrast between the movements of the live action Wray and the stop-motion animated Kong, to be discerned. As a result the shot approximates the illusion of spatiotemporal proximity, repeatedly staging the moment that Kong touches Darrow, while also guaranteeing spatiotemporal distance and the impossibility of contact: Darrow and Kong are both there but 'not there' – that is, never there in the same space/time. This allows us to make a case for the 1930s audience's awareness of the presence of this special effects practice – prompted not least by the fact that Kong cannot exist as a being in the real world – that informs their reading of such moments: an equivalent, then, of the digital literacy audiences bring to their viewings of contemporary digital effects movies.

The 1930s special effects depict these moments between Kong and Darrow with a duality that signals both the terrifying-but-titillating touch and its simultaneous reassuring impossibility. Bellin links this articulation directly to the film's racial politics, arguing that the composite process shots,

> participate in the film's halting recognition that it is playing with fire: Kong never *really* touches Wray, yet it is imperative that the film produce the illusion that the boundary between black and white [and, we might add, between 'Primitive' and 'Civilised', 'Ancient' and 'Modern'] has been overcome. (2005: 37, emphasis in original)

In Bellin's interpretation the overcoming of the barrier between black and white is intended to signal for white audiences an ultimate kind of horror, and the scene's staging thus confirms for Bellin the film's inherent racism.[10] However, we can complicate this reading by drawing on Donna Haraway's work on ethnography. In her theorisation of first contact with the ethnographic object, and the anticipation and anxiety focussed around it (in both its nineteenth- and twentieth-century permutations), Haraway suggests that ethnography's desire for knowledge of, but fear of proximity to, the Other – of contamination by the Other – produced a 'drama of touch' (1989: 149). This was fraught with risk but also offered the possibility of being 'brought into touch with [one's] origin and nature' in a fulfilling, life-affirming way (152).[11] The static two-shot at the centre of the sequence does not simply or only present the spectacle of a horrifying encounter with the Primitive Other, but in its proximate framing and careful staging also offers the spectacle of an exploring, inquisitive, playful prehistoric creature (while Darrow's presence partly functions to indicate his unusual size and underscore his status as a fantastical being). The interactions between Darrow and Kong are certainly dramas of touch, charged by racist, colonial and anthropological fears of miscegenation, of mixing across race and evolutionary time (and in the fictional world of the film, species), but as dramas of touch they are also charged by the affirmation that can be accessed through that contact.

The co-presence of redemptive and destructive possibilities in the ethnographic conception of 'first contact', and the way in which it is literalised in the co-presence inherent in the film's compositing practice – its aligning of stop-motion bodies and profilmic bodies as if in the same space – help problematise too straightforward, or straightforwardly negative, a reading of Kong's interactions with Darrow. One of the things that we have discovered already in preceding chapters is the extent to which digital imaging, combined with the audience's knowledge of its nature and presence, can generate connotations which feed back into or qualify in some way our reading of other aspects of a scene. What is clear from the current discussion is that the stop-motion animation and celluloid compositing deployed in the 1933 film can work in similar ways. The encounters between Kong and Darrow risk simplistic interpretation, not least because of all the screaming Fay Wray gets to do: Bellin, for example, characterises them as 'a pattern of alternating, screen-filling close-ups swooping in to Kong's frankly leering face and Darrow's cringing reaction' (2005: 21). But this description elides the detail of Kong's stop-motion animation as well as the point of view structures at work in these scenes. Through close scrutiny of the interplay between the stop-motion processes and other stylistic decisions, these scenes can be opened up to a more complex reading. I want to illustrate this with brief reference to two more of these encounters, before we compare how the Jackson remake manages its own intersection of issues of representation, characterisation and 'special effects'-assisted realisation.

The 1933 Kong's arrival at the sacrificial altar where his newest 'bride' has been strung up precipitates a cut to a medium close-up of Darrow looking from side to side as she struggles to free herself from the altar bonds. She looks up at Kong, speechless, as if unable to verbalise or process what she sees, and a reverse angle follows, dollying quickly into an extreme close-up of Kong's eyes. In his frequently illuminating essay on the film, Noël Carroll muses that 'it is hard to tell whether the rapidity of the camera movement here is meant to register Darrow's shock at first seeing Kong, or vice versa' (1998: 137), but the sequence's construction makes this clearer than Carroll suggests. This first close-up of Kong's face is *Darrow's* point of view, cued by the preceding medium close-up of Darrow looking up out of frame towards Kong's spatial position, and followed by a similarly scaled shot of Darrow screaming in response to what she has seen. The rapid dolly into the extreme close-up of Kong's face expresses Darrow's subjective experience (panic, shock) at this moment of meeting, but the second part of the sequence demonstrates that this shot says more about Darrow's fears (and the cultural discourses that might inform them) than about the dangers Kong actually poses. Back in long shot, Kong moves forward, pounding his chest to declare his arrival, but then pauses and drops his arms, looking at Darrow. Another close-up of Kong's face follows, this time a static shot, in which he slowly shakes his head, opens and shuts his mouth and raises and lowers his eyebrows, while slightly averting his eyes. A close-up of Darrow shows she is still terrified, twisting her body away from Kong and screaming. Kong's reaction is played out in long shot; he hesitates, scratches his torso, moves to beat his chest then changes his mind, each time seeming to pause in response to a scream. What this description immediately yields is an impression of a tentative Kong whose pauses indicate an alertness to Darrow's responses. The second close-up of Kong's face is notably divested of indicators of subjectivity, slightly angled from the left so that Kong is no longer looking directly into camera, and without a dramatic dolly-in: this shot is *not* from Darrow's point of view. In order to argue that the scene characterises Kong as a sexual predator – that he is, 'as it were, giving Darrow "the look"' (2005: 40), Bellin has to conflate the two close-up shots – the subjective dolly-in from the first part of the sequence and the eyebrow waggling shot from the second. Dismantling this conflation and taking the second close-up shot on its own allows another explanation to come to the fore. The sexualised, objectifying look Bellin is insinuating would conventionally draw together eyebrow waggling with a simultaneous direct look at the object of desire, but Kong's eyes are averted, and he is combining eyebrow movements with head shakes and mouth movements. Enacting all these simultaneously indicates he is either experimentally attempting a combination of expressions, or mimicking Darrow's own widened eyes, shaking head, and screaming mouth movements, in order to try and communicate.[12]

We see evidence of this attentive and tentative Kong in other of the pair's encounters, once again embodied in the relationship of the detail of Willis O'Brien's stop-motion animation to point of view structures. After Kong has vanquished the T-Rex he turns back to Darrow, who has been pinned under a felled tree trunk. As he leans over her, the long shot of the scene is abruptly interrupted by a fast dolly into a close-up of Kong's face, and a reverse angle fast zoom into a close-up of Darrow's screaming, recoiling body.[13] Back in long shot Kong sits back on his haunches, looking around, as if unsure what to do in the light of Darrow's reaction. Here we are presented with further views that help to evoke Darrow's subjective experience, though they are not point of view shots; as before, their placement in the sequence points up the distance between the level of her fear and Kong's *actual* actions. Next, Kong swings his arms in a pausing gesture, then gingerly lifts the branch off Darrow, and tentatively nudges her into his cupped hand, eliciting more screams from the terrified woman. As he picks her up a second close-up, this time static, depicts his face as he watches her, while reverse angles of Darrow clutched between his fingers help evoke his perspective. As in the sacrificial altar scene, Darrow's subjective terror at this looming ape's features is conveyed with a dollying close-up of his face, which is then re-presented in a static close-up that under-cuts Darrow's subjective perspective. Earlier, Kong was not leering but trying to communicate; here Kong is not leering but watching, and waiting to see if Darrow calms down.

Close textual analysis of these sequences reveals the detailed features O'Brien invests in Kong, the hesitation gestures, the watchful pauses, the tentative behaviour that contrast so sharply with Darrow's extreme, hysterical fear. This is not to deny that such situations would not be frightening, but that the specifics of the stop-motion work provide an opportunity to consider the proportionality of Darrow's response in relation to Kong's actions. While others have cited the way that O'Brien invests Kong with fighting moves from wrestling and boxing as the humanising factor in Kong's characterisation (Erb 1998: 116), for me it is in these smaller moments of hesitation, patience and care that one finds the complexity and humanising impulse in Kong's representation. It is these smaller 'phrases' of animated behaviour, and the point of view structures in which they are situated (and to which they contribute), that encourage a partial alignment with Kong that will be crucial in generating pathos as Kong is shackled and then shot down in the final reel, and which complicate a reading of *King Kong* as only manifesting racist fears of the Primitive or African American 'Other'. These positive elements of Kong's characterisation also connect to other aspects present in the later New York sequences, that encourage a critical distance on Denham's attempts to make a spectacle of his captive 'monster', and which invite a complex emotional response to Kong's subsequent rampage and annihilation.[14]

Special effects thus play a key role in the tension between less and more progressive elements in the 1933 film. In the retelling of *King Kong* for a new socio-cultural moment, what is the relationship between the 2005 film's special effects – this time digital – and its systems of representation? The 2005 scene of first contact at the sacrificial altar allows us to begin to answer this question. All we see at first is Kong's hand, and as it moves towards Darrow, two shots from her optical point of view emphasise his giant size, underscoring the dangers of this close encounter. In both point of view shots a wide angle lens is digitally simulated, exaggerating the distance between the background and foreground. In the first shot Kong's right hand moves from the background into a fore-ground close-up and lands on the ledge on which Darrow is restrained with an audible boom, shattering several rocks on impact in an illustration of his size and heft. In the second shot the wide angle lens effect distorts the edges of the image as Kong's fingers reach out beyond the foreground plane and the frame edge. A cut to a position from just behind Darrow shows her stretching to avoid Kong: the camera then cranes above her to frame Kong's enormous fingers touching, and then caressing, her hair next to her face.

While the caressing brings to mind the sexualised investigation of Darrow by Kong that the stripping scene in the original seems to threaten, it also establishes some key differences. The 1933 Kong is dexterous enough to pull some bits of dangling clothing from Darrow's inert form but ends the sequence with more blunt gestures, such as prodding and sniffing. In contrast the 2005 Kong is able to separate some strands of Darrow's hair in between his fingers, an action that, given the thickness of his digits, demonstrates a striking but believable precision of touch, thanks to highly detailed digital animation and compositing. The detail of the action is achieved by meticulous digital compositing of Kong's fingers and strands of Darrow's hair; the *delicacy* of the action radically undercuts the cumulative expectations generated by the preceding shots of Kong's threatening heft. Here the drama of first contact (complete with Darrow's terrified screams) is presented and then undercut, resolving into a moment of non-violence, of gentle tactility: an attempt at haptic connection. The original film's strategy of subtly undercutting the pitch of Darrow's reaction to Kong is here extended and foregrounded.

Here then, the 'transcending' of the 1933 film's staging and special effects practice we observed earlier in the chapter finds its mirror in the remake's extension of the original's quest to give its prehistoric protagonist sympathetic qualities. The 2005 equivalent of the scene in which Fay Wray's Darrow is stripped and prodded offers further illustration, in the dynamic between the pair and in Kong's realisation, which develop in tellingly different ways to the original. The scene begins with a ground-level long shot in which Darrow attempts to slip away from a momentarily distracted Kong. As Darrow sprints towards the camera Kong's giant fist thumps down into the extreme fore-ground of the shot to stop her. Darrow turns in medium close-up and runs away from the camera only to be cut off again by Kong's other fist, slamming into the background plane. Darrow tries a different route, but Kong blocks her path: the camera tilts up to reveal Kong's face in a medium close-up, bearing down on Darrow as he begins to frown and growl. A crane shot from above Kong moves with him as he leans towards Darrow, and her fear, shown in close-up, prompts a further escape attempt that catches Kong momentarily by surprise. These initial shots have much in common with the 1933 film; composition emphasises the difference in size between Kong and Darrow and camera movement conveys Darrow's subjective experience of the giant ape bearing down upon her. A key difference, however, is the steadiness of Darrow's gaze: she uses her eyes to monitor where Kong's attention is focused, in order to decide on the direction in which she will run, and to check his reactions to see if she can risk another escape attempt. This watchfulness pays off by briefly catching Kong out, but it also opens up the possibility of communication between them, as the rest of the sequence illustrates.

Darrow is corralled to a standstill and has tripped backwards, falling into a vulnerable position on the ground. Kong towers above her in long shot, and begins to emit abbreviated roars, punctuated by softer fist thumps into the rock by her feet. A cut into a close-up of Kong occurs as he shouts plaintively; Darrow sits up, meeting his gaze, the reverse angle held long enough to catch her expression as it shifts from trepidation to puzzlement. A long shot frames them as they look at each other; Kong's movements are careful and slow, his fists always slightly at a distance from Darrow. Darrow gets to her feet, her eyes locked to Kong's; more truncated roars can be heard off-screen, and the camera tracks into close-up to catch another moment of quizzical calculation flit across Darrow's face. A reverse angle shows Kong shifting position, growling and raising his eyebrows, his expression one of concern before he utters another reproachful roar. A shot-reverse shot pattern has developed, then, but one devoid of terrified screams. In striking contrast to the 1933 Darrow's reactions, which included throwing her head to the side, squeezing her eyes shut, and fainting, here Darrow meets and maintains Kong's gaze. Moreover, the rhythm of Kong's short roars and growls resembles a non-verbal attempt at vocal communication, one that the conscious, alert Darrow is evidently trying to translate. With language unavailable as a means to interact, Darrow – who in this film was working as a vaudeville dancer before the voyage – resourcefully reciprocates in the most appropriate manner: using her body. In a bold move she suddenly jumps up and taps Kong on the nose, before 'playing dead' on the ground. The stunned Kong complains, but instead of stopping Darrow repeats the action, this time segueing into a section of her vaudeville show, which provokes laughter from Kong. The importance of reading the scene as communication is signalled by the way in which it is presented: the two are mostly filmed in a shot-reverse shot pattern of the kind conventionally used in dialogue scenes, with close-ups showing their faces as each struggles to understand the other.[15]

The original Kong's attempts at communication, subtly suggested in 1933, become the basis for a transformed sequence here. The scene is divested of its sexual overtones, the risk of exposure of Darrow's body no longer the focus, the child-like play of the 1933 Kong now a more 'adult' appetite for vaude-ville entertainment, while Kong's attempts to communicate take the form of a much more sophisticated array of directed bodily gestures, controlled roars and targeted looks. Darrow's fears for her safety are not constantly at a hysterical pitch, and she manages to remain conscious, lucid and resourceful when confronted by Kong. Here the moment of actual touch is initiated by Darrow in her first surprise nose jab, and when Kong becomes too boisterous in his own playful nudges, she uses a blocking move and a firm commanding 'No' to stop him. This is a more progressive construction of female agency and composure than the 1933 version offered, but it depends on a Kong that is characterised and animated quite differently than in the original. Aside from its aim to produce an exciting spectacle, the animation of Kong is informed by two impulses – to make him a more completely sympathetic figure, and to point away from his digitally constructed nature by making him convincing and 'authentic'.

The progression in this scene illustrates some of the ways in which this is attempted, through the narrative design of the interaction but also the special effects work. Kong's expressions and movements are partly informed by actor Andy Serkis's performance, which was captured by an intricate motion and facial performance capture rig and combined with detailed key frame anima-tion. As in other films featuring digitally generated protagonists, Serkis's performance capture contribution was at the heart of publicity about *King Kong*'s technical achievements. The actor's description of his work is reveal-ing of what motivated both Serkis's approach to his performance and the detail of Kong's characterisation in the finished film. In media interviews Serkis made much of the fact that his performed movements were informed by close observation of gorillas in the wild, as a way to reach towards an authenticity rooted in Nature rather than Culture, in real-world fauna rather than fantasy.[16] This is clearly indicative, then, of a desire to animate Kong as a sympathetic animal rather than either a horrifying monster, or the object of conflicted emotions that Kong represented in the original film. Nevertheless, what is most noticeable is not the veracity of Serkis's physical emulation of authentic gorilla movements but the series of human expressions the digital animators invest Kong with (using Serkis' contribution as a key reference). The close-ups provide the opportunity for the spectator to contemplate the resulting moments of technological achievement – which are also moments of expressive digital performance; that is, of a mode of digital characterisation that will have consequences for the representation of the island's other inhabitants.

These expressions – querying, expressing frustration, warning, and later, amusement – contribute to the psychologisation of Kong-as-character, and thus to his reception as possessing a cohesive form of personhood. The range of emotions identified even in this scene is important – this is a character who can be animated in a much more detailed way than in the original film, and who in the world of the film wants to be expressive and nuanced in his exchanges with Darrow. As a result, the digital Kong is constructed as an anthropomorphised animal to try to understand and communicate with, an indication that the filmmakers want to invoke not outdated, imperialist notions of capture and conquest, but contemporary discourses of ecological responsibility and ethical conservation.[17] The capacities of digital imaging technologies thus enable a recuperative strategy that positions Kong as a much more explicit locus for sympathy and identification, and creates the circumstances in which the film can establish a transformed narrative trajectory for Kong and Darrow. The 2005 film is as fascinated with 'transphotographic contact' (North 2008: 1) as the 1933 version is, but our relationship to the 'drama of touch' is elaborated and modified in comparison. As Jackson's remake progresses, touch becomes not a fascinating danger but a reciprocal process between the pair that is protective, respectful, companionable, and communicative; hands shelter (Kong) or entertain (Darrow) as both stumble towards a simple sign language. The filmmakers' construction and dramatisation of Kong, 'authentically' animal-like but simultaneously 'human' in his behaviour, is a substantial extension of the humanising animation strategies that were evident in the 1933 film. The intricate realisation of his communicative personhood, alongside the film's placement of Kong in the role of action hero and protector, is successful to the extent that the 2005 film is 'safe' to imagine a narrative trajectory for Darrow and Kong that is familiar from the romance genre. They will meet, learn to communicate with each other, spend time together, even, rather surprisingly, share a moonlit skate in a park in the middle of the city, before finally the obstacles to their pairing are re-imposed. Indeed the iconography of romance is strikingly overdetermined in the skate scene – locked gazes, dancing, and affectionate touches all unfold in an implausibly quiet, deserted setting (given that armed forced have mobilised in the city to capture Kong) lined with fairy lights. Another indication, then, of the film's investment in constructing Kong as a locus of recognisably human feeling and interaction, but one which is matched by the film's investment in constructing him as a site of advanced, sophisticated, modern high technology.

DIGITAL PROTAGONISTS AND QUESTIONS OF REPRESENTATION

Earlier I noted that nineteenth- and early twentieth-century primitivist discourse depended on a conception of indigenous peoples as temporally distant from the 'civilised' explorers that discovered them, and resulted in a rhetoric of temporal distancing. A form of temporal distancing is also enacted in the 2005 film's relationship to its predecessor, an implied assertion of the 'primitiveness' of the nuanced stop-motion animation and compositing strategies readable in the remake's emphatic transformation of iconic scenes via the latest digital technologies. I have also suggested that Jackson's film wants to distance itself from the more problematic aspects of Kong's characterisation in the original, to replace 1933 representations with 2005's more progressive depictions. Thus digital Kong's construction as a thinking, feeling, significantly anthropomorphised being, and his simultaneous function as the signifier of the virtuosic digital achievement of that construction. But while the presence of digitally constructed, detailed characterisation contributes to a more progressive depiction of both Kong and the Darrow/Kong relationship, it has less positive effects elsewhere. In the process of constructing the central protagonist as a 'civilised', 'modern', Kong, the 2005 filmmakers have to set him in opposition not only to the island's predatory fauna (in relation to which he can become the chivalrous hero), but also to the human occupants of the island. This is where we find the less positive ramifications of the remake's recuperation of its prehistoric monster-hero. In the final section of the chapter, I want to once again adopt a comparative approach to show how this aspect of the 2005 transformation of the original *King Kong* is not quite as transformative as we might expect.

In the 1933 film, the first meeting of the ship's crew with the indigenous tribe is presented as a tense but lightly humorous scene. On hearing drums and chanting, Denham's team approach the ancient wall, concealing themselves behind some tall grass. Denham parts the foliage and sees a ritual dance staged on the steps of the entrance gates, performed by figures dressed as gorillas and watched by a large, chanting group wearing grass skirts, headdresses, painted faces, and carrying spears. Denham exclaims 'Holy mackerel, what a show!' and proceeds to set up his camera in the open, hoping aloud that he manages to shoot some footage before he is seen. The tribal leader spots him, and approaches the group, angrily addressing them in an unfamiliar dialect. The ship's captain knows the language, and negotiates their safe passage out of the village, but not before the tribal leader's desire to make Darrow a 'Bride of Kong' has been made clear. Denham's first look at the ritual is conveyed by a reverse angle long shot that approximates Denham's distanced position. The long shot permits a spectacular scale of action, but also has depersonalising effect, making it difficult to pick out individual expressions in the massed crowd. In this way the camera's distance from the action is initially aligned not only with Denham's actual location but with the position Denham wishes to adopt in relation to what he sees; his response 'Holy mackerel, what a show!' designates the view as spectacle, to be photographed rather than engaged with.

His use of colloquialisms continues throughout the scene, indicating a refusal to take the situation entirely seriously that implies an imperialist sense of superiority. As the scene progresses, long shots are inter-cut with medium close-ups that provide the opportunity to consider the expressions of the woman at the centre of the ritual who is being readied to become a Bride of Kong; they also give us some access to the tribal leader's focus of attention. Our initially close spatial and epistemic alignment with Denham is broken down by such presentational strategies. Denham's attempts to film without being seen, to objectify (and thus remain separate from) the indigenous people are dashed by the tribal leader's move to communicate with the Western interlopers. Soon he is being forced to converse with the figures in his intended 'picture', the ship's captain's command of local languages permitting an unexpectedly two-way interaction. The 1933 film certainly posits the islanders – and, to a lesser extent, Kong – as 'primitive' in relation to the emphatic modernity of the American explorers, with their cameras, guns, gas-bombs, cities and fighter planes, implying that a Modern vs. Primitive dichotomy underpins these representational choices. But in providing some access to the interiority of individual islanders – and Kong – at certain moments, and in occasionally highlighting the intrusive and ultimately destructive effects of Denham's quest, the original film also problematises the imperialist principles its plot might seem elsewhere to enthusiastically enact.

Denham remains a figure of imperialist opportunism in the 2005 remake, but the presentation of the first meeting with the islanders reveals that the film adopts an attitude towards the indigenous people that is markedly different from the original. The explorers walk tentatively through an apparently deserted village strewn with skulls and skeletons. A child appears suddenly in front of the surprised group, silent, inexpressive, and unsettlingly still: she raises her arm and points a long finger towards them, but does not speak. Denham tries to charm the child by forcing a bar of chocolate into her hand, but as he takes hold of her arm she bares her teeth, hisses and bites him. Indigenous women suddenly appear in every doorway and recess in the settlement, huddled together, watching the group with staring, blood red eyes. Equally quickly, male islanders surround the team and move at bewildering speeds to assault their new captives; Denham, Darrow and Driscoll are soon forced to watch in horror as the islanders begin to smash in the skulls of their travelling companions. As in the original, Denham's actions are remain the catalyst for the first meeting with the islanders, but here his colonialist presumptuousness is underlined by his aggressive attempts to get the child to accept chocolate, and Driscoll and Baxter's requests that he leave the child alone. Notably, in the 2005 film there is no possibility of verbal interaction with the indigenous people; in contrast to Kong's communicative interactions with Darrow that will follow, here no common language is found, and rather than attempting to forge a dialogue, the islanders simply attack the explorers with brutal weapons. The 'primitiveness' of the indigenous peoples is asserted in these violent confrontations, which the crew with their modern automatic machine guns inevitably win (Denham and his group are rescued at this point in the film by a contingent of sailors from the ship who shoot indiscriminately at the islanders until they fall away). Communication is replaced by exchanges of violence, the use of which is 'justified' by the filmmakers' decision to construct the islanders as dumb and murderous beings, unlike Kong, whose capacity for meaningful interaction will make his incarceration and death register as unjust in comparison. The camera work underscores the sense of threat in the sequence, and thus its representational choices: the 1933 scene's static framings are replaced by swish pans and crash zooms at canted angles, while the soundtrack develops an expressionistic, asynchronous style, combining the moaning wind with human and animal screeches and discordant notes. The camera effects are not tied directly to a particular character's optical point of view, but seem to represent the travelling party's collective subjective response to the unsettling aspect of the deserted dwellings, and their subsequent terror at the male islanders' murderous attack. Smaller details also contribute to the much darker tone of the 2005 scene: as the child raises her arm and straightens her wrist a brief click is audible which, though non-diegetic, gives the distinct aural impression of a snapping or clicking bone, a sound which invokes the iconography of the zombie or cannibal movie. The child's protector, revealed in a doorway, is a haggard old woman with hooked nose and crooked teeth whose appearance calls up related associations with witches and ghouls.[18] In these ways the audio-visual narration seems to be 'infected' with the subjective horror the group experiences. This is only one of several sequences in which the indigenous people are similarly presented. Later, at Darrow's sacrifice ritual, swish pans and crash zooms return and drums beat in increasingly frantic rhythms as the unwilling Darrow is tied up and lifted onto a ledge some distance away from the wall. Close-ups capture the islanders in trance-like states, frozen rigid or vigorously shaking their bodies, rolling their bloodshot eyes, wailing, panting and hissing, while dressed in accoutrements drawn from various tribal costumes.

If there is a real-world referent for this indigenous community's appearance, behaviours and rituals, the filmmakers choose not to clarify this, through dialogue or any other means. Such details provide only an introduction to the range of strategies the film employs to dehumanise the indigenous tribe. Kong's revelation of sensitivity and expressiveness moves his representation much closer to that of the white explorers than theirs. The islanders, performed by flesh-and-blood actors, register as substantially less 'human' than the digitally generated Kong; indeed they arguably constitute the 'real' horror in this horror re-make. The differentiation between Kong and the islanders is underscored by their comparative relationships with their local environments.

The human inhabitants are in a kind of exile on the other side of the ancient wall, alienated from the verdant abundance of the rest of the island. They eek out a brittle existence on dried fish, surviving in makeshift shacks perched on a barren shelf of rock between the wall and a treacherous coastline. In stark contrast, Kong's lush jungle habitat on the island, much of it digitally generated or composited, provides a varied, unpredictable terrain that is teeming with life. His expressive features, dynamically 'authentic' motions and vibrant, glossy fur contrast with the islander's inscrutable expressions, predominantly grey skin, and spasmodic physical movements. The indigenous people of Skull Island are the antithesis of Kong's sensitive and heroic characterisation and his elevated status as digital spectacle. The 1933 film's underlying dichotomy between Modern and Primitive has not been dismantled; rather, in 2005 Kong himself has been 're-classified' as 'Modern', with the indigenous island community occupying the designation of 'Primitive' even more emphatically than before, in the service of shoring up Kong's new position.

In the 2005 *King Kong* the filmmakers were faced with the challenge of constructing a Kong figure who would be believable, sympathetic and compelling despite being 'virtual' – that is, a digitally generated being. In taking up the challenge, the filmmakers assigned characteristics to Kong that overturned his 1933 role as a monstrous, if also sympathetic, racial Other. But in doing so, the racist construction was relocated elsewhere, projected, that is, onto the indigenous people, thus bearing out bell hooks' observation that primitivist narratives and representations *still* circulate in contemporary mass culture (1992: 25). In analysing the recuperation of Kong, then, we must look beyond the technical and artistic achievement of the digitally generated figure himself, and trace the ripple effects of his transformation across the rest of the film's representations, ripples that reposition Darrow as a self-possessed agent in the narrative, but that also intensify the 'othering' of the indigenous islanders. This chapter has offered developed analysis of a film that very self-consciously locates itself in a history of special effects practice, and that wishes to offer itself as a modernising transformation of Cooper and Schoedsack's original *King Kong*. In order to assess the film's success in this endeavour, it has been crucial to understand the complex visual and epistemic operations of the original film's special effects practices, as well as those of the remake. The practices of historicisation elaborated in this chapter have been grounded in the textual detail of the films themselves. In both cases, the articulation of the Kong body has consequences not only for the staging and characterisation of Kong himself but for others in the films' fictional worlds. The implications for analysing digital imaging practice as it pertains to the construction of the digital protagonist are clear: we must not look at the digital body – its digital construction, its correspondences, its character consistency – in isolation, but in relation to the structures of characterisation, narration and representation in which it is embedded. The next chapter will intensify this focus on the ways in which digital imaging contribute not only to narrative or aesthetic elements but also to the politics of contemporary cinematic representation.

NOTES

1. A number of films in the contemporary period do this quite self-consciously, albeit in different ways, such as *Tron: Legacy* (Joseph Kosinski, 2010), which references the early digital effects that appeared in the ground-breaking *Tron* (Steven Lisberger, 1982), the homages to celluloid rear projection in films as wide-ranging as *Sin City*, *Knight and Day* (James Mangold, 2010), and *Resident Evil: Afterlife*, and the homage to early trick effects in *Hugo* (Martin Scorsese, 2011).

2. Featurettes show Jackson talking about the original but also demonstrating one of Willis O'Brien and Marcel Delgado's articulated armatures used in the original Kong stop-motion puppet.

3. Indeed in the remainder of the T-Rex fight sequence the camera continues to mimic Kong's powerful, frenetic twists and rolls as he struggles and succeeds to best the T-Rex.

4. Irony and pathos will be generated by the contrast between Kong's command of his native island and his increasingly desperate predicament at the film's end, trying to find the highest point in New York city from which to escape the armed forces, and in doing so becoming a target for the fighter planes which will pick him off the Empire State Building.

5. My conceptualisation of this process is informed by Richard Slotkin's notion of the hero's 'regeneration through violence' (1992: 8) and Steve Neale's seminal essay, 'Masculinity as Spectacle: Reflections on Men and Mainstream Cinema' (1983: 2–16).

6. Bellin goes into some detail about this context. For further reading in this area, see Donald Bogle (2000), Miriam Hansen (1991) and Grace Elizabeth Hale (1999).

7. See Fatimah Tobing Rony (1996) and Rhona Berenstein (1996) for further accounts of these films. Cooper and Schoesdack had made several films that capitalised on this ethnographic impulse using footage obtained on expedition to put indigenous communities and wild animals on display: *Grass: A Nation's Battle for Life* (1925), documenting an Iranian nomadic tribe's migration, *Chang* (1927), concerned with an indigenous family and various wildlife in jungle in Thailand, and Schoesdack's solo project, *Rango* (1931), shot in the tropical forests of Sumatra. Storylines about 'exotic' lands and apes or indigenous peoples as threatening surface in early films like *The Lost World* (Harry O Hoyt, 1925), and in sensationalised form in jungle horror and jungle adventure films that grew in popularity in the late 1920s and 1930s, such as *Ingagi* (William Campbell, 1930), *Trader Horn* (W.S. Van Dyke, 1931), *The Blonde Captive* (Clinton Childs et al. 1931), and *Bring 'Em Back Alive* (Clyde E. Elliott, 1932).

8. Bellin is the first to note that there are factors that complicate his reading of the film, and the final part of his chapter is an interesting document of his ambivalence about some of these factors, particularly in relation to the work of Willis O'Brien; in this regard in particular, the chapter makes for a compelling read.

9. See Goldner & Turner's account of the special effects work in *The Making of King Kong: The Story Behind a Film Classic* (1975: 94–5).

10. It is worth noting here Bellin's acknowledgement that his critical position assumes 'the perspective of the dominant – in this context, white – culture in the creation, circulation and reception of fantasy films' (2005: 45).

11. According to the racist conceptualisation of indigenous peoples as 'primitive' and thus representing access to the past and to humanity's origins.

12. As a sidebar, the fact that this 'eyebrow waggling' close-up is so often misinterpreted by critics as a sexual look is partly related to the use of an animatronic head in the shot, which with its rigid and very simplistic replication of facial movements simply did not permit the same level of expressive sophistication as O'Brien's stop-motion animation of Kong.

13. The designation of close-up in this analysis is somewhat problematic, given the disparate sizes of the characters' bodies, but is based on shot scale in relation to the body in each case.

14. For example, consider the snatches of conversation the film presents as the audience waits for the Kong show to start, in particular the woman who has come expecting a condescending ethnographic or jungle film not unlike the kind discussed earlier in the chapter, featuring 'darling monkeys and tigers, and things'; it is also clear that the press photographers' flashbulbs cause Kong to think Ann is under attack, and thus precipitate him breaking his chains as he tries to protect her.

15. The background of Darrow's reaction shots also has a relevant metaphorical function: initially only the rocky ground is visible, communicating her trapped state, but as she progresses to a standing position the backdrop of the island, the sea and the horizon beyond overturn this sense of Darrow being 'caught', and operate as a visual metaphor for her openness.

16. See for example staff article (2006), 'King Kong – We talk to Andy Serkis, the man who played Gollum, about how wild gorillas inspired his new film role,' in *BBC Wildlife* 24.1: 60–3.

17. Notice how Darrow develops a limited sign language with Kong in the subsequent sunset scene, opening another channel of communication that is full of potential. For contemporary audiences it may evoke the experiments to teach sign language to primates that garnered public interest in the 1960s, 1970s and 1980s.

18. The elderly woman will reappear as the high priestess officiating at the ritual sacrifice of Darrow, her garb augmented by a makeshift, web-like headdress that intensifies these connotations of witchery.

CHAPTER 5

Representation and the Digital

One of the strands of enquiry that has emerged in this book is the staging of the profilmic body in relation to digital elements of the frame, and the connotative potential inherent in such staging. Another strand of enquiry, made explicit in the preceding discussion of *King Kong*, and equally pressing in those films which use the profilmic body as a canvas for direct digital manipulation, is the relationship of digital imaging deployments to questions and practices of representation. In this Chapter I want to bring these two strands together in an extended analysis of *300*. In particular, I will suggest that the ways in which digital imaging mediates and frames the profilmic body in *300* have a direct correspondence to the film's preoccupations, its engagements with questions of genre, and the politics of its representations. In an era when the most explicit uses of digital imaging are found in blockbuster entertainment, and digital effects are promoted only in terms of their contribution to a film's entertainment value, I will argue that we must recognise, and analyse, the part digital imaging plays in the ideological operations of these mainstream texts.

DELINEATING THE BODY

300 is based on a Frank Miller graphic novel of the same name (1998), a fictionalised account of the 480 BC Battle of Thermopylae in which a small number of Spartan soldiers and Greek allies, led by the Spartan king Leonidas, held off a massive Persian army before being outflanked and killed. The film opens with the tale of Leonidas's origin, told in an extended montage sequence that establishes the mode of narration and visual style that the film will adopt. The sequence is an effective, and efficient, introduction to the values and principles that will define the idealised Spartan body, and immediately demonstrates

Figure 5.1 Still from *300* (Warner Bros / Legendary Pictures / The Kobal Collection): A high contrast 'look' and attenuated vista in the shot where baby Leonidas is inspected for flaws.

the way in which digital imaging works to intensify our experience of that body.

Brief shots economically convey key stages in the king's early life – a brutal fight practice with his father, bloody Spartan combat training, the solitary rite of passage called the 'time in the wild' – accompanied by a sonorous male narrator who repeatedly affirms Leonidas's grounding in traditional Spartan values: 'From the time he could stand he was baptised in the fire of combat . . . taught never to retreat, never to surrender.' At the start he is a baby being inspected for flaws, in danger of being flung into a ravine if he fails the inspection. A high angle over-the-shoulder shot bears down on the baby in close-up as the Spartan elder holds him over the cliff edge; the drop and the risk of imminent death are emphasised by canted, low reverse angle shots from the bottom of the ravine, the skulls of less fortunate babies coming into sharp focus in the foreground (see Fig. 5.1). These early shots point up the child's vulnerability and passivity, but as the sequence progresses the growing Leonidas displays a range of gestures of resilience and determination. During combat training with his tall, muscular father, a series of low angle shots emphasise the father's monolithic physical superiority over the skinny boy, but also the crouching, agile readiness of Leonidas's postures and the defiant, resolute upward swing of his heavy sword. In the next sequence this maturing determination results in a reversal of power relations articulated through a new spatial relationship between the boy and a young adversary: the boy king pushes down onto his opponent (and the spectator) in a low angle close-up, an over-the-shoulder reverse angle showing his battered victim. Leonidas is framed above him as aggressor and victor, his swinging fists now successfully connecting with their target. These shots map out the youth's transformation into a warrior in a procession of physical postures and gestures that illustrate his growing stamina, agility and self-assurance, a procession that is made significantly more conspicuous by the digitally manipulated qualities of the cinematic image itself.

The opening displays the film's signature 'look', which replaces a more graduated naturalistic style with a high contrast between lit and shadowed portions of the frame, giving a two-dimensional, graphic quality to relatively static compositions (see Fig. 5.1). Director of Photography Larry Fong explains that this results from the film's attempt to replicate the visual 'style and compositions' of the graphic novel, including colours and visual textures (in Williams 2007: 14). Digital imaging technologies are integral to the realisation of this aesthetic goal. The digital intermediate was used to impose a very particular colour grading process on the images, which Fong describes as '"crushing" the blacks and the high end and ramping up the midrange and contrast, and then desaturating the entire image' (16). This approach brought out deep reds and blacks but dampened other colours in order to approximate the graphic novel's artwork. The film's various digital effects vendors also used the novel's look as a constant reference point. Art director Grant Freckleton of Animal Logic comments that the graphic novel

> was textured and had bits of paint splattered this way and that. You could almost see the paper texture coming through the paint. We didn't want to lose the texture of the graphic novel, and we wanted to avoid the crisp, digital feel that is always a giveaway to work that's been done on a computer . . . [we] came up with a look that was obviously not a photograph, but not quite a painting; it was something in-between. (in Fordham 2007: 67)

This post-production image processing and its replication of the artistic style of the source material also crucially foregrounds the bodies, poses and actions of its characters.

The hard-edged, 'crushed' tonal quality of the resulting images 'outlines' bodies, picking out their musculature in detail as well as delineating them from the background of each shot. The static nature of the frame is also important in this regard, and not simply as a replication of the graphic novel's presentation style; shots are stilled or slowed so that the arrangement and poses of bodies within them is emphasised. Such practices render the shots declarative rather than 'documentary' in purpose; each shot becomes a *tableau vivant* in which framing and thus spatial relations, physical attitude and movement (whether frozen or in motion) are isolated for contemplation. During the sequence which depicts Leonidas's combat training, at first it is his father's extremely muscular body that is picked out by the high contrast between lighter and darker areas of the frame, the adult soldier's upright presence associated with the stone pillars emerging out of the shadows behind him, communicating his immovable strength and fighting skill. In contrast the skinny Leonidas is punished for his combat failings by a backhanded clout that sends him flailing to the ground. In the subsequent shots, however, the contours of the boy's body are picked out instead, his resilience and determination in the face of defeat communicated in his crouched, battle ready pose.[1] These lower angle shots now align the boy with the stone pillars, indicating a reaching towards the older soldier's stature and combat success that qualifies Leonidas's squatting gait as one of readiness rather than fear. The presence of the rather monolithic, impassively upright figure of the father in the sequence presses the point home: young Leonidas will have to rise, physically and mentally, to the challenge of being a Spartan king.

The post-production digital image processing works with the static framing to foreground the developing boy-king's gestures and postures of growing resilience, stoicism, and martial athleticism, making sense of his progress to kingship as a progress towards becoming a fully-fledged warrior *body*. This effect is most pronounced in the final initiation stage of the Spartan training – the teenage boy's 'time in the wild' and his life-threatening confrontation with a giant wolf. Composition and the digitally achieved play of light and shadow allow the confrontation to be silhouetted against the pale night sky, outlining the antagonists' physical attitudes as they circle each other, watchful and poised to strike. Unfolding in wintry moonlight, an intensified visual contrast is produced as each shot becomes a graphic intersection of blacks (rock, shadows) and insipid whites (snow, sky, the boy's skin). Leonidas's fatal spear thrust into the wolf is similarly captured in a static framing or *tableau vivant* that foregrounds his physical extension in sharply contrasted light and dark areas, the wolf's death convulsion visualised as a large black shadow that brings the boy's lit body into further relief. The narrator's declaration at this moment, that 'his form was perfect', reveals a visual interest in the body's physical assertions that is in keeping with the entire opening's visual and metaphorical emphasis on the maturing warrior's postures and gestures. These culminate in Leonidas's triumphant return from the wilderness to claim his throne, depicted in another, literal, *tableau vivant*; like his father, Leonidas now stands tall against the stone pillars of Sparta, fellow warriors bowing and prostrating themselves before him. The specificities of bodily display and physical attitude, emphasised through the aesthetic attributes of the digitally enabled high contrast image, generate very precise connotations here. This kind of aesthetic 'marking out' of corporeal shapes and poses will become increasingly important as the narrative develops, as the confrontation between the Spartans and the Persians is dramatised across the body. But before exploring this in more detail, I want to place *300* in context, in terms of genre and in relation to other films that display similar aesthetic characteristics.

STAGING THE BODY

In attempting to create a moving image that registered somewhere between a photograph and a painting, *300*'s visual effects team deployed post-production processing but also replaced location shooting with filming on a blue-screen stage, with digital matte paintings and digitally animated 2-D and 3-D artifacts (dust, cloud, snow) added later to provide the backgrounds. These digitally inserted set extensions and artifacts frame the action but have a painterly quality that is unapologetically non-naturalistic. In this regard *300* is similar to a number of other films that have emerged since the late 1990s, which use blue- or green-screen shooting to allow different settings to be constructed digitally around the actors in post-production.[2] These films are most often characterised by an overt visual stylisation that explicitly references previous visual cultural forms. Overt stylisation also partially circumvents the difficulty of achieving naturalistic-looking composites of digital and live action elements, while mobilising connotations about the composited environment and the bodies it stages. For example, *Sky Captain and the World of Tomorrow* (2004) manifests its alternative 1939 as an amalgamation of motifs from pre-1960s science fiction cinema and 1930s and 1940s fashion, news media, technologies, adventure serials and comic books. A soft-edged, luminescent filter and a sepia-toned colour palette invokes the faded, softened edges of old photographs. In each of these films, the manner in which the profilmic body is staged by digital compositing and in relation to digital environments is meaningful in a particularised way. For example, the digital compositing strategy in *Sky Captain* is deliberately palimpsestic, refusing to fully stitch together image planes which are themselves compositionally flattened out. In this visual field, the profilmic characters appear to be living out their adventures literally as if across the pages of a comic book: this adventure will be strictly 'boy's own', returning its hero and heroine safely at the end of the narrative.[3] *Sin City* (Frank Miller and Robert Rodriguez, 2005) closely replicates the black and white illustrated frames (and occasional flash of colour) in Frank Miller's *Sin City* graphic novels (1991), using a monochromatic tonal range that eradicates most greys and produces a high contrast, hard-edged look appropriate to its homage to Miller's graphic style but also to the lighting aesthetic of film noir. In contrast to the compositing strategy in *Sky Captain*, the various planes of the image in *Sin City* are carefully arranged to achieve compositional depth, helping to create a much stronger sense of a three-dimensional diegetic space. The profilmic body is carefully and emphatically anchored in this space, moving through and interacting with the environment in ways that emphasise weight and momentum. A persistent foregrounding of the visceral consequences of impacts with the environment and with other bodies is achieved through the digital colourisation of isolated elements of the frame: blood, cuts, plasters and

scars glow red or a stark, fluorescent white against the monochrome articulation of the storyworld. In a violent film world in which innocent bodies suffer
in profoundly physical ways as a result of the machinations of others, venge-
ance is partly justified through a digital aesthetic that underscores the visceral-
ity of that suffering.

In keeping with its generic lineage, *300* stages the body through specific
modes of digital compositing. However, the differences from, as well as the
similarities with, the way that *300*'s cinematic antecedents staged the body are
instructive. Along with its Ancient Greek setting, it is *300*'s preoccupation
with the spectacle of the heroic male body that locates it in the generic tradition of the historical or ancient world epic (Neale 1983; Hark 1993).[4] Films
like *Ben-Hur* (William Wyler, 1959) and *Spartacus* (Stanley Kubrick, 1960)
enacted a large-scale, extravagant, exhibitionist version of history while also
acclaiming the spectacular nature of the terms of their own production. Derek
Elley argues that the spectacles they provided were 'merely the cinema's own
transformation of the literary epic's taste for the grandiose, realised on a sufficient scale to impress modern audiences' (1984: 1). Vivian Sobchack has
gone rather further, however, memorably calling the post-war historical epic
'cinema tumescent', a 'perverse and inflated display of autoerotic spectacle . . .
swollen with its own generative power to mobilize the vast amounts of labor
and money necessary to diddle its technology to an extended and expanded
orgasm of images, sounds and profits' (1995: 282).[5] This engagement of cinematic technologies in the historical epic to produce certain kinds of excess
was crucial in achieving product differentiation in relation to other post-war
cinematic output (Neale 2000: 85).[6] *300* emerges at an equivalent moment in
current mainstream cinema, at which exhibitionist digital effects – rather than
large-scale real-world sets and thousands of human extras – are perceived as
differentiating a film from other products in the marketplace.[7] In the light of
this continued studio and press preoccupation with 'special' digital effects, and
the generic tradition of visual extravagance of which they are a part, it is not
surprising that *300* adopts an exhibitionist visual style. The film relies heavily
on overt uses of digital effects, not to recreate a naturalistic vision of an ancient
world but to generate a hyper-stylised, excessive visualisation of events. This
is an aesthetic mode that has consequences both for the representation of the
Spartan heroes *and* their Persian foes, and is thus key to what we might call the
film's 'body politics'.

To begin to think about this, let us look at the sequence in which King
Leonidas and his 300 soldiers leave Sparta and begin to march to the battle-
front, a sequence in which what is shown and what is heard reveals the film's
developing ideas about bodies. In a field of golden corn just outside Sparta's
walls the now-adult Leonidas (Gerard Butler) bids farewell to his queen while
his troops begin their march. As he moves to join his men the voice-over

intones, 'There's no room for softness, not in Sparta. No place for weakness. Only the hard and strong may call themselves Spartans.' In the foreground Queen Gorgo (Lena Headey) turns her troubled face away from the departing group and towards the camera as the voice-over repeats, 'only the hard . . . only the strong'. In the next shot the 300 traverse a valley, unaware of a figure watching them from behind a tree, a figure that is nearer to the camera, and whose silhouette reveals a substantially deformed back. A cut into a close-up of the figure's hand reveals that this, too, is deformed. Slow motion shots of red capes and marching Spartans are followed by a long shot in which the men dip into a valley, as the voice-over returns to affirm, 'We march. For our lands, for our families, for our freedoms, we march.'

The words of the voice-over, and the shots with which they are juxtaposed, are revealing. As Queen Gorgo turns towards the camera, determinedly suppressing her emotions at the painful moment of parting, the voice-over's assertion that there is no room for softness and weakness appears to affirm her Spartan stoicism in the face of her husband's fatal mission. But the words' occurrence with her presence in the foreground of the shot has another effect. Dominant, conservative constructions of femininity as 'soft' and 'weak' are called up and associated with the sole woman in the frame so that they can be explicitly and literally 'left behind' – with her, static in the foreground – by the men moving purposefully into the background of the shot. The voice-over then uses repetition and vocal emphasis to underline the qualities the departing soldiers share: 'Only the *hard*. Only the *strong*.' The emphatically corporeal nature of these categorisations refers to the characteristics of the Spartan male body that the film has already repeatedly presented, its marked musculature – clearly defined through the digital post-processing of the image – generating associations with both strength and 'hardness'. The sequence itself reaffirms this correlation by subsequently returning to slow motion shots of the 300's naked, muscled torsos as they march. The first appearance of the deformed Ephialtes (Andrew Tiernan) in this context is significant. A soldier hopeful, Ephialtes' physical deformity later prevents him from joining the Spartan forces, and in his anger at what he sees as an unjust rejection he turns traitor. Here he is a mysterious unidentified silhouette; alongside his hidden viewing position this makes his watchfulness potentially threatening. His silhouetted body shape is in marked contrast to the Spartan male physical norm the film has quickly established, and which has been outlined for us literally by the digital colour grading. Failing to clarify who or indeed what this silhouette is, the sequence subtly conflates potential villainy with physical deformity. Interestingly, here and in the rest of the film, the voice-over does not refer to Ephialtes' onscreen presence, remaining silent on the subject of this body that so emphatically transgresses the corporeal characteristics the voice-over espouses. The sequence thus presents bodies that are not Spartan male (that is, female; deformed) in order to re-present Leonidas's men as the physical embodiment of heroic martial endeavour.

The voice-over mutually reinforces the images through its extravagant rhetoric as well as its selective silences, thus contributing to our reception of the muscular, digitally delineated Spartan bodies we see. Voice-over narration is a familiar element in the post-war historical epic: the 'sonorous – and patriarchal – "Voice of God" narration' promised 'epic scope' while signalling the safe 'pastness of the past' (Sobchack 1995: 281), but was also a residue of the epic movie's origins in literature (see Elley 1984). In *300* the extravagance of the voice-over narration matches the hyperbole of the film's digitally intensified visual presentation, making this not so much 'History' writ large as a mythic tale of male heroism. Indeed, the framing story within which the narrator is located explicitly offers the story as myth: the narrator Dilios (David Wenham) is a Spartan warrior known for his story-telling skills who takes part in the first phases of the fighting, but is injured, and as a result sent back before the battle reaches its conclusion, expressly instructed by Leonidas to tell such a dramatic version of the events that Spartans and other Greeks will be galvanised into further action against the Persians. The narration we hear and see are parts of Dilios's inspirational speech to the Spartan army as it prepares to go back into battle against the Persian armies and Persian king Xerxes (Rodrigo Santoro) at Plataea, one year after the Battle of Thermopylae that *300* depicts. While the temporal positioning of the narration locates the three hundred's fight within a larger temporal canvas, identifying it as key to the Greeks' ultimate success against the Persians (and thus positioning it as 'History'), the voice-over's employment of repetition and exaggeration to rhetorically mythologise the Spartans' heroic feats and the 'monstrosities' of the Persian hordes has a particularly corporeal emphasis. Equally, however, the voice-over is also concerned to convey the principles for which these Spartans have mobilised. During the initial stages of the Spartan march the narrator declares the men are marching for their lands, families, and freedoms, a word that recurs several times in the film. The voice-overs of post-war historical epics were often preoccupied with the theme of freedom, within films that have been interpreted as displaying variously Cold War, anti-communist or liberal sentiments to contemporaneous audiences (Neale 2000: 90–1). *300*'s voice-over narration characterises the Spartans as heroes fighting to safeguard democratic freedom for future generations, the Persians 'barbarian hordes' attempting to thwart this aim. This has led some commentators to interpret the film as displaying pro-George Bush or anti-Iran sentiments,[8] but while the dialogue's assertions about the Spartans as democracy's protectors might have contemporary cultural and political resonance, Rudolf Maté's 1962 account of the battle, *The 300 Spartans* (said to have inspired the young Frank Miller), was equally insistent on this point at a quite different cultural-historical moment, as Derek Elley has observed (1984: 74). In my view, *300*'s 'politics' are more readable in its representational dynamics than in the overtly politicised rhetoric of its voice-over narration.

The film's hyperbolic visual presentation depends in large part on digital set extensions and highly stylised backdrops, which erect a peculiarly non-naturalistic *mise-en-scène* around *300*'s protagonist-bodies. Animal Logic provided digitally generated skies to drop behind the blue screen filmed footage, produced by combining moving images of real clouds with digitally manipulated 'coffee stain' patterns, which according to art director Grant Freckleton 'gave the audience a visual cue that they were looking at stylized imagery, rather than something that was striving to be realistic' (Fordham 2007: 67). This overt stylisation signals that *300* will not depict events naturalistically, but also permits a communicative level of expressiveness in the background elements that define the landscape and the space within which the action will develop.

Attention to the detail of these digital environments' construction is necessary to register the meanings they put into play. In the concise opening sequence, which shows Leonidas's origins and progress to an adult warrior, digital backdrops and set extensions quickly establish an atmosphere that frames the events themselves. Painterly, turbulent skies form the backdrop for the vetting of baby Leonidas and for Leonidas's emphatic beating of his boxing competitor, setting a melodramatic tone that corresponds to the potential or actual violence of the scene (see Fig. 5.1). Later in the sequence as Leonidas and the wolf circle each other, our sense of the surrounding landscape is extremely limited; digitally generated environmental elements produce a pared-away setting of distant moonlit hills and snowy fog that communicates Leonidas's isolation and vulnerability at this moment of danger. When Leonidas later takes leave of his wife low-lying, thunderous clouds and a rising hill on the left of the frame prevent the eye from perceiving the full extent of the valley; frame right, mountains soar beyond the top of the frame, forcing the men to detour left through the cornfield and curtailing the optical reach of the viewer. In the Spartans' subsequent encounter with Arcadians keen to join forces, the two groups meet on a slope, the variable incline forcing them towards each other. Framed from a low angle, the hillside interrupts a view of the full extent of the landscape behind it, while the blaze from the setting sun obliterates much of the remaining detail of the mountains beyond. Glowering clouds gather close behind the men, completing a digital set extension that, as in the other examples above, lends the depicted situation a claustrophobic, sombre quality.

From the distant buildings of Sparta framed behind Xerxes' approaching messengers, to the thousands of Persian troops spread across the terrain at Thermopylae, *300* presents digitally generated landscapes that are painterly, softened by the synthetic effects of shallow focus, and often swathed in smoke and brooding clouds shot through with wide beams of digitally inserted light. But as the previous paragraph implied, composition and the visual design of these digital backdrops combine to noticeably limit the spatial extension of each shot, an effect even more pronounced during the battle scenes, when the geological formations of the Hot Gates, the gorge where the Spartans make their stand, constrict the space of action even further. Such landscapes express a sense of accumulating foreboding at the task awaiting the Spartans, which, once undertaken, offers no escape. The digital background elements in *300* do not simply establish a visual 'mood', then; they also foreshorten the horizon and their landscapes' apparent reach, creating a sense of enclosure and demarcating a space of action that is much more limited than one might expect. This is a significant visual contrast to the extended vistas of the post-war historical epic, which were often filmed in bright sunlight to emphasise the breadth and reach of the real-world landscapes on which the casts of hundreds, if not thousands, acted out their conflicts. This is the style of presentation in films such *Ben-Hur* and *The 300 Spartans*, and was more recently reproduced in *Troy* (Wolfgang Petersen, 2004). Indeed, Sobchack notes that this quality of extended space is normally integral to the historical epic, translating 'the sense of temporal *magnitude* and the existential *weight* of being in historical time into visible size and scale and quantity and extravagance' (1995: 294, emphasis in original). In this way such films intensify their affective impact, as extended space stages the experience of momentous history, and '"being caught up" in and "swept along" by social events not of one's own making are translated into massive surges of movement – from buffalo stampedes to revolutions to the Exodus' (294). Eschewing the extended vistas of the traditional historical epic, *300* constructs instead a series of claustrophobic, enclosing environments for its Spartan heroes: its account of the clash of one nation with Xerxes' many nations is mapped, not onto a giant canvas stretching out as far as the eye can see, but onto a small, attenuated space. This works thematically, of course; in their attempt to prevent the Persians from invading Greece, the Spartans will occupy the narrow gap between the Hot Gates, and this will also be the confined space in which they die. But in demarcating a limited space of action in this way, the 'massive surges' of competing forces Sobchack resonantly describes are also transcribed into a smaller arena, and reconfigured as competing bodily forces. As the following analysis will show, the manner in which the film arranges, choreographs and presents its opposed bodies in these particularised, digitally constructed spaces reveals the extent and nature of *300*'s underlying body politics.

At the Spartans' arrival at the Hot Gates, notions of distance and proximity, knowledge and power are introduced through the performers' relationship to the digitally generated *mise-en-scène*. The sequence begins by framing the Spartans from above in a high angle long shot as they walk through the Hot

Gates, the narrator asserting 'into the mouth of Hell, we march'. The camera's spatial orientation is shared by the crippled Ephialtes, who is lit by the sun at the top of the Gates while the Spartans tread in darkness at the bottom of the towering corridor of rock. The Spartans' progress is depicted in closer framings before the initial composition returns, Ephialtes still watching them pass far below him. As the voice-over repeats, 'Into Hell's mouth, we march', the camera tilts upward and pans to reveal the amassed Persian fleet at sea: during the pan, digital imaging generates rocks, sea, ships and roiling sky, but also simulates wide angle lens distortion, 'bending' the extreme edges of the image. Dilios, who is still part of the 300 at this point in the film, Captain (Vincent Regan) and Leonidas briefly discuss their hopes that the approaching squall will catch the Persians unawares, and it seems their hopes are answered, as a second sequence shows the Spartans cheering gleefully as they witness Persian ships capsized by the turbulent sea. Cutting between close-ups of the shouting men and a striking long shot that frames the Spartans clustered on the tip of the Hot Gates, the enormous crushing waves and collapsing ships playing out beyond them, the sequence categorically confirms that the Persians have experienced a punishing setback. But the visual presentation of the digitally composited and generated environment, in relation to the pro-filmic bodies within it, once again qualifies our reading of events.

Both vistas offered in this scene are dramatically foreshortened, replaced by a sea view that is dark, visually busy and which fills virtually the entire frame. In the second long shot in particular, the horizon is severely limited, ships and the sea itself appearing to rise up towards the Spartans rather than extending away into the distance. The strikingly curtailed visual reach of the vistas points towards their evident artifice, producing a strong sense of *trompe l'oeil* that makes them register almost like an artificially constructed, painted panorama. The circular panorama, invented by Robert Barker in 1789 and proliferating in urban centres in the nineteenth century as painted wraparound displays of battles, natural wonders and 'exotic' locations, enabled a kind of expanded vision by offering spectators an extended view and 'an ambulatory ubiquity' (Crary 1988: 22) often not practically achievable outside its walls. The pano-rama thus produced the impression of a fictional omniscience for the spectator, as Norman M. Klein suggests:

Your individual ego commands the horizon (or pretends it does) . . . Inside the panorama, you exceed your place; you exceed boundaries. You feel for a moment the success of overcoming. (2004: 185)

This sense of omniscience, of overcoming, and its inherently illusory nature, is something the film seems interested in invoking at certain points for narra-tive ends. The legible artifice of the 'panoramas' *300* offers is central to this strategy. For example, the notion of the panorama in concert with the artifice of the digital backgrounds expands, beyond the literal, the implications of the storm sequence in which the Spartans behold the Persians in trouble at sea. Like in the spatial arrangement of the panorama, the Spartans subject their troubled opponents to their triumphant gaze from a detached vantage point above the Hot Gates. At a safe distance from the boiling sea, the Spartans cheer, roar and punch the air, relishing their momentary victory. Certainly these men are experiencing the 'success of overcoming', but the artifice of the digital background and its enclosing nature – sea and sky looming oppressively on the Spartans' seemingly safe position – tempers the extent to which we share the Spartans' sense of their superiority over the Persians.

Permitting a participant to subject a large field of view to his or her gaze – and in this way enjoy a sense of empowerment – the nineteenth century painted panorama simultaneously revealed this empowerment as an illusion through its evident artificiality. In the same way, during the storm the Spartans' assumption of an omnipotent, triumphalist position is subtly undermined by particular configurations of camera position and digital backdrop that foreground the artifice and the foreshortened nature of the horizon they are contemplating. Haunting the scene is the implication that this disengaged, distant viewpoint on events will *not* characterise the rest of their conflict with the Persians, which will instead be defined by the extreme proximity that these curtailed digital horizons are already pointing towards. It is significant, too, that in the high angle 'bird's eye view' of the Spartans entering the Hot Gates in the scene preceding the storm, Ephialtes has followed an old goat trail to obtain a higher, more informative viewpoint. His successfully undetected subterfuge qualifies the Spartans' sense of a secure, superior perspective on the Persians' manoeuvres. Indeed the shot prefigures the Spartans' fate: Ephialtes will later lead the Persian king Xerxes to the same goat trail, precipitating the Spartans' defeat.

These claustrophobic, enveloping skylines thus have a narrative function that extends beyond this particular sequence. From the bright, slightly more expansive vistas of the Spartan homeland via the smoke filled, indeterminate spaces of the burnt out village that the Spartans pass through and the cloudy cliff-top on which they sleep during their march, a motif of progressive enclosure develops, culminating in the three hundred's last stand in the narrow Hot Gates.[9] At the same time, the notion of an empowered, elevated viewpoint that has been invoked in this early sequence continues to have currency as the narrative progresses. Later it is Xerxes who will mistake a lofty, disengaged vantage point for an empowered position, surveying his troops' progress from his camp and his enormous throne. The film does not share Xerxes' panoramic vision at these moments, but registers his efforts to publicly assert a mastering gaze over events. The hubris that lies behind such attempts is jolted by the Spartans' persistent battlefield successes, and it is significant that the film ends with a literal traverse of this viewing distance that Xerxes relies upon, as Leonidas's final, heroically assertive spear throw manages to make contact with a horrified and momentarily chastened Persian king.[10]

The claustrophobic, enclosing digital environments of the film culminate in the Hot Gates, a confined space that brings the opposed forces into close proximity with each other, and with us. The attention to the body encouraged by the digitally produced high contrast aesthetic here foregrounds physical attitudes and bodily interactions that are highly communicative. After rejecting Xerxes' first offer to surrender, the Spartans find themselves face to face with their enemy. An extreme long shot momentarily captures the Persian's first charge on a large canvas, the continuous line of glinting, tightly packed Spartan shields hinting at the composure and impenetrability of their defensive position.[11] This shot is followed by a shallow focused extreme close-up of the tip of a Spartan spear, still and ready, its closeness to the camera conveying the physical immediacy of the imminent clash of bodies. The compositional simplicity of these early images contrasts with the visual density of what follows. Three consecutive medium close-ups depict the roaring crowds of Persians as they hurl themselves forward, weapons and shields waving. In each shot they literally thrust the Spartan line to the edges of the frame, and a subsequent close-up shows Spartan feet losing ground. Two further shots of advancing Persians follow, before another shot of Spartan feet being pushed back. The absence of a precise shot-reverse shot pattern underlines the Persians' forward momentum, raising the spectre that they will break the Spartan line. The struggle for momentum and for purchase between the opposed forces plays out in a series of close-ups that emphasise physical exertion and mental determination as each side pits all their strength against the other; faces grimace, battle cries vent forth, feet scrabble to keep their footing under the pressure. Each mass of soldiers pushes itself into the other, bodies themselves giving form to the line of battle. And then the Spartan line simply stops, halting the Persians' progress. The border not only stands firm, but actively repels: Spartan shields slam Persian bodies backwards in unison, and when the Persian soldiers move forward again, they are skewered – partly by their own forward momentum – on newly levelled Spartan spears. Once again this is shot in close-ups from a range of angles, the thump of the line of shields as they impact and the wet 'shunk' of each spear penetrating Persian flesh repeated on the soundtrack, the regularity of the sounds and images indicative of the military manoeuvre's efficacy.

During the fray the protagonists are again circumscribed visually, by the walls of the Hot Gates, the masses of bodies filling the foreground, and the shafts of light and smoke that obscure the precise coordinates of the battleground. The digital set extensions and backdrops operate as an architecture that centres and frames the body as the locus of attention. This corporeal focus is then intensified by the persistent use of close-ups, many digitally enhanced to give the detail of penetrating spears, severed limbs and sprays of blood that vividly convey the violence of bodies meeting, resisting and being breached. The epic's surging forces are reconfigured as competing bodies at the ground level in a confined space, the defence and attempted incursion of national borders played out in the collision of opposed warrior bodies.

In battle, as in the montage showing Leonidas's journey from infancy to manhood, progress is communicated by a series of body positions fore-grounded by the visual presentation of the sequence, which includes the delineating digital colour grading and the attenuated digital backgrounds. During the first phase of this initial confrontation such postures and gestures are presented in close-ups or medium close-ups, in a rush of profilmic flesh and movement. The Spartans repeatedly reassert their battle-ready shield-raised pose, a posture of resistance and intactness that communicates stasis as immovability. The sequence develops a rhythmic alternation between differ-ent body poses and movements, as a series of three shots from the middle of the sequence illustrates. The first is a close-up of a cluster of Spartan spears plunged into the Persian line, composition in depth emphasising the controlled simultaneity of the multiple thrusts while the high contrast image and lighting design, along with the camera's close proximity, allows Spartan musculature to be picked out in detail, multiplying the connotations of force in the shot. This uniformity of purpose and action is contrasted with the uneven Persian line in the second shot, the angled frame underlining the way in which their spears, shields and bodies are pointing confusedly in different directions. In medium close-up a Persian staked through with a spear doubles over, his eyes widening with shock before he slumps towards the bottom edge of the frame. In shot three, his trajectory to the ground is confirmed, as his prone body is trampled by Spartan feet in a dark, cluttered, low angle close-up.

The spear thrust gesture, distilled to its basic elements – arm propelled forward, spear and limb united in direction, rigidity and force – and mul-tiplied within the frame, efficiently conveys the penetrating power of the Spartan-in-motion. Elsewhere in the sequence the sword slash has a similar connotative impact, both gestures repeatedly deployed with deadly, effec-tive regularity against the oncoming hundreds. Contrastingly the Persian body – its lack of purposeful direction, its stilled pose of shock and pain as its forward momentum is stopped by a Spartan spear, and its consequent physi-cal collapse – is forced to perform its disempowerment in a static posture and then a moving gesture of defeat. This is repeated throughout the sequence, as spear thrusts result in stilled postures of fatally penetrated, brutally folded Persians, and gestures of physical overthrow as Persian bodies are propelled backwards, limbs extended, into dying falls.[12] The repetition of these Spartan and Persian actions and body postures – brought into sharp focus through the camera's close proximity to them – cumulatively asserts the power relations which they convey (*this* group of Persians will not succeed) and importantly, too, the mental attitudes they reveal: the Spartans' repeated thrusts signal their unfailing determination and resilience, the folding and backward flight of the Persians displays a lack of literal stability that hints at a deeper lack of motivation (these are slaves forced to fight by Xerxes, rather than free men fighting for their own land). This repetition occurs across shots and within shots: digital compositing combines with a telephoto lens to visually compress several Spartan spear thrusts or falling Persians into the same frame and the same shallow space of action. Crowded bodies mean digital backdrops are only visible at the edges of the frame, conveying very little sense of surroundings or spatial depth. As I have indicated, such tactics are part of the film's presentation of a series of digital environments that close in on the Spartans, producing a limited space of confrontation and an intensified awareness of the violent clash of bodies that fill the frame. At the same time, the compressed shots and the cumulative effect of a succession of views multiply the signifiers of Spartan strength and Persian weakness, the Persian bodies penetrable, conceding, and weak, the Spartans strong, forceful, and effective.

In the battle's second phase, digital imaging is employed to stress this differentiation between Spartan and Persian, through the figure of Leonidas himself and his presentation using 'speed-ramping', a form of digitally constructed variable speed slow motion. Persian numbers are thinning, and in an extended take Leonidas bursts out of the Spartan ranks and strides forcefully through the battlefield, each swing and spear-plunge lethally dispatching another foe. The take begins as a medium long shot, Leonidas stepping forward into the mêlée with his spear straight and ready as the Persians approach. A crash zoom reframes him in a medium close-up as he hurls a Persian over his shoulder, then zooms back out to a long shot as he pulls his arm back ready for a spear thrust. Another crash zoom turns the shot into a close-up, capturing his grimace of exertion as he begins the thrust, followed by a crash zoom out to a medium shot that catches the moment that the spear impales an approaching Persian. The long shot frames Leonidas's assertive, controlled attack, surrounded with whirling, compromised Persian bodies. During his spear thrust Leonidas's pose appears controlled, his feet anchored on the ground, increasing the movement's force and accuracy, while his Persian victim is lifted into the air, divested of purchase. The closer views (combined with precise costuming decisions) pick out the detail of Leonidas's musculature and determined facial expressions, but fail to individualise the Persians in the same way.

These digitally constructed crash zooms were achieved by mounting three cameras very close together, each focused on the same focal point but using three different lenses, the rig moved on a dolly to follow Leonidas's

Figure 5.2 Still from *300* (Warner Bros / Legendary Pictures / The Kobal Collection): King Leonidas impales a Persian in a speed-ramped sequence.

movements. Using digital morphing to move between the footage captured at different focal lengths and angles, synthetic zooms were produced within the tracking shot without damaging the impression of continuous action. Their effect, combined with the shifts between slow motion speeds which are also a feature of the shot, distil Leonidas's extended spatial penetration of the field of battle into a series of emphatic postures and gestures of mastery (Purse 2011: 66–8), removing scrappy intermediate movements from Leonidas's trajectory into the battlefield.[13] All superfluous action is pared away, and instead his attack comprises only declarative killing motions, the digitally enabled presentation throwing into relief the moment of each dispatch. Postures and gestures of attack are foregrounded within a continuous, fluid flow of motion that attests to Leonidas's physical control, strength and agility. In contrast, the crash zooms elide the Persians' energetic forward motions, reducing them to a series of death throes that are fixed in extreme slow motion. As each step in his trajectory of violent overcoming is repeatedly slowed, stilled, and brought close to the spectator through the digitally mediated sequence, the projective force of Leonidas's body is verified by the flailing gestures of death enacted by his Persian victims, and the exaggerated sprays of digital blood that issue from their broken bodies (see Fig. 5.2). The oncoming Persians never push Leonidas back on his heels; instead his unrelenting momentum, emphasised by the digital articulation of the sequence, overwhelms them. This is epitomised by the moment that a Persian running full pelt at the king is stopped dead by his shield, the Persian ricocheting off its surface in slow motion while the Spartan simply absorbs the impact, lowers the shield, and waits for his victim to fall. At this striking point in the king's offensive, extreme slow motion produces a *tableau vivant* that captures both the Persian's death fall – the physical embodiment of his battalion's collapse – and Leonidas's paused, poised and unmarked body, the symbol of his physical integrity and implied impenetrability. Thus motifs of resistance and assault, notions that define the larger conflict over land and sovereignty between the Greeks and Persians, are enacted by bodies; national borders come to be represented by skin and musculature, resistance physicalised in the struggle for purchase of pressing forms, penetrability vividly enacted as a breaching of corporeal integrity: limbs slashed, torsos bloodily speared.

The lowering of the shield is also a performative gesture, intended to convey a nonchalance that only the most accomplished warrior could afford; a gesture, then, that acknowledges that Leonidas is on display, to the Persians, and to his own men. At various points during the battles Leonidas is filmed in this way, his naked, muscular torso the focus of the shot as he enacts gestures of defiant resilience in slow motion, the digital post-processing of the image picking out the vivid flesh tones framed by the brilliant red of the cape. Moreover the deployment of digital imaging technologies, to increase the rapidity of shifts between different slow motion speeds without sacrificing the seamlessness of the image, is crucial in drawing attention to the athleticism of the Spartan's movements, allowing intense contemplation of the workings of different muscle groups as the warrior body extends, stretches, exerts and physically asserts itself with energy and force. These stilled moments that capture mid-gesture or declarative posture do not dissipate the spectator's sense of that body's momentum and force, but bring them into more focused view. Here the spectator is invited to echo the narrator's assertion early in the film that the Spartan's 'form' is 'perfect'. If the Spartan soldiers' gestures and postures communicate their heroic, determined action, the visual display of their bodies becomes the badge of their physical integrity, diegetically (for the purposes of boosting morale and de-motivating the enemy) and extra-diegetically (visually constructing and affirming the heroic body). The nakedness of the Spartans – fighting only in leather shorts, forearm and shin guards, red capes, shield and helmet – is a somewhat extreme way to indicate their physical resilience and fighting skills, but is indicative of the deliberate nature of the film's strategy of corporeal display.

The film's emphatic presentation of the body and concern with physical display is mirrored within the fictional world by both parties in the battle. The Spartans strut like peacocks and direct assertive looks towards the enemy; the Persian generals and their leader Xerxes wear heavy jewellery, and are raised on gilded platforms designed to demand their enemies' upturned gaze. When the first Persian general (Patrick Sabongui) arrives to instruct the Spartans to lay down their arms, the moment is staged as an exchange of looks. In a shot-reverse shot sequence Leonidas and his men persistently return defiant gazes in response to the increasingly vehement attempts by the general to stare them down, attempts cut short by a Spartan spear thrown across the space of the look, which kills the general and initiates the fighting. These physical exhibitions and exchanges of looks connect *300* to action cinema in both its contemporary form and in its historical manifestations such as the Western and the historical epic. The display of the male hero's body – poised for action, or defiant in defeat – is as central an ingredient of the Western as it is of more recent action films. Although such representations draw on 'those Christian traditions of representation which offer up the suffering white male body as spectacle', in these male-dominated genres in which friendships between men are often prized above heterosexual union, bodily display and its invitation of the gaze of other male characters can also generate connotations of homo-sexual desire (Tasker 1993: 74). Steve Neale has discussed the ways in which these genres have historically worked to suppress such readings: to prevent the male body from being 'marked explicitly as the erotic object of another male look', Neale explains, that look 'must be motivated in some other way, its erotic component repressed' (1983: 8). Framing the exchange of male looks within a situation of conflict helps the spectator to read other male characters' looks as fearful, hating or aggressive rather than desiring (12). Following the same principle, the most protracted exchanges of looks in *300* occur on the battlefield, between enemies, and dialogue and voice-over narration charac-terise these as aggressive and driven by battle hunger. However, the extreme emphasis on the display of the naked or partially nude form throws into ques-tion whether the film succeeds in suppressing homoeroticism in the manner described by Neale.

This tension between admitting and suppressing the homoeroticism inher-ent in the Spartans' insistently displayed bodies finds particularly striking illustration in the visual articulation of the 'beautiful death' that the Spartans wish for and finally achieve. The phrase, carefully emphasised at various earlier points in the voice-over narration, conveys that it is the public, dis-played nature of this death that defines it as a worthy annihilation in the midst of battle against a mighty enemy. But it also has a sexual connotation, recalling *la petite mort*, the 'little death' that follows the male orgasm. This beautiful death arrives in the Spartans' massacre by a digitally generated mass of Persian arrows, a fittingly hyperbolic end expressed in a spectacular image of bodily display and penetration. The dead Leonidas lays prone, eyes unseeing, arms outspread, in a jumble of shields and dirtied red Spartan capes. Arrows have pierced every inch of his body, their excessive number an asserted reassur-ance that the Spartan king has only been felled because a superabundance of force was deployed. The medium close-up frames Leonidas directly from above, presenting his musculature to view even at the point of death, while the shallow space of the flattened composition is an apt conclusion to the

progressively confined spaces within which the film placed its Spartan warriors. Perspective has been artificially exaggerated in the shot, so that the
arrows extend outwards from Leonidas's body towards the edges of the frame.
Compositionally this creates a myriad of sightlines that direct attention back to
the centre of the frame and back to Leonidas. As the camera cranes upwards
into a long shot, more and more similarly angled arrows come into view, intensifying this effect. The 'bird's-eye' view of the scene, which has drawn in other
Spartan corpses, shields, and out-flung capes, emphasises the staged nature of
the shot, which pictures a terrain of posed bodies carefully interleaved with
shields and other bodies rather than a naturalistic depiction of soldiers felled
as they fought. This self-conscious composition is a final demand to behold the
Spartan body, the shot's attempt at immortalising through display (alongside
the commemorative voice-over) also evident in Leonidas's Christ-like outstretched pose. However, the careful arrangement of Leonidas's body, head
thrown back and multiply penetrated, also evokes the many representations of
Saint Sebastian as a youthful male nude, pierced by arrows, in paintings from
the Renaissance onwards – representations which resonate with such homoeroticism that Sebastian has been claimed more recently as a gay icon.

STAGING OTHERNESS

The corporeal display of the muscular male body is too important to the
construction of the Spartans as heroic figures to be avoided, so rather than
anxiously policing the connotations of homoeroticism the Spartans' nudity
and costuming might generate, the film utilizes a strategy of ironic pop cultural reference to frame their presentation. The Spartan outfits – naked save
for shorts skimpy enough to be read as leather cod-pieces, and the 480 BC
equivalent of shiny knee-high boots – correspond to Frank Miller's vision of
Spartan clothing from the graphic novel, but are significantly more revealing
than the historical Ancient Spartans' chest plates, skirts and shin guards. As
such these costumes are not gestures towards historical accuracy, but instead
are generically and ironically inspired, referring to the iconography of gay
pornography and particularly the 'leather man' sub-culture,[14] as well as the
Italian sword and sandal films starring Steve Reeves (himself an important
gay icon).[15] Spartan dialogue is similarly heavy with doubled connotations,
and certain turns of phrase seem to equate combat with sexually aggressive
interactions: Leonidas instructs the Persians to 'come and get [it]' and later
predicts a night-time Persian assault with the words 'we're in for one wild
night'. Such knowing rehearsals of the possibility of homosexual interaction
are accompanied by explicit verbalised disavowals: it is the Athenians who are
allegedly 'boy-lovers', not the Spartans (a remarkable historical inaccuracy

among several the film perpetuates), and it is the Persians, not the Spartans, who according to Leonidas's insinuations fight like women.[16] The heterosexuality of the Spartans must further be 'guaranteed' by their war cries and the emblematic scene of enthusiastically thrusting sexual intercourse between Leonidas and Queen Gorgo.[17]

This process of disavowal also leads the film to project the spectre of 'deviant' sexuality squarely onto the Persians, part of the wider project to construct the Persians as Others, and a process enabled partly through digital manipulation of the image. When Leonidas comes face to face with Xerxes, the Persian king arrives on a platform carried by at least a hundred men that takes the form of a giant gold staircase, lion statues at its base, antelopes and a golden sun functioning like an inverted proscenium arch that frames Xerxes at the summit. A long shot initially pictures the platform in its entirety, before a cut to a medium close-up permits a more detailed contemplation of Xerxes himself. While clothing is limited to a gold-encrusted cod-piece, Xerxes is draped in a disproportionate amount of jewellery, an adornment usually worn only in particular areas – neck, wrist, and so on – now present across every inch of skin. The grandiloquent display of jewellery calls attention to Xerxes' wealth and stature, but also his narcissism; while the Spartans display their bodies as a group and for military ends, the emphasis on decoration here hints at a more self-regarding impulse in the Persian king. Equally, alongside a lack of evident musculature, the jewellery marks Xerxes out as different from the Spartans, acting as one of several signs of femininity inscribed onto his body, the others being his pierced ears, eye make-up and lipstick. The facial piercings and the gold bands strapped around his neck and torso, resembling a collar and chains, also subtly suggest the iconography of sadomasochism. In this way, costume and make-up quickly link Xerxes to dominant conceptions of 'aberrant' sexual practices and effeminacy. As the sequence progresses, this process of 'othering' Xerxes is furthered by the digital effects that help stage the shot-reverse shot interaction between the two kings. False perspective and digital compositing create the illusion that Xerxes is unusually tall in comparison with Leonidas, while digitally enlarged pupils make his human features appear strange. Xerxes' head is oversized in some of the composite shots, a literalisation of his God complex that constructs both his size and his egotism as physical mutation. Indeed, mutation becomes a through-line in the depiction of the Persians across the film, their human ranks extended with a variety of monstrous figures achieved through a combination of practical and digital effects. The 'Immortals', whose grimacing Japanese Samurai war masks hide teeth sharpened to fangs and warped, wizened faces, fight alongside a deformed, scarred giant whose triangular ribcage protrudes from his chest; elsewhere, the executioner who puts failing generals to death on Xerxes' orders is a grotesquely obese figure whose arms have been replaced with bloody saws. This representational strategy finds its most emphatic expression in Xerxes' private quarters, where Ephialtes is seduced into becoming a Persian ally.

As Ephialtes makes his way through the softly lit interior, a series of point of view shots show the objects of his fascinated gaze in close-up. Red drapes frame a range of mostly female performers, some dancing, others playing instruments, still others seemingly engaged in sexual foreplay or performance. Women draped in little apart from jewels cavort with each other in the half-darkness of the rooms, while a partially digitally constructed transsexual paraplegic watches from the shadows. Two women kiss in profile in front of Ephialtes, but as they turn towards the camera in close-up the previously unseen halves of their faces are revealed as significantly deformed. None of the women speak, but we hear breathy female gasps and groans. The rhythms of the women's gyrations, the drums on the soundtrack, and the pace of editing increase in line with Ephialtes' growing arousal, which seems to climax with his assent to Xerxes' request that he betray Leonidas.

The interior of Xerxes' private quarters could have been imagined and populated in a number of alternative ways, not least because the scene is not in the graphic novel, but the film settles on a highly sexualised milieu where voyeurism, sexual display as performance and female homosexuality combine in the attempt to provide a titillating spectacle. At the same time, the association of these sexual practices with each other and with physical disability invokes conservative notions of sexual 'deviancy' that are attributed to Xerxes and his followers. In addition, the conflation of activities and bodies evident in Xerxes' quarters is in emphatic contrast to the Spartan corporeal and behavioural model proffered by the film. In this context the Spartan body, already presented as an 'ideal' of a 'traditional' muscled masculinity, is troublingly established as a norm against which Xerxes, the other Persians and Ephialtes are located in opposition. Ephialtes' final request to Xerxes before he kneels before him as his ally is telling in this regard: he wants a uniform, a costume, that is, that will help him to achieve the uniformity of appearance that defines the Spartans in contrast to the Persians. The film's digital colour grading has emphasised the similarity of overall shape and muscle structure and the identical red capes shared by the Spartan soldiers, their uniformity of appearance linked to their effectiveness as a fighting unit and epitomised by their phalanx formation. But in relation to the Persians, the same colour grading process creates a contrast between the shadowed and illuminated lines of the body that delineates the diversity of their physical appearances, and their difference from the Spartan 'ideal'. In the light of Ephialtes' frustrated dream to be accepted as a Spartan, his excited exploration of Xerxes quarters, and his exhilaration in finding others who do not conform to the Spartan's physical ideal enjoying themselves and each other, is poignant. But the film does not attempt to explore these sentiments, nor attempt to naturalise the physicality on display, instead moving it into the realms of the 'exotic' and the fantastical. The first figure Ephialtes sees in Xerxes' private quarters is a lyre-playing half-goat, half-man in the foreground – a striking and fantastical spectacle of mutation constructed through digital compositing which is indicative of the tenor of the imagery the sequence will offer. There is no narrative justification for the extreme representations mobilised in this scene, which shockingly conflate monstrosity, physical disability and homosexuality. Such conflation, evident here and in the representation of Xerxes more generally, seems to enact a process Robin Wood has identified, whereby non-normative social or physical attributes, activities or lifestyles are 'repressed (though never destroyed) in the self and projected outward in order to be hated and disowned' (1986: 73).[18] In this way, for example, the homoerotic undertones in the film's presentation of the Spartans as heroic, masculine warrior bodies are recuperated through contrast with the vehement communication of the Persians' otherness.

As the preceding analyses illustrate, digital imaging deployments contribute directly to these designations and visual articulations of normativity and otherness. There is also a racial aspect to the structures of othering the film is engaged in: the Spartan army are all played by Caucasian actors,[19] whereas the Persian army is multi-ethnic, with actors presenting a range of South-Asian, East-Asian and African appearances. Hyperbolic dialogue references to the ethnic diversity of the 'thousand nations' under Persian command are followed by a series of scenes where multi-ethnicity seems to be conflated with a multiplicity of monstrous figures – from gigantic digitally generated rhinoceroses and elephants and body-painted, horned soldiers, to the 'Immortals' referred to earlier. These blatantly monstrous representations are accompanied by a number of more insidious digital interventions into sound and image: the voices of Xerxes and his messengers are digitally altered to make them deeper and more otherworldly, while the Persian emissary visiting the Ephors (Sparta's priests) has eyes that glow impossibly in the dark as the light fades from the shot. Such alterations to image and sound contribute to the conflation of racial difference with monstrosity and the fantastical. As these examples demonstrate, the sexualised, gendered and physicalised othering exemplified by the scene in Xerxes' private quarters intersects with, and mutually reinforces, a racial othering that is also deeply problematic. Digital and practical effects combine to construct or in some cases 'piece together' the monstrous figures of the Persian army and Xerxes' retinue, such as the half-man, half-goat in Xerxes' quarters, the saw-armed executioner, and Xerxes' own oversized body. At the same time, the contrasting physical integrity, power and uniformity of the Spartan body are also delineated by digital effects, through post-processing and the digital slow motion and zooms discussed earlier.

DIGITAL ENTERTAINMENT ALIBIS

The director has suggested that this deeply problematic series of representations should be seen in the context provided by Dilios' narration:

> The framing device was our justification for the exaggerated visual style . . . It made a lot of our aesthetic choices feel natural. Our storyteller gave us an 'out' where we could imagine, 'If I was an ancient Spartan and I was into the story being told, this is how I would imagine it.' That shaped a lot of our imagery. (in Fordham 2007: 69)

This is a disingenuous position, offering the framing story as an 'alibi' for fantastical verbal and visual representations that this chapter has found to be racist, disablist and homophobic. Other alibis offer themselves too, although they are equally disingenuous. Reactionary elements of the film could be blamed on the source material, although this fails to take into account the fact that adaptation is by its nature a series of choices. In addition, implicit in the detailed marketing by the filmmakers themselves about how digital technologies made the film possible, is the claim that this is first and foremost digital entertainment, so that the focus of media, audiences' and critical attention should be the aesthetics of the overt digital effects deployments on show, rather than the epistemic and ideological issues at stake in digital imaging practices across the film. As we have seen, it is not *300*'s expressive, excessive, stylised mode in itself that is at issue, but the reactionary purposes to which it and the more imperceptible deployments of digital imaging are put. And while it may be relatively easy to pull apart proffered alibis in the context of academic discussion, it is more difficult to intervene into the publicity and press discourses that circulate around such digital event movies in the public domain.

Much of the current scholarship on digital imaging technologies in cinema steers a path away from the question of the politics of representation. While certain strands of cinema filmed on digital formats, like movies inspired by the 1990s *Dogme 95* movement, or the virtuosic real-time cinema of *Russian Ark* (Alexander Sokurov, 2002), have led to claims that the digital has initiated an aesthetic democratisation (Rombes 2009: 27), the equivalent claim cannot be made for cinematic representation. As this chapter and Chapter 4 have demonstrated, digital imaging can be heavily complicit in the operations of cinematic representation. Politically retrograde representations enabled by digital imaging such as those found in *300* are quite common in recent mainstream cinema. We might mention the casual racism of characters like Jar Jar Binks (voiced by Ahmed Best) in the *Star Wars* prequels or the racist and homophobic construction of the robot characters who provide 'comic relief' in the *Transformers* franchise, for example; the multi-ethnic stereotypes used in the depiction of the supernaturally shape-shifting assassins in *Elektra* (Rob Bowman, 2005); or the hyperbolic digital rendering of the monstrous femi-nine[20] in a raft of movies such as *X-Men: The Last Stand* (Brett Ratner, 2006), *Beowulf* (Robert Zemeckis, 2007), and *Stardust* (Matthew Vaughn, 2007). Press responses to films such as these that are steeped in digital effects empha-sise them as digital entertainments, and use this as a reason not to take the films 'too seriously'. But whether the filmic decisions at issue are unthinking or intentional, they contribute to the perpetuation of familiar, and familiarly problematic, representational hierarchies within popular cinema. Indeed, the digital permits a new order of insidiousness, its interventions into the image as invisible as the filmmakers wish to make them. Presented with imaging technologies that can generate any moving images imaginable, many film-makers and visual effects artists working in this area of cinema are falling back on tried, tested and deeply reactionary representations. In the media rush to congratulate, and the academic rush to understand and account for, the latest developments in mainstream cinema's utilisation of digital technologies, we must not leave behind our interpretive or political responsibilities. This is one of the reasons why it is so important to locate digital imaging practice within a wider film's narrative, epistemic and representational structures, in an analyti-cal approach that is as alert to the ideological as it is to the digital.

NOTES

1. This clenched pose is soon repeated in the context of victory, as the still-young Leonidas celebrates his victory over a boxing adversary, the posture again etched out in the contrast between bright and darker lines on the body, this time against a skyscape that will become a familiar aspect of the framing of the Spartan body later in the film.

2. George Lucas's *Star Wars* prequels (1999, 2002, 2005), particularly the first film *Episode I – The Phantom Menace*, demonstrated that this technique was viable to use across a whole movie at least in terms of producing an acceptable level of photorealism. As the required technologies became more affordable and produced more satisfactory visual results, a rash of these films emerged. Films like *Sky Captain and the World of Tomorrow* (2004), *Sin City* (2005) – and outside of the US, Japan's *Casshern* (Kazuaki Kiriya, 2004) and the European co-production *Immortel (ad vitam)* (Enki Bilal, UK/France/Italy, 2004)

3. Interestingly Kerry Conran's film was marketed very much as a visual experiment: much was made of the fact that he had constructed the film (or, more accurately, a 'demo' clip for prospective funders) on a home computer set-up. This, then, is another example of a mode of anti-coherent digital compositing able to flourish in a space where experimentation is tolerated.

4. This form appeared in early incarnations in films like *Cabiria*, (Giovanni Pastrone, 1914), *Intolerance* (D.W. Griffith, 1916), *The Ten Commandments* (Cecil B. DeMille, 1923) and *Ben-Hur: A Tale of the Christ* (Fred Niblo, 1925), and *The Last Days of Pompeii* (Ernest B. Schoedsack, 1935) before re-emerging after the Second World War to become a popular cycle until the early 1960s, consisting of films such as *Alexander the Great* (Robert Rossen,

1956), *Spartacus* (Stanley Kubrick, 1960) and *Cleopatra* (Joseph L. Mankiewicz, 1963) and later versions of *The Ten Commandments* (Cecil B. DeMille, 1956) and *Ben-Hur* (William Wyler, 1959).

5. Sobchack also implies a gendering of cinematic technologies and cinematic spectacle that there isn't space to address in a study of this kind, but which bears further scrutiny in relation to the discursive positioning of digital effects work in the trade press.

6. Neale notes that this strategy places the historical epic alongside other large-scale films of the post-war period that used 'new technologies, high production values and special modes of distribution and exhibition to differentiate themselves both from routine productions and from alternative forms of contemporary entertainment, especially television' (2000: 85). Similarly one of the ways in which extravagant displays of digital imaging technologies achieve product differentiation is in their self-conscious pointing towards the mobilisation of money and technical skill that brings them into being.

7. We might also note that in economic terms the advent of digital imaging technologies and artificially intelligent synthetic 'extras' has done away with the need for such extravagances.

8. See for example Eagan (2007), Sarris (2007) and Ebert (2008a).

9. We might note that this motif is replicated in the depiction of the Spartan Queen's political fight to convince the council to send more troops to the Hot Gates; in scenes without much digital intervention, the darkened rooms and narrow side streets where Queen Gorgo must privately negotiate are constructed using 'real-world' sets. Views into and out of these spaces are persistently obscured by shadows or foreshortened by the scores of Spartan cloaks hanging across them to dry.

10. At two different instances the Spartans' battlefield resilience prompts shots of Xerxes shuddering at his losses from a high vantage point.

11. It is notable that this shot also provides an enclosing digital backdrop – the sky and the horizon are excluded from the image, a high angle camera position taking in only the battlefield and the Hot Gates.

12. Equally the sword slash produces shorn, stilled Persian appendages and sliced-open bodies spinning away from the blade.

13. For a more detailed technical account of how this sequence was achieved, see Fordham 2008: 76 and 109.

14. Pamela Church Gibson noted as much in her keynote speech at the *Dressing Rooms: Current Perspectives on Fashion and Textiles* conference, Oslo University College, Norway, 14–16 May 2007.

15. In films like *Le fatiche di Ercole* (Pietro Francisci, 1958), *Gli ultimi giorni di Pompei* (Mario Bonnard, 1959) and *La guerra di Trioa* (Giorgio Ferroni, 1961).

16. *300*'s revisionist approach to the Spartans is evident elsewhere: the version of the *agōgē* the film presents does not correspond to the real process Spartan boys were expected to go through; more generally Spartan society was highly undemocratic.

17. The film's significant expansion of the Queen's role in comparison with the graphic novel is worth noting in this regard. In the novel the Queen suggests Leonidas take his 300 personal bodyguards with him but does not know in advance his plan for them, while in the film the Queen has much more agency and knowledge, advising Leonidas in his strategy, and in his absence fighting a political battle to bring more troops to him. The shape these narrative details takes make clear the purpose of this larger role however – to pay lip-service to a progressive construction of expanded feminine agency while foregrounding the wife as a guarantee of the hero's heterosexuality, a function familiar from the action genre (Tasker 1993: 16). Despite her political negotiations the Queen is

predominantly depicted in domestic space, and the scene showing the couple's lovemaking before Leonidas's departure is reduced to a series of slow motion thrusts that foreground penetration and replicate a dominant active/passive conception of the gender binary (also evident in the spear thrusts and penetrations, and the construction of masculine and feminised bodies, on the battlefield). In appearance and action Queen Gorgo is the least visually or behaviourally excessive representation in the film, but her body is also subjected to excessive treatment, the repeated object of political insinuation and a physical rape that exceeds narrative motivation. I am grateful to Pamela Church Gibson for a stimulating discussion on this point.

18. See also Benshoff 1998.
19. A group of British actors were employed to play the Greek warriors.
20. Here I am referring to Barbara Creed's formulation, set out in her book *The Monstrous-Feminine: Film, Feminism, Psychoanalysis* (1993).

CHAPTER 6

The Digital in Three Dimensions

One of the central arguments of this book has been that we should not let the presence of a particular technology skew the process of interpretation, that we should look at the relationship of filmic elements to each other in the context of the whole, whether that 'whole' is a shot, a sequence, a scene, or a film. This final chapter's focus on a digital delivery technology, Digital 3-D (D-3-D), might appear at first glance to prioritise technology above the interpretive process. In fact, what follows is an attempt to bring interpretation back into the frame in the often heated debates about this recent digitally assisted return of stereoscopic cinema. To explain why such an intervention might be necessary, I want to spend a little time contextualising 3-D's most recent resurgence.

Digital technologies technically made 3-D's reappearance possible, but the economic imperatives of the entertainment industry made it happen. The digitisation of large parts of the film production process, what Bernard Mendiburu calls 'full digitisation from glass to glass – from the camera's to the projector's lenses', created the circumstances in which many of the problems inherent in analogue 3-D image capture and projection could be minimised (2009: 7),[1] but the film industry encouraged this 3-D renaissance for clear economic reasons. Despite D-3-D adding at least 25–30 per cent to below-the-line production costs (Winters Keegan 2008: para. 10), it offered the opportunity to differentiate once more the theatrical cinema-going experience from domestic HD, surround sound home cinema viewing, and thus to charge an increased ticket price (Winters Keegan 2008, Porges 2008). It also provided a critical bargaining chip to force reluctant exhibitors to stump up the cost of conversion to digital projection, something that film distributors had been pushing for some time (Porges 2008). The long trailed and heavily publicised release of *Avatar* (2009) in 3-D was the appropriate calling card. It generated a significant increase in the number of US digital screen conversions, which grew from 2,000 by the end of 2006 (with under 500 3-D enabled) to over 6,000 digital screens by the end of June 2009 (and just under 2,500 3-D enabled) (Karagosian 2009).[2] That trend has continued (although it is expected to peak by mid-2012): by July 2011 50 per cent of US cinema screens (over 11,000) had converted to digital, with the number of 3-D screens reaching around 7,000. Worldwide digital screen conversions now stand at 46,000, with 65 per cent 3-D enabled (Karagosian 2011).[3] Press and industry commentators continue to deliberate about whether this iteration of stereoscopic cinema will remain popular and profitable enough for studios to continue to produce movies in D-3-D.[4] Indeed it is possible that, by the time this book comes into print, the question will be settled one way or another. Thomas Elsaesser suggests that D-3-D has already served its purpose, continuing the tradition of theatrical release serving as a 'shop window' for ancillary markets (2011), and certainly 3-D televisions, broadcasting content, video games and game console add-ons are now very much in the marketplace, at the same time that theatrical venues are welcoming in other kinds of spectators, those for various forms of stereoscopic 'expanded cinema', such as music concerts, operas, theatre and dance performances.

What will remain open, I suspect, is the media debate about the films themselves, frequently carried out under sensationalist, polarising headlines like 'Why I Hate 3-D (And You Should Too)' (Ebert 2010) and 'No, your eyes aren't deceiving you – 3-D really is a con' (Kermode 2010). The debate is often framed in terms of quality, but risks conflating issues of technology, technical competence, cultural value, and artistic expression. 3-D's somewhat chequered history has always brought together these competing issues. The technological feat of projecting stereoscopic images cleanly was persistently challenged in previous 3-D 'boom' periods by poor screen quality, and dual projector systems not being properly synchronised at either the point of image capture or projection, creating a difficult and sometimes painful viewing experience for audiences (Hayes 1989: 54). The lack of continuity of practical stereoscopic experience in filmmakers and crews additionally generated some 3-D effects that were challenging for the eye to accommodate (Lenny Lipton in Zone 2005: 22). And many of the films produced in previous booms fell foul of cultural distinctions about 'high' and 'low' culture. In the 1950s, for example, the studios' rush to capitalise on the success of the independent stereoscopic film *Bwana Devil* (Arch Oboler, 1952) while minimising financial risk generated a slew of cheap, often poorly scripted or achieved, genre 'B' movies (Mitchell 2004: 209). The revival of many of these films in the early 1970s was accompanied by a series of pornographic 3-D movies initiated by the success of *The Stewardesses* (Al Silliman Jr., 1969) (Hayes 1989: 68–88). In the subsequent 1980s stereoscopic phase genre movies once again predominated, such as the Western *Comin' At Ya!* (Ferdinando Baldi, 1981), horrors such as *Jaws 3-D* (Joe Alves, 1983) and *Friday the 13th Part III* (Steve Miner, 1982), and the science fiction fantasy *Spacehunter: Adventures in the Forbidden Zone* (Lamont Johnson, 1983). These B-movies and genre films frequently exploited to the full 3-D's most well known but often pilloried trick: the 'emergence' effect, whereby objects appear to be thrust out of the screen and into the audience space, generating an affective shock but one with a particular reputation for kicking audiences out of imaginative engagement with a film, or for offering cheap thrills instead of narrative complexity.

Opponents of D-3-D cite such 'gimmickry' as one of their key objections to the format (Kermode 2010: para. 5; see also Ebert 2008b: para. 1–3), and certainly a variety of contemporary 3-D films have continued this eye-popping tradition, sending items such as swords, axes, and even severed heads careering towards the spectator in the likes of *My Bloody Valentine 3D* (Patrick Lussier, 2009), *Piranha 3D* (Alexandre Aja, 2010), *Resident Evil: Afterlife* (Paul W. S. Anderson, 2010), and *Drive Angry* (Patrick Lussier, 2011). We can find the emergence effect in other kinds of movie too, in blockbusters like *Pirates of the Caribbean: On Stranger Tides* (Rob Marshall, 2011), and in animated children's films such as *G-Force* (Hoyt Yeatman, 2009) and *Cloudy With a Chance of Meatballs* (Phil Lord and Chris Miller, 2009), where its intended use is primarily comedic. But it is most prevalent in those films we might expect to rely on 'cheap shocks': the 'B-genres' of horror and exploitation. 3-D in this context is simply the newest tool in such films' endeavours to continue the sensationalist shock tactics of their 2-D peers and predecessors, in a revival of 1970s exploitation and horror genres that has been going on for almost a decade.[5] This example also suggests why we should be wary of claims that 3-D is changing the kinds of films being made. Roger Ebert makes this assertion in a 2010 opinion piece:

> I'm not opposed to 3-D as an option. I'm opposed to it as a way of life for Hollywood, where it seems to be skewing major studio output away from the kinds of films we think of as Oscar-worthy. Scorsese and Herzog make films for grown-ups. Hollywood is racing headlong toward the kiddie market. Disney recently announced it will make no more traditional films at all, focusing entirely on animation, franchises, and superheroes. I have the sense that younger Hollywood is losing the instinctive feeling for story and quality that generations of executives possessed. (2010: para. 1)

The problem with Ebert's argument is that the trends he identifies were already in evidence well before 3-D re-emerged in the digital era as a viable format for theatrical release. One thinks of the ongoing run of animated children's films prompted by the phenomenal success of *Toy Story* (John

Lasseter, 1995), or the digital effects franchises spawned by the *Matrix* (Andy and Larry Wachowski, 1999, 2003) and *Lord of the Rings* (Peter Jackson, 2001, 2002, 2003) trilogies, or indeed the longevity of the superhero cycle, whose recent history could begin at any number of points in the last fifty years, with *Superman* (Richard Donner, 1978), *Batman* (Tim Burton, 1989), or *X-Men* (Bryan Singer, 2000). As Kristin Thompson points out, franchises and the genres that appeal to potential franchise fans, such as children's book series or comic book hero movies, are with us not because of a 'withering of scriptwriters' inspiration' but because studios are multimedia conglomerates that want to maximise their ancillary markets, and to mitigate against losses and stabilise profits in an era of accelerating costs (2007: 4–6).

Ebert's distinctions, between Martin Scorsese, Werner Herzog and 'the kinds of films we think of as Oscar-worthy' on the one hand and Disney's 'animation, franchises, and superheroes' on the other, and between the auteur or grand master of cinema Ebert implies and 'younger Hollywood', suggest a cultural bias, a prioritising of 'high' cultural products over 'low'. Several reviewers and commentators make similar distinctions in their reviews of Herzog's *Cave of Forgotten Dreams* (2010) and Wim Wenders' *Pina* (2011). Cultural bias is explicit in, for example, the opening sentence of Ann Hornaday's review of *Cave of Forgotten Dreams* for *The Washington Times*, in which she remarks dryly that 'it's about time the technology reached the hands of an artist' (2011: para. 1). The distinctions being made seem to have a chronological aspect, presenting Herzog's and Wenders' films as maturations of 3-D film practice: so A. O. Scott of *The New York Times* is moved to declare, 'Those who dismiss the format as the industrial gimmick (and excuse for price gouging) that it frequently is may need to reconsider now that a handful of certified auteurs have given it a try' (2011: para. 1), while for *The Times'* Kate Muir, *Pina* represents the moment that 3-D 'grew up and became a sophisticated medium' (in Ross 2011: para. 1). Here, as at other points in its history, 3-D is rhetorically situated at a distance from notions of filmmaking artistry and a film canon. But D-3-D's more obviously commercial deployments are also marked as the 'primitive' forerunners of the more 'civilised', more 'artistic' forms of 3-D filmmaking now emerging. I do not wish to underplay the extent to which each iteration of 3-D has necessitated a re-learning of stereoscopic cinema's technical demands and artistic possibilities for filmmakers, so that more 'expert' deployments of 3-D might arrive later in any 3-D cycle. But narrativising D-3-D as a progression from 'primitive' to 'artistic' film practice may be to fall into the same trap as early historians of cinema's first decades. Initial histories characterised early cinema primarily as a primitive forbear of the classical narrative cinema that would later predominate. The work of Gunning, Gaudreault, Elsaesser et al. in the 1980s and 1990s complicated this account and proposed new, more nuanced ways of understanding early cinema's forms and impulses.[6] We similarly need to complicate the nascent narratives about D-3-D, particularly those circulating in media culture.

The nuances of Ebert's ongoing discussion of 3-D, which is by turns strident and thoughtful, are lost when they circulate second hand in media discourse, reduced to simplistic oppositions between advocates and opponents of 3-D, 'good' or 'bad' 3-D films, 'good' or 'bad' genres, 'worthy' or 'unworthy' subject matter, artistic tours de force or artistic failures. It is this polarised rhetorical landscape, coloured as it is by 3-D's reported histories of dubious technological and artistic achievement, into which this chapter wishes to intervene. In a review of *Pina*, Leslie Felperin suggests that 'the latest 3-D technology is good for a lot more than just lunging knives and fantastical storylines' (2011: para. 1). Rather than allow the assertion to lead us back into a polarised discussion around 'quality' 3-D films, it is better to read statements such as this as an invitation to look more closely at D-3-D: to see that there may be more to D-3-D than its most obvious effects; to be open, that is, to D-3-D's full potential as one of the tools of artistic expression.

DEPTH AWARENESS AND VISUAL NARRATION

> Inasmuch as aesthetic issues may be looked at in isolation . . . there is no inherent reason why 3-D *had* to emphasise emergence so insistently . . . stereoscopic still photography had something of a different bias.
> (Paul 1993: 336, emphasis in original)

Stereoscopic cinema's mode of delivery is also a tangible part of its aesthetics. Both 2-D and 3-D cinema use framing, composition and focal length to change by degrees the spectator's spatial relationship to the objects and phenomena presented on screen, and to modify the spectator's perception of the relative depth of the diegetic space. But 3-D has another 'tool' at its disposal, one that depends on human beings' binocular depth perception. Our eyes are roughly 2.5 inches apart, and generate overlapping images of what is being viewed from slightly different angles, which are then interpolated by our brain into a single composite image. The distance between the eyes is called the interocular, and the extent of the overlapping of the images is called parallax. Parallax is one of the methods used by the human brain to judge depth and volume.[7] In stereoscopic cinema, the extent of parallax can be controlled by the filmmakers, who can vary the distance between the two cameras and hence the notional distance between our eyes (the interocular distance) to lend volume to objects, to lend an increased sense of depth to the image, and to locate objects either at the screen plane, or in front or behind it.[8] For example, the emergence effect is achieved by lending a screened object extreme negative parallax, so that the object appears to extend beyond the screen and into the audience space. Correspondingly, positive parallax will place screened objects 'behind' the screen (Lipton 1982: 92–5). In addition to framing, composition and focal length, then, 3-D cinema can use negative or positive parallax to encourage in the spectator a more pronounced sense of depth, and of spatial relationships within the film world. This heightened depth awareness can have a highly affective impact on the spectator, particularly in the case of the much maligned 'emergence' effect already mentioned. Even though certain strands of 3-D filmmaking tend towards this stylistic flourish, 3-D movies do not have to use significant negative parallax as a matter of course, as William Paul makes clear in the epigraph at the top of this section. Indeed Paul's words remind us that there are other options for a 3-D aesthetic, and that negative and positive parallax can be – and in fact already are being – deployed in more subtle registers. This also means that we need to understand the heightened depth awareness that 3-D fosters not in terms of 'on' or 'off', present or absent, but in terms of degrees of awareness that fluctuate over time. In the 3-D movie the foregrounding – in more or less pronounced manner – of spatial configurations interleaves with other elements of audio-visual narration to produce meaning. Some of the same questions we have asked about digital imaging thus pose themselves afresh in the face of digital 3-D filmmaking: when does the presence of D-3-D's spatial foregrounding matter? When does the spectator's awareness of it matter? How does the presence of D-3-D's spatial foregrounding bear on the processes of meaning making and interpretation?

In *Tron: Legacy*, Sam Flynn (Garrett Hedlund) is searching for clues to his father's disappearance. His father Kevin Flynn (Jeff Bridges) was a genius computer programmer and head of computer software company Encom who went missing with no explanation twenty-five years before. Sam finds a secret backroom in his father's old video game arcade, sits at a computer console, and gets converted into data and transported inside the mainframe computer his father was working on when he disappeared. After the transition, colour is the first sign that things are somehow different. Sam is sitting at the same computer console, apparently in the same room as before, but the colours are darker, the contrast sharper, the palette more monochrome than before. Prompted outside by a loud noise and bright light, Sam bursts out of the building (a cleaner, sharper version of the arcade's real-world facade) and runs towards the camera as it tracks into a medium close-up. A brief side angle follows, before a point of view shot of Sam's view of the street: neon lights and rain-swept surfaces glitter in an artificial night. The street stretches almost impossibly back into the distance. After a reverse angle of Sam, a closer view of the arcade frontage tilts up to take in the building's now towering height: it was, we are invited to calculate, a shorter building in the real world. Sam runs into the crossroads outside the arcade, muttering 'This can't be happening', the camera spinning around him as he views this unfamiliar world. Buffeted by a sudden rush of air, he looks up: some kind of hover ship approaches from above. A harsh glare from the ship's lights obscures a full view of the vehicle as it lands right over Sam's position, but it is a black, muscular-looking machine behemoth. He seems to realise his predicament ('Oh man, this *is* happening') and makes a run for it, but the street surface has turned into hexagonal units, most of which have dropped away from him, leaving him stranded on a small cluster of hexagonal blocks. Two visored soldiers from the hover ship collar Sam, noting 'This program has no disc – another stray', and he is strapped into the lower section of the ship in between a row of equally shackled, inexpressive humanoids that we will shortly learn are manifestations of computer programs. As the ship takes off Sam looks down through the transparent surface on which his feet are secured, the camera above him sharing his perspective on the depths beneath. A reverse angle from below shows the ship rising steadily, Sam and the other prisoners visible through the transparent floor. Then a wider high angle shot that looks down on the rising ship: as the ship begins to move down the street at rooftop level, the camera tilts upwards to take in an extensive view of this neon, skyscraper filled cityscape.

In this first sequence in the mainframe computer environment *Tron: Legacy* uses D-3-D as a key indicator to signal the shift from the real world to the artificial world. The signalling is subtle at first, but grows more pronounced as the sequence develops, in line with Sam's increasing understanding that he has been transported into a digital universe. When Sam bursts out of the arcade towards the camera, the resulting close-up uses a small amount of negative parallax to bring his face out of the screen towards the audience, underlining Sam's spatial separation from the arcade door he has run from. In the shot at the crossroads, the camera circling around a bewildered Sam, he is placed at the screen plane while positive parallax makes the streets look as if they extend far back behind him. This and other shots in the sequence employ positive parallax for the same purpose that the initial close-up of him used negative parallax: to underline Sam's planar separation from his surroundings, both literally and metaphorically. Sam feels out of place, *is* out of place (he is a user, not a program, so should not be in the computer environment), and we experience that with him through increasingly conspicuous use of negative and positive parallax. In addition it is worth noting that across the sequence the extent of positive parallax used is much more pronounced than the negative parallax. In combination with perspectival leading lines (both building edges and neon strip lights) that pull the eye into the image, this more emphatic use of positive parallax creates a strong sense that the universe Sam now occupies is extensive, perhaps boundless, its buildings taller, its streets longer, than the real world. The artifice of this world is sensed not just through what is shown (black tower blocks, an unnatural-looking darkened sky with stars arranged in grid-like formations) but through the mismatch between the way depth cues function in *this* cityscape and how they work in the real world Sam has come from. Since we have already seen Sam moving around the real city in earlier scenes, we are primed to make such a comparison. There, depth cues functioned naturalistically, detailed gradations in texture, definition and colour giving a strong sense of a city environment that corresponds spatially and perceptually with our own real world experience. In the new world Sam occupies, the use of positive parallax and perspectival leading lines to suggest structures that gradually recede away from the camera is at odds with the contrapuntal functioning of other depth cues such as texture gradient (where objects further in the distance lose definition and textural detail) and atmospheric perspective (where objects further in the distance appear paler and bluer due to atmospheric particles). For example, in Sam's point of view of the street, and the later wide shot of the ship against the cityscape, the buildings retain sharp definition for several blocks further than we might expect before their neon lines suddenly become bluer and less distinct: there is no gradation in the depth cues, just an apparent significant shift from one distance to another at a certain point, a phenomenon at odds with the depth cues provided by the gradually receding perspective lines. The impression of this world's non-reality is thus created in a number of different ways. Parallax effects are used subtly and sparingly, and do not stand on their own, but work with other facets of depth perception and elements of composition to generate meaning.

Tron: Legacy is not the only film to use alterations in stereoscopic depth cues to signal a move between worlds. *Coraline* (Henry Selick, 2009) takes up this strategy in a highly developed way, to distinguish between the young title character's subjective experience of her real, everyday world, and the 'Other World' she discovers. Cinematographer Pete Kozachik explains:

> Henry wanted 3-D depth to differentiate the Real World from the Other World, specifically in sync with what Coraline is feeling. To do that, we kept the Real World at a reduced stereo depth, suggesting Coraline's flat outlook, and used full 3-D in the Other World. At first, full 3-D opens up a better world for Coraline, but when things go bad, we carefully exaggerate stereo depth to match her distress. (2009: para. 25)[9]

What emerges in Kozachik's account is that the spectator's experience of those different depth cues is at the heart of the strategy's intended power. In their research for the design of stereoscopic aspects in relation to story, Kozachik comments, 'We found that a setting receding deeply behind screen [*sic*] creates a sense of space and freedom and is more effective at evoking pleasant feelings than bringing everything out into the theater . . . Sometimes we did the opposite, crowding images into theater space to invoke claustrophobia or discomfort' (2009: para. 26). As Kozachik implies, 3-D has the capacity to articulate a fictional space and then make us experience that space to varying degrees of consciousness using the depth perception processes we employ in the real world to assess spatial configurations and relationships. This allows filmmakers to 'design in' corporeally felt, space-dependent sensations – such as expansiveness, claustrophobia, vertigo and so on – that are directly experienced by the spectator rather than imaginatively inferred by a two-dimensional representation. We find our place in the spatial configuration being manifested in the cinema, in front of and behind the screen, and that finding-a-place generates meaning. But while 3-D's effects depend on depth perception processes developed in the real world, these constructed spatial configurations do not have to correlate directly to our real-world experience of space (the only exception being those effects which create physical discomfort as a result of poor stereoscopic design). As Thomas Elsaesser points out, in *Coraline*'s case '3-D doesn't serve to recreate spatial plausibility or the semblance of reality. It does the opposite, stealthily reinstating two-dimensionality or working with Cubist distortions and other effects of formal alienation' (2010: para. 23). This opens up the possibility (grasped enthusiastically by *Coraline*'s filmmakers) of using 3-D effects in complex ways for artistic purposes, a possibility enhanced by the digital tools which now allow filmmakers highly developed, detailed control of almost all aspects of 3-D cinematography. Elsaesser rightly argues that we need to think of 3-D 'not as a tool of the cinema of attractions, nor as a technique for propelling objects towards us from the depths of space . . . [but as] an element of a new and comprehensive cinematic narrative, one embedded in flowing, elastic, hybrid space' (2010: para. 23). In the second half of this chapter, I want to look at a particular case study film in more detail, to explore some of these possibilities of 3-D cinema, and specifically the role stereoscopic design can play in the production of a film's meaning.

CINEMATIC SPACE IN *HUGO* (2011)

'The secret was always in the clockwork.' (Hugo's father)

Martin Scorsese's *Hugo* (2011) is adapted from the illustrated book *The Invention of Hugo Cabret* by Brian Selznick (2007). Set in Paris in the 1930s, the film tells the story of Hugo (Asa Butterfield), a young orphan who lives in the walls of the Gare Montparnasse. He uses skills learned from his clock-maker father (Jude Law) to keep the station's clocks running on time, while avoiding the orphanage by keeping out of sight of the station inspector (Sacha Baron Cohen). He is also trying to fix an automaton (a wind-up mechanical man) which he and his father had worked on together, using clockwork machine bits pilfered from the station's toy shop. Caught stealing by the shop owner Papa Georges (Ben Kingsley), he is summarily divested of the pocketbook in which he kept his workings on the automaton. Hugo enters an alliance with the shop owner's goddaughter Isabelle (Chloë Grace Moretz) to get his pocketbook back. They gradually uncover that Papa Georges is in fact the early filmmaker Georges Méliès, who had fallen into obscurity years before and was presumed dead in the First World War. The automaton is one of his inventions, donated to a local museum at the traumatic moment when Méliès gave up filmmaking, and linked to Hugo's own traumatic moment: the loss of his father in a fire at the museum. Calling on a local film historian to assist them, Hugo and Isabelle help Méliès reconcile with his past and bring him back to the public eye, and to public acclaim.

The film opens with an image of the internal workings of a clock, cogs and mechanisms whirring and clicking in regulated motion. A slow dolly forward moves the spectator gradually closer to the beautiful intricacy of the machinery at work, before a graphic match over a cross-fade constructs night-time Paris's cityscape as another intricate moving machine. The spokes of the central clockwork cog have been replaced by streets that fan out from the Arc de Triomphe, streets that pulse with light, movement, and energy. Once again the camera slowly tracks forward, before a cut to a daylight city vista brings the Eiffel Tower into a closer view (where previously it was only in the distance). Thus begins a mobile long take which pans across the cityscape, tracks forward and pans right and down towards the Gare Montparnasse, the railway station that will serve as the hub, as it were, within and around which narrative events will circulate. The camera continues its journey through space – there has been no cut since the closer view of the Eiffel Tower – and violins pick out a regular, train-like, up-and-down movement on the soundtrack as the seemingly airborne camera approaches the station at speed. It plunges into the railway station along a platform, train carriages and passengers embarking and disembarking on either side, people glimpsed briefly through billowing steam before they disappear from view behind the film frame. Entering the main station concourse the camera pushes through the bustle of travellers and shopkeepers before tilting upward and forward towards a large clock above the station's main entrance. Dollying closer and closer to the clock face, the camera comes to rest on the 'four' of the clock. The close-up reveals that the apparently solid numeric symbol is in fact a hollow in the shape of the number, opening up an unanticipated space behind the plane of the clock face. Within that space, a face is now visible; it is Hugo, looking out onto the bustle of station life unfolding below.

The film's first shot highlights the clockwork machinery's smooth motion and each cog's shining surface. This is clockwork as beautiful machine, a mystery that the camera glides closer to. The cross-fade is slow, streaks of light making the machinery's centre glow as if by magic, before the transition completes to show us that the streaks are automobile movements traced along Parisian thoroughfares. Paris glitters, lit up, another beautiful machine brought to life by the human beings that move around its inanimate structures. The cross-fade thus establishes a relationship between the energies of clockwork motion and human movement through the city, between the mechanical and the social, between the illusion of movement created by machines, and the bustle of life itself. This series of thematic relationships will animate the film's narrative and its visual aesthetics, but also locates *Hugo* in a historical and cultural moment with a specifically ambivalent attitude toward machines. It is the era of clockwork's magical ability to bring mechanical objects to life in the name of entertainment, and of cinema's equally entrancing ability to combine sequential still images into the illusion of moving life. But it is also the era of steam engineering, industrialisation, urbanisation, and technologisation, a modernity in which the machine is both wonder and menace. As Peter Brooker notes, '[t]hough some commentators welcomed the image of a new modernized future, most tended to bemoan the speed, turmoil, anonymity and loss of human association modern urban life entailed' (2002: 18). Urbanisation and industrialisation had created mass societies compressed into city environments that offered anonymity rather than community. Life accelerated as telegrams and telephones increased the pace of communication; trains, trams, and automobiles had sped up the pace of urban existence and increased the risk of bodily injury, as *Hugo* reminds us in several ways, for example the scene where Isabelle almost gets trampled underfoot by a crush of rail travellers, and the recreation of the real Gare Montparnasse train derailment in Hugo's dream. And the First World War had only recently showcased horrifyingly efficient technologies of death, returning soldiers shell-shocked and with missing limbs, visible 'proof' of technology's destructive potential.[10]

All this might seem far removed from *Hugo*'s child-centred narrative, yet a closer look reveals that the film is rooted in these ambivalent ideas about modernity and machines. For example, the station master's braced leg is a visual reminder of war's destructive machinery: as he tells the flower seller Lisette (Emily Mortimer), it was 'injured in the war and it will never heal'. The brace is a mechanical support but one that is temperamental at best, prone to jamming in awkward positions and catching on things, and it does not prevent him from walking with a limp. More generally, the city reveals its unpredictable nature in the sudden death of Hugo's father in a museum fire, the boy's equally sudden rehoming in the walls of the railway station with his drunken uncle (Ray Winstone), and the uncle's unexpected disappearance and subsequent death. This child protagonist is the epitome of the alienated urban dweller, his orphan status divesting him of agency, social standing and indeed social visibility, despite his existence at the centre of the railway's bustle. In the opening sequence the camera's track forward into a rush of embarking and disembarking passengers offers a visceral illustration that the station will serve as a microcosm of a turbulent urban existence. In Walter Benjamin's musings on the modern city he noted 'the role of the urban masses in shielding an asocial person from discovery' and the equally important impulse to subject the crowd to scrutiny (Dimendberg 2004: 22). We find these notions of anonymity and surveillance echoed in Hugo's repeated attempts to use crowds and unexpected spaces within the station to evade the ever-watchful station inspector, but also the easy manner with which the station' inspector categorises Hugo as just another orphan (and the fact that being identified as such is enough to bring you under suspicion of a standard but arbitrary list of petty offences). Georges Méliès too finds anonymity in this milieu, although for different reasons than Hugo.

The first shots of the film also introduce a further concept. Snow begins to fall over Paris, negative parallax bringing it slightly in front of the screen so that it lends volume to the space of the film world, a strategy commonly used in 3-D movies to replicate atmospheric perspective, but employed with specific intent in this sequence.[11] Falling snow will return as a motif later in the film, but its function here is to draw our attention to the depth of the onscreen space, to encourage us to experience its three-dimensionality, just before the camera begins its first forward movement through that space. Billowing steam is employed for the same purpose when the camera moves inside the station structure. At the outset, then, as the narrative begins to gain momentum, the stereoscopic design of the shot foregrounds the importance of our engagement in the spatial coordinates of the film world. This primes us to think about space not in the abstract but in *experiential* terms. Notions of space also connect the film's first oblique references to the technology that has a privileged place in its machine/human thematic framework: cinema. Once inside the station, the sequence visually quotes from film's very beginnings. The camera view of train carriages, passengers, and steam recalls the Lumière brothers' *L'arrivée d'un train en gare de La Ciotat* (*Arrival of a Train at La Ciotat*, 1895), an iconic moment in early cinema, and one that *Hugo* will return to a number of times. In the camera's journey through the air and into the station, it also visually echoes the 'phantom ride' films of the early 1900s, which were achieved by mounting the camera onto a moving train (Christie 1994: 18).[12] These are references designed not simply to refer us to cinema and its history in a generalised sense: instead they represent some of cinema's earliest attempts to lend an impression of three-dimensional space to the moving image. Jan Holmberg explains:

> early tracking shots were not used so much for rhetorical purposes or
> narrative emphasis, but rather, as Yuri Tsivian puts it (1994, p. 207), to

offer a stereoscopic view, activating the profilmic space. 'Stereoscopic' is used here as a metaphor but also almost literally. In the early teens, commentators often used the term stereoscopic as a synonym for deep focus, [while] . . . both inward and outward movements were perceived as stereoscopic or three-dimensional, as evident from contemporaneous reports. These movements could include tracking shots but also characters in the film moving along the depth axis of the image. (2003: 137, 138–9)[13]

Phantom rides, the Lumières' *Train*, and D-3-D: each uses movement or staging along the depth or 'z' axis to enhance our experience of film space. Before we see a directly represented reel of film, or a camera or film theatre onscreen, then, this sequence introduces cinema not just as a technology per se, but as a technology that has this power to animate space for us.

Why this emphasis on the articulation of cinematic space? The beginning of an answer lies in how we are introduced to the central protagonist, Hugo. I've noted already that we discover Hugo inhabiting an unanticipated void behind the number four on a clock face: indeed the camera encourages us *not* to anticipate this space by homing in on the centre of the clock face before reframing *at the last moment* to bring the number four into close-up. In addition, positive parallax is applied to the portion of the image that sits behind the clock face so that it seems to extend behind the plane of the screen, to increase the unsettling sensation that one's grasp of the spatial coordinates of the station has been momentarily knocked. It is the first in a series of moments across the film at which hidden spaces reveal themselves: points at which the spectator is forced to reconsider the configuration of the space they are engaging with. Two of these follow soon after our first sighting of Hugo. After becoming worried that the station inspector will spot him behind the number four, Hugo steps back from the other side of the clock face and runs along a dark, pipe lined corridor, down a ladder, along another corridor, through a small doorway, down a spiral slide, across an expanse of metal flooring, through the spokes in a slowly turning giant cog, up a spiral staircase and down another short corridor to the back of another clock. The whole journey is shown in a single long take,[14] but with no hint of how these tunnels link to the outside: as a result, the spatiotemporal continuity the long take provides is undercut by the impossibility of confidently mapping the network of spaces Hugo is negotiating. The effect is more pronounced when we see Hugo back in these tunnels after his first, hostile encounter with Papa Georges, during which Georges calls 'Thief!' and Hugo is forced to make his escape with the station inspector in hot pursuit. This time there is no long take, but the relationship of these spaces within the station's walls to the public layout of the station is even less clear. Dark shadows hide many spatial cues from view, and as the sequence progresses positive parallax exaggerates the depth of the tunnels, clock pendulum shafts and stairwells, making them stretch away into the distance as if the space behind the walls is preternaturally more extensive than it should be. Stereoscopic design and other compositional elements combine to prompt us to conclude that, like the innards of a clockwork machine, the innards of the station walls are unfathomable to the untrained eye, a spatial mystery impossible to unpick. Hugo is the specialist, the clock-maker's son who knows the secret of the tunnels, and for whose energy the tunnels provide a conduit. This is a labyrinth constructed by industrialisation, disturbing in its spatial uncertainties (which have been underscored by positive parallax), mastered by a small boy. And yet our experience of Hugo's connected network of inner sanctums is unsettled, uncomfortable. If the articulation of cinematic space in these sequences expresses Hugo's wily competence and potential within the walls of the station, it also implies that these spaces are not as safe, not as master-able, as Hugo might want them to be.

Stereoscopic design helps develop this implication further in the mapping of Hugo's relationship to the outside world: both the station's public world and that of Paris. The foundation for this strategy is the film's decision to present that world to us from Hugo's spatial perspective. *Hugo* Steadicam operator Larry McConkey confirms that 'Scorsese wanted most of the images to suggest Hugo's perspective, which meant a lot of low angle shots' (in Hope-Jones 2011: 64). It also means high angle shots as Hugo watches the lives of the station's regular inhabitants – the bookseller (Christopher Lee), the café owner (Frances de la Tour) and her admirer (Richard Griffiths), Lisette the flower seller – unfolding below, and corresponding reverse angles that show Hugo's reactions to what he sees. In shots from Hugo's perspective, the view is frequently partially obscured by whatever clock face Hugo is concealed behind: equally in the reverse angles Hugo's face is often blocked by parts of the clock structure (see Fig. 6.1). Hugo is persistently depicted in this way, his visage or his view blocked by window frames, doors, tunnel grilles, and, when caught by the station inspector, even the bars of a prison cell. This type of partial obscuring of the image by something that is slightly out of focus is particularly noticeable in 3-D because it is experienced as a conspicuous, undesirable interruption of the spectator's visual field. As a result, even as Hugo nimbly slips out of sight, and smiles in amusement at the narratives of romance and friendship playing out in front of him, the spectator experiences his spatial orientation as uncomfortable. Hugo has freedom of movement within the labyrinthine station walls, but the presentation of that freedom underscores the reality that he remains separated, blocked off, literally barred from the social spaces of interaction he observes. In this way the film's literalisation of alignment with Hugo as a stereoscopically expressed spatial alignment thematises perspective, converting it to a spatialised figure through which the film's

Figure 6.1 Still from *Hugo* (GK Films / The Kobal Collection): Hugo watches life go by from behind a station clock face.

concerns can be introduced and elaborated. Our experience of that spatialised figure encourages us to recognise and share in Hugo's confinement, and to root for his faltering progress towards a rewarding social integration.

A later sequence provides a poignant example of how the film sustains and modulates this spatialised figure. When Hugo trails Papa Georges from his shop in order to get his prized notebook back, he is momentarily flummoxed by the fact that in order to do so he will have to leave the familiar environs of the station. As he plucks up the courage to follow Papa Georges out through the station entrance, his hesitation is aptly represented by a wide shot of a very small Hugo dwarfed against the flat expanse of columns and doors that make up the entrance wall. The shallow depth of field, shallow composition and frontality of the shot lend it a flatness that interrupts the relatively deep stereoscopic compositions to which the film has accustomed us up to this point.[15] It is a flatness that connotes impenetrability, indeed encourages us to *feel* that impenetrability, a spatialised figure that moves us beyond a straightforward registration of the actor's performance of hesitation to begin to consider the character's reasons for this pause; economic disadvantage, a lack of social experience, perhaps an uncertainty about the geography of the world beyond the station. Once Hugo has crossed the threshold, the diegetic space reacquires depth, first in a reverse angle shot that shows both he and Papa Georges walking away from the station and towards the camera, then in shots of Parisian streets which emphasise diagonal perspective lines. Having experienced with Hugo the seeming impassability of the boundary between the station and the Paris beyond it, we feel a corresponding relief as the space beyond the screen opens back up. The moment exemplifies one of the ways in which the film predisposes us to feel positive about Hugo's attempted progress towards greater penetration of the social spaces beyond the station's walls. This is important because as the film goes on, Hugo's secret domain becomes less viable, less secret, and less sustaining. It cannot answer Hugo's musings on what his function in the world might be, or fill the void left by his father, or protect against incursions by both friendly visitors (Isabelle) and unwelcome guests (the station inspector). In this, Hugo shares an affinity with the man he will come to know well, George Méliès. Both are, in their own ways, hiding in the station, incomplete after having suffered a traumatic loss.

Our first introduction to Papa Georges is revealing, simultaneously of the character's predicament and of the way in which stereoscopic design underpins our sense of that predicament. Hugo is looking down from a clock face located in one of the station's quieter areas, and Georges appears in the void of the clock face's number four (a passing reference to the manner in which we first encounter Hugo which serves to hint at the link between the two characters). A track in from Hugo's spatial perspective frames Georges from above, stationed at the counter of his *Confiserie et Jouets* ('Sweets and Games') shop, then a lower angle cranes into a frontal framing of the shop front, Georges in the same position, stock still, chin resting on hand. A close-up illustrates that, while he is unmoving, his eyes are darting this way and that; an extreme close-up catches the moment his eye alights on the clock face Hugo hides behind, introducing the possibility that he might know Hugo is there. After a reverse-angle shot of Hugo watching intently from the clock, a shot from Hugo's optical point of view reveals Georges winding up a toy mouse and letting it run across the counter. If he does know Hugo is behind the clock, it follows that this demonstration might be *for* Hugo. A girl we will later learn is his goddaughter Isabelle appears, chats briefly with her godfather, and departs: then Georges looks like he is napping, the mouse lying inert on the counter in front of his hands. Hugo climbs out of the nearest tunnel grille and slowly approaches the counter. He is just about to make away with the clockwork mouse when Georges shoots out a hand to grab him, holding him firm. Thus begins the interrogation that will end with Georges depriving Hugo of his precious notebook.

The explicit narrative detail in this sequence is minimal: we learn that Georges is the toyshop owner, that he has been monitoring Hugo's pilfering of clockwork parts for some time, and that Hugo has an as yet unexplained fixation on acquiring clockwork mechanical parts by any means necessary. But the visual presentation tells us more. The high angle shot of Georges' shop front from Hugo's position shows us that the walls between which the shop sits, the sign above the counter, and the counter itself are all on the same structural plane, with Georges behind that plane, which creates the impression that he is pinned behind the counter of his own shop (see Fig. 6.2). This impression is strengthened by the lack of a visible exit or entrance (we later learn the shop has a side entrance not visible from the front). In the closer view that follows, the camera moves to a frontal framing, flattening the dimensionality of the vibrant clutter of clockwork toys and other trinkets that surround Georges, but from which he is spatially isolated. As I signalled in my earlier discussion of the moment Hugo hesitates to leave the station in his pursuit of Georges, frontality registers much more strongly in 3-D. This is partly because we expect the 3-D image to have depth, and partly because in the three and a half minutes before George is introduced, the composition and stereoscopic design of *Hugo* has emphatically and persistently emphasised depth. Frontality and shallow depth of composition become features of our encounters with Georges at his shop for much of the early part of the film. Further examples include a frontal shot of the shop at the end of a corridor as Hugo approaches it to steal the mouse, and, in a subsequent scene, Georges framed from behind as he pulls down the shutters on his shop for the day, a large opening hours sign which is pinned to the shutters reducing the sense of spatial depth even further. The actor's physical performance in the shots of the shop press home

Figure 6.2. Still from *Hugo* (GK Films / The Kobal Collection): George Méliès 'pinned' behind his shop front.

the possibility that the lack of depth within the image might be a metaphor for a lack of energy or engagement in Georges' life. Across both initial shots of the shop front, Ben Kingsley as Georges maintains the same posture: he is the very picture of stillness. While the character's stillness might have a pragmatic explanation at one level, an attempt to entrap errant young thieves by convincing them he is napping, it registers at another level as a withdrawal from life, from the hubbub of the station crowds: a kind of living death. The film flags this association with deathliness in later scenes. For example, when Hugo follows Georges home, we discover Georges lives next to a graveyard. To get to his house one must pass through the graveyard along a path lined with statues. The statues, an addition by the filmmakers to the graveyard featured in Selznick's book, explicitly bring together associations of stillness and death just metres away from George's doorstep.

It is human interaction that breaks the frontality. Hugo's dialogue scenes with Georges across the shop's counter dissect the seemingly shallow space in angled shot-reverse shot patterns which move from close-ups to wider shots in a way that invests the space of the shop and its immediate environs with a growing impression of depth. Just as the depiction of the shop progresses from an impression of two-dimensionality to three-dimensionality, so Georges' life acquires extra dimensions through his developing association with Hugo, a person in whom Georges recognises his own enthusiasm for and skill with clockwork mechanisms and other inventions. Through the interaction of careful stereoscopic design with other elements of *mise-en-scène*, the film uses cinematic space to express at both metaphorical and literal levels the situations of its two most central characters, and to spatially animate *Hugo*'s thematic emphasis on the magic of machines that bring things to life. Both Hugo and Georges are pinned behind barriers, planes that obscure them, and that limit their ability to participate fully in the rush of life represented by the energy of the station's comings and goings. Both need to 'reconnect', to find a way to be brought back out into the open, from 'flatness' into 'depth', to rediscover their place in the wider world. This fate is only achievable for either character when personal connections begin to intersect, cogs metaphorically meeting and meshing together to bring them out into the open.

Thus we begin to see why the film opens not with a traditional establishing shot but with a clockwork mechanism. If a clockwork machine, the automaton, functions as the film's central narrative mystery (how does it connect Hugo and Georges? Who built it? How does it work? What will it 'say'?), clockwork mechanisms more generally operate as a potent analogy for the processes of socialisation that will complete both characters. Dialogue makes this explicit on two occasions. When Hugo and Isabelle in a private moment muse about their role in the world, Hugo says that when he was younger, 'I'd imagine the whole world was one big machine. Machines never come with any extra parts, you know. They always come with the exact amount they need. So I figured, if the entire world was one big machine, I couldn't be an extra part. I had to be here for some reason.' The second occasion is at the end of the film when Hugo is finally apprehended by the station inspector, in a chase that leaves the automaton broken to pieces on the railway tracks. Just as Hugo is about to be swept off to the orphanage, Georges arrives and claims ownership of Hugo, welcoming him into the Méliès family. As they walk away together arm in arm, Hugo refers to the automaton, saying, 'I'm sorry, it's broken'. Georges replies, 'No it's not. It worked perfectly!' The only way to make sense of this assertion is to see it as a recognition of the automaton's role as a mechanism for social connection, rather than just a machine, which has worked 'like clockwork' to bring Hugo and Georges out of their stillness back into life, and to bring about a reconstitution of the family unit.

The patterning of the movement from flatness to depth that expresses Hugo's and Georges' rhyming narrative trajectories also characterises the presentation of the developing status of Méliès' filmmaking across the film. For Méliès at the start of the film, his history as a filmmaker is a suppressed and painful memory, the only trace of which are flat drawings on sheaves of paper shut away in a box. But by the end of the film he has remembered the vitality of his filmmaking years, reanimating them in his mind, and embodying them for the audience amassed to celebrate his life's work. For Hugo, Isabelle and the extra-diegetic audience too, there is a literal as well as metaphorical movement from a two-dimensional awareness of Méliès' work to a three-dimensional appreciation of it. We first learn more about Georges' past as a filmmaker when Hugo and Isabelle read from a book of film history written by the fictional film scholar René Tabard (Michael Stuhlbarg). In the book are two-dimensional still images from various films from cinema's first three decades, which are brought to life onscreen as the children begin to imagine each photograph as a moving image sequence. Tabard takes Hugo and Isabelle to his office where he shows them more still images from the films and of Méliès at work, but their understanding – and ours – only develops three dimensions when we are transported into Tabard's flashback of his encounter with Méliès at the filmmaker's production studio.

A frontal shot of the glass-lined studio's exterior is followed by an interior shot which constructs a scene from a 1903 Méliès film, *Le Royaume des feés* (*Fairyland: A Kingdom of Fairies*). Four actors – three sea nymphs and a sea king – pose atop a scenery 'flat' in front of a painted backdrop. Three more sea nymphs stand in front of the flat, and a further painted flat stands closer to the camera. Lobster men, additional sea nymphs and other characters walk on from screen left between the nearest stage flats, while in the near foreground live fish are swimming. The shot is held for several seconds, the better for the spectator to appreciate Méliès' careful use of planar layering to create an illusion of depth (albeit in a non-naturalistic mode), an appreciation underpinned by the stereoscopic presentation, which holds the different layers at spatially distinct planes. The camera itself breaks the illusion by tilting left and up, beginning to pull apart image layers as it deviates from Méliès' famously frontal camera placement. As the flashback progresses, shots from different angles dissect the space of production, so that we discover the live fishes are in fact in a tank in front of Méliès' camera, and are invited to scrutinise the practical reality of other elements of the illusion, from the scenery flats to costumed performers to Méliès' multiple production and performance roles. Two-dimensional images acquire metaphorical depth as we discover how they were constructed by flesh and blood actors and material elements of staging. A similar process occurs in Méliès' own flashback to his heyday as a filmmaker, later in the movie. Once again there is a shot that mimics the framing in Méliès' 1905 film *Le Palais des Mille et une nuits* (*The Palace of the One Thousand and One Nights*), followed by shots which dissect the space of production from different angles. This time crane shots and mobile forward tracking shots circle different parts of the set and the studio, so that the layered scenery flats that construct the scene being filmed are legible as separate planes. These literal and metaphorical movements from two dimensions to three culminate in Méliès' presentation of his works at the gala celebration of his career. At the point in the narrative when Méliès has, with Hugo, achieved a more engaged and deeper connection to the world and those around him, the film strikingly chooses to convert the originally two-dimensional Méliès movies into 3-D.

At one level the presentation of Méliès' work in 3-D works for the narrative resolution, expressing the fullness of his contemporaries' admiration for his *oeuvre* as well as the fullness of the fictionalised Méliès' own situation, head of a newly reconstituted family into which Hugo, a fellow inventor and trick enthusiast, has been welcomed. But the sequence also functions at another level that speaks to how *Hugo* wants to position itself in relation to both cinematic history in general and stereoscopic cinema in particular. The sense of spatial depth encouraged in the stereoscopic presentation of Méliès' films generates an experience in which our awareness of the planar layering Méliès used to construct his spectacular images is held in tension with the resulting illusion, an illusion which joins together Méliès' original vision with a contemporary 3-D spectacle. Both illusions are achieved through emergent cinematic technologies, their simultaneous presentation in this sequence an invitation to contemplate this comparability of film technology, film spectacle and illusionistic endeavour at different ends of cinema history. In its homage to Méliès' achievements, its attempt to 're-animate' his films and their trick effects for a new generation of potential cinephiles, *Hugo* self-consciously locates itself within the same history of cinematic illusionism, connecting its stereoscopic practice not to previous 3-D cycles but to the filmmaker most popularly associated with initiating a cinema of attractions and a tradition of special effects that still persist today.

As the analysis in this chapter has demonstrated, *Hugo*'s stereoscopic strategies foreground visual style in the service of the film's work on character, its thematic movement from separation to belonging, and its evocation of Paris as the Modern City *par excellence*. Locating its characters in a dynamically three-dimensional cinematic space, *Hugo* deploys stereoscopic design to animate spatialised figures which are central to our experience and understanding of the narrative and its setting. In that sense, in a story about cinema's beginnings, *Hugo* throws into relief, in more than one sense of that phrase, the expressive potential of one of cinema's most recent technological iterations. This is an important move in the context of the current cultural and media debate, sketched at the beginning of this chapter, about whether D-3-D is doing something really new, has not yet reached maturity, or has already become exhausted. By explicitly connecting itself to a history of cinematic illusionism rather than the often derided history of 3-D cinema, and by attempting to showcase a relatively sophisticated stereoscopic practice which moves forward narrative, action and character in subtle and complex ways in addition to providing pleasurable spectacle, *Hugo* represents an intervention into these ongoing debates about D-3-D's value, and about its artistic potential in the mainstream.

NOTES

1. There are, however, still difficulties that come from imperfections in stereo capture of live action, which need to be corrected in post. See Sylwan 2009 for an informative discussion of the challenges and opportunities D-3-D presents at every stage of the production pipeline.

2. See also Robertson 2008; Cielpy 2010.

3. This increase in 3-D enabled screens was crucial to avoid enforced shortened runs and thus attenuated box office returns as 3-D releases competed for the same screens (see Thompson 2009: paragraph 15 and Cielpy 2010: paragraph 11).

4. Kristin Thompson's insightful series of articles titled 'Has 3D Already Failed?' (Thompson 2009, 2011a, 2011b) on the *Observations on Film Art* blog are an invaluable introduction to such discussions.

5. This revival includes remakes and homages like *The Texas Chainsaw Massacre* (Marcus Nispel, 2003), *Planet Terror* (Robert Rodriguez, 2007), *Death Proof* (Quentin Tarantino, 2007), *The Last House on the Left* (Dennis Iliadis, 2009), *I Spit on Your Grave* (Steven R. Monroe, 2010) and *Machete* (Ethan Maniquis and Robert Rodriguez, 2010).

6. This reconsideration of early cinema was driven by the 1978 FIAF Brighton Project on Early Fiction Film and the scholarship that emerged in its wake. See Fell 1983, Gunning 198; Gaudreault and Gunning 1989; Elsaesser 1990; and Strauven 2006.

7. Parallax is the most effective binocular depth cue, in that it requires two eyes to operate. Monocular depth cues – which allow us to judge depth with only one eye – include linear perspective, retinal image size (where the real size of an object is known, the object viewed is compared to this size), overlapping (where an object overlaps another it is closer to us), and atmospheric perspective and texture gradient, which I will discuss below.

8. It is worth noting that the digital 3-D production line includes (usually bespoke) software packages to calculate and control the interocular distance and other aspects of 3-D composition, and playback facilities for viewing rushes in 3-D, alongside digital post-production processes which provide a further opportunity to correct 3-D effects in post.

9. David Bordwell makes some initial comments about the results of *Coraline*'s 3-D design in his blog post 'Coraline, cornered' (2009).

10. While art movements such as the Futurists and the Vorticists celebrated technologisation and the possibilities machines had introduced, several commentators noted the shock of modernity, including Georg Simmel in his 1903 essay 'The Metropolis and Mental Life' (2002: 11–19), and Walter Benjamin's 1939 essay 'On Some Motifs in Baudelaire' (1968: 155–200). Art of the period reflected on this ambivalence towards modernity, and the effects on people's mental and social wellbeing, from Virginia Woolf's novel *Mrs Dalloway* (1925) to Max Beckmann's pre- and post-First World War paintings like *Die Strasse* (1913) and *The Night* (1919).

11. Artefacts with negative parallax floating through the air (clouds, snow, rain, etc.) are used to underline the stereoscopic nature of sequences in various films including *A Christmas Carol* (Robert Zemeckis, 2009), and *Harry Potter and the Deathly Hallows: Part 2* (David Yates, 2011).

12. Examples of the phantom ride film can be found at the British Film Institute's Screen Online archive (link active as of February 2012, registration required), http://www.screenonline.org.uk/film/id/1193042/.

13. In the complete passage, Holmberg gives an example of 'stereoscopic' being used as a metaphor in a 1912 issue of *Moving Picture World*: 'The photography is perfect and finely

stereoscopic; the coloring just enough to seem natural and make one forget that it is hand painted' (2003: 138).

14. In fact this is an illusion: there are a number of digital compositing 'cheats' which create the impression of a seamless long take. See Seymour 2011.

15. With some significant exceptions which I will shortly address.

Conclusion

Contemporary mainstream cinema increasingly incorporates a wide range of digital interventions, some overt, some less easy to discern, and others simply invisible to the naked eye. In this way, even while promotional discourses still use the term, digital imaging technologies deployments have extended far beyond the designation 'special effect', while at the same time audiences are increasingly aware of the digital's screen presence and something of the techniques being employed. Emerging from a conviction that such circumstances might well require a modified form of film analysis, this book has asked how we might read the digital elements of the cinematic frame, and how we might quantify their impact on the meanings generated within a particular image, moment, scene or film. Simply put, do our interpretive strategies or conclusions change in the presence of the digital?

I have argued strongly against trying to answer these questions by artificially isolating the digital from other filmic elements. This position might have seemed strange given the book's title, which explicitly names the digital as its subject. However, the study emerges from a desire to develop a critical approach to contemporary mainstream cinema that is able to take appropriate account of recent developments in film style which include, but are not wholly constituted by, digital imaging. At its best, film analysis engages with the materiality of a particular film moment by seeking to understand the interplay of all evident cinematic elements: to isolate or prioritise the digital within such a process risks unbalancing the act of analysis and its outcomes. Digital imaging must take its place alongside a myriad other filmmaking technologies and techniques in the production of meaning, and so digital image elements must be seen in context, in relation to and as part of (rather than separate from) narrative structure, characterisation and performance, *mise-en-scène*, cinematography, and so on. This refusal to elevate the digital's aesthetic and epistemic influence above other filmmaking practices permits critical reflection on media accounts of digital effects, and the film industry's commercially driven attempts to valorise digital imaging as a transformative 'high' technology. It also represents a form of resistance to the idea, cyclically mooted by commentators since the early 1990s, that digital imaging technologies are irrevocably altering cinema.

Interpretation draws its evidence from cinema screen and soundtrack, from what has been presented and the manner of its presentation. Digital imaging technologies have certainly transformed the basis of a range of filmmaking processes, but what we encounter on the screen remains familiar. It is still useful to talk of elements of *mise-en-scène*, even where some of those elements are digital, or to discuss shot scale or point of view even if the camera is a notional one whose position and path is constructed inside a computer, since the filmic conventions themselves are still evident in the finished film. As an important strand through this study has worked to point out, there are significant continuities between 'pre-digital' modes of narrative filmmaking and current forms that incorporate digital imaging, which problematise claims of digital's newness. It is noteworthy that while digital imaging technologies have the capacity to transform the nature and characteristics of the cinematic image, at present mainstream narrative cinema persists as a cluster of familiar aesthetic, narrative, representational and presentational conventions; rather than overturning them, digital imaging technologies work in the service of, or directly replicate them. Narrative cinema is not usurped but propagated in a filmmaking process that draws on more recent tools alongside older practices and technologies. However, as we have seen, digital imaging's inherent plasticity also offers a space for experimentation that is beginning to be grasped at the playful margins of mainstream cinema. The directionality and future extent of such experimentation is as yet unclear, but the same interpretive strategies I have argued for elsewhere in the study find productive application in relation to these developments.

This book has espoused an interpretive model which sees digital elements as simply one of the building blocks in the wider systems working across a sequence, scene or film. Each case study has provided a developed example of how this can be achieved, making the case for a versatile analytical approach that is always alert to the digital's potential to be relevant to interpretation. At the same time, such an approach must be grounded in a developed understanding of what digital imaging is capable of communicating, in its 'mimicry', its objecthood, its compositing, and its own digital-ness. Part of this project has been to illustrate the importance of moving away from reductive conceptions of digital effects to a more sophisticated and flexible understanding of how digital imaging might contribute to meaning. The case studies investigated here have sought to signal the multiplicity of digital interventions into the image and the diversity and complexity of their epistemic consequences, while resisting the temptation to provide a survey or taxonomy that would soon be out of date.

While digital imaging's most explicit deployments generate moments of 'effects' spectacle, the full range of deployments, from imperceptible to exhibitionist, also work in the service of narrative, as Chapter 1 began to explore, and the rest of the study has illustrated in contexts ranging from action and fantasy, to dramas operating in a more naturalistic mode, to the recent emergence of digital stereoscopic cinema. Indeed, as Chapter 3 made clear, visual, narrative, and character coherence is still prioritised over other options the digital might offer in mainstream narrative cinema, thus making redundant any approach that considers digital elements only in terms of their status as technology. Chapter 2 argued for digital imaging's capacity to offer a versatile metaphorical function that can inform narrative action, characterisation and thematic structures in complex ways, a capacity revisited in Chapters 3 and 4 on the digital protagonist, and in Chapters 3, 4 and 6 in relation to the spatialised, digital staging of the profilmic body. Chapters 4 and 6 confronted the manner in which cinema in the digital era often historicises its own digital imaging technologies in relation to earlier moments in cinema history or special effects history, a process which has its own implications for meaning, and for how we might think about those previous histories. Digital imaging is now one of cinema's representational tools, in both senses of that word, and the study has investigated how digital imaging works with other filmic elements to construct difference and identity. Chapters 4 and 5 focused on the complexities and politics of digitally assisted representation in detail, in the process reaffirming the fact that filmmaking decisions are a product of culture and ideology alongside technological and economic pressures.

In this manner, the detailed textual analyses elaborated in these case studies have revealed the intricate ways in which digital deployments contribute to and often extend or intensify the workings of audio-visual narration, narrative design, characterisation, staging and performance. Across the case studies, the impossibility of discussing the connotative impact of a digital element in isolation from a film's wider epistemic structures has become apparent, but so too has the necessity to be attentive to how digital imaging functions in each case, in order to achieve a fuller interpretive account. This validates the seemingly paradoxical basis of the project – to focus on the digital in film in order to demonstrate a model of close textual analysis that engages with digital imaging alongside, rather than to the exclusion of, other filmmaking practices. The study makes a case for a mode of film analysis that sees the digital as part of the cinematic whole, while allowing for the complexities of digital imaging's epistemological effects within its larger interpretive endeavour. In doing so, it makes a case for a critical engagement with the digital in film that is informed by an alertness to questions of representation and cultural politics as well as to questions of style and meaning. The case studies contained within these pages begin this project; I hope it is one that others will want to continue, matching the complex possibilities of digital imaging's communicativeness with an analytical versatility of our own.

Bibliography

Abramowitz, Rachel (2010), '*Avatar*'s animated acting', *Los Angeles Times* (18 February), last accessed 11 April 2012 at http://articles.latimes.com/2010/feb/18/entertainment/la-et-avatar-actors18–2010feb18.

Balcerzak, Scott (2009), 'Andy Serkis as Actor, Body, and Gorilla: Motion Capture and the Presence of Performance', in Scott Balcerzak and Jason Sperb (eds), *Cinephilia in the Age of Digital Reproduction: Film, Pleasure and Digital Culture Vol. 1*, 195–213.

Barker, Martin (2011), 'Playing with Gollum: Uncovering the Cultural Life and Transnational Travels of a Complex Character', *Scope: An Online Journal of Film and Television Studies*, 19 (February), 1–34 (PDF pagination), last accessed 6 April 2012 at http://www.scope.nottingham.ac.uk/article.php?issue=19&id=1251.

Barnes, Brooks (2011), 'As 3-D Falls From Favor, Director of *Transformers* Tries to Promote It', *The New York Times* (21 June), last accessed 15 January 2012 at www.nytimes.com/2011/06/22/business/media/22transformers.html?_r=1.

Barthes, Roland (2000), *Camera Lucida: Reflections on Photography* (1980), trans. Richard Howard (1981), New York: Hill and Wang.

Barr, Charles (1963), 'CinemaScope: Before and After', *Film Quarterly*, 16.4 (Summer), 4–24.

Bazin, André (1997), 'Will CinemaScope Save the Film Industry?' (1953), in Bert Cardullo (ed.), *Bazin at Work: Major Essays and Reviews of the Forties and Fifties*, trans. Alain Piette and Bert Cardullo, Routledge: London, 77–92.

— (2005a), 'The Ontology of the Photographic Image' (1945), in *What is Cinema? Volume 1*, trans. Hugh Gray (1967), Berkeley: University of California Press, 9–16.

— (2005b), 'The Myth of Total Cinema' (1946), in *What is Cinema? Volume 1*, trans. Hugh Gray (1967), Berkeley: University of California Press, 17–22.

— (2005c), 'The Evolution of the Language of Cinema' (1950–55), in *What is Cinema? Volume 1*, trans. Hugh Gray (1967), Berkeley, Los Angeles and London: University of California Press, 23–40.

BBC Wildlife staff article (2006), 'King Kong – We talk to Andy Serkis, the man who played Gollum, about how wild gorillas inspired his new film role', *BBC Wildlife* magazine, 24.1, 60–3.

Bellin, Joshua David (2005), *Framing Monsters: Fantasy Film and Social Alienation*, Carbondale: Southern Illinois University Press.

Belton, John (1992), *Widescreen Cinema*, London: Harvard University Press.

— (2002), 'Digital Cinema: A False Revolution', *October*, 100, 98–114.
— (2008), 'Painting by the Numbers: The Digital Intermediate', *Film Quarterly* 61.3 (Spring), 58–65.
Benjamin, Walter (1968), 'On Some Motifs in Baudelaire' (1939), in Hannah Arendt (ed.), *Illuminations*, New York: Shocken Books, 155–200.
— (1972), 'A Short History of Photography' (1931), *Screen*, 13.1, 5–26.
Benshoff, Harry M. (1998), *Monsters in the Closet: Homosexuality and the Horror Film*, Manchester: Manchester University Press.
Berenstein, Rhona J. (1996), *Attack of the Leading Ladies: Gender, Sexuality and Spectatorship in Classical Horror Cinema*, New York and Chichester: Columbia University Press.
Bernadelli, James (2002), *Spider-Man* film review (3 May), last accessed 28 March 2005 at http://www.reelviews.net/movies/s/spider-man.html.
— (2004), *Spider-Man 2* film review (30 June), last accessed 6 April 2012 at http://www.reelviews.net/php_review_template.php?identifier=713.
Bogle, Donald (2000), *Toms, Coons, Mulattoes, Mammies, and Bucks: An Interpretive History of Blacks in American Films* (1973), London and New York: Continuum International Publishing Group.
Borde, Raymond and Chaumeton, Étienne (1996), 'Towards a Definition of *Film Noir*' (1955), in Alain Silver and James Ursini (eds), trans. Alain Silver, *Film Noir Reader*, New York: Limelight Editions, 17–25.
Bordwell, David (1985), 'Widescreen Processes and Stereophonic Sound', 'Deep Focus Cinematography', and 'Technicolor,' in David Bordwell, Janet Staiger and Kristin Thompson, *The Classical Hollywood Cinema: Film Style & Mode of Production to 1960*, London: Routledge and Kegan Paul, 358–64.
— (1992), *On the History of Film Style*, Cambridge, MA: Harvard University Press.
— (2006), *The Way Hollywood Tells It: Story and Style in Modern Movies*, Berkeley and Los Angeles: University of California Press.
— (2009), 'Coraline, cornered', in *Observations on film art* blog (23 February), last accessed 23 August 2011 at http://www.davidbordwell.net/blog/2009/02/23/coraline-cornered/.
— (2011), 'Pandora's digital box: In the multiplex', *Observations on film art* blog, last accessed 1 April 2012 at http://www.davidbordwell.net/blog/2011/12/01/pandoras-digital-box-in-the-multiplex/.
Branigan, Edward (1985), 'Color and Cinema: Problems in the Writing of History' (1979), in Bill Nichols (ed.), *Movies and Methods: An Anthology*, Berkeley and Los Angeles: University of California Press, 121–43.
Brooker, Peter (2002), *Modernity and Metropolis: Writing, Film and Urban Formations*, Basingstoke: Palgrave Macmillan.
Bukatman, Scott (1999), 'The Artificial Infinite: On Special Effects and the Sublime', in Annette Kuhn (ed.), *Alien Zone II: The Spaces of Science Fiction Cinema*, London and New York: Verso, 249–76.
— (2003), *Matters of Gravity: Special Effects and Supermen in the 20th Century*, Durham and London: Duke University Press.
— (2011), 'Why I Hate Superhero Movies', *Cinema Journal*, 50.3 (Spring), 118–22.
Buscombe, Edward (1985), 'Sound and Colour' (1978), in Bill Nichols (ed.), *Movies and Methods Volume II*, Berkeley: University of California Press, 83–92.
Caillois, Roger (1983), 'The Detective Novel as Game' (1941), in Glenn W. Most and William W. Stowe (eds), *The Poetics of Murder: Detective Fiction & Literary Theory*, trans. William W. Stowe, New York: Harcourt Brace Jovanovich, 1–12.
Caranicas, Peter (2011), 'Birns & Sawyer stops renting film cameras: Legendary equipment

house switches to all-digital line', *Variety* (18 October), last accessed 1 January 2012 at http://www.variety.com/article/VR1118044669?refCatId=3683

Carroll, Noël (1998), '*King Kong*: Ape and Essence' (1984), in Noël Carroll, *Interpreting the Moving Image*, Cambridge, New York and Oakleigh, Melbourne: Cambridge University Press, 118–42.

Child, Ben (2007), 'Should all CGI be banned?', *The Guardian* online film blog (14 November), last accessed 27 April 2009, at http://www.guardian.co.uk/film/filmblog/2007/nov/14/shouldallcgibebanned.

— (2012), 'Does *Avengers Assemble* deliver the Hulk we have been waiting for?', *The Guardian* (13 April), last accessed 15 April 2012 at http://www.guardian.co.uk/film/filmblog/2012/apr/13/avengers-assemble-hulk.

Christie, Ian (1994), *The Last Machine: Early Cinema and the Birth of the Modern World*, London: BBC Educational Developments.

Church Gibson, Pamela (2007), 'Masculinity in the New Millennium: Spectacle, Performance, Dress and Identity', keynote speech at *Dressing Rooms: Current Perspectives on Fashion and Textiles* conference, Oslo University College, Norway, 14–16 May.

Cielpy, Michael (2010), 'Resistance Forms Against Hollywood's 3-D Push', *The New York Times* (2 August), last accessed 23 August 2011 at http://www.nytimes.com/2010/08/03/business/media/03-3d.html?_r=1&hpw.

Comolli, Jean-Louis (1985), 'Technique and ideology: camera, perspective, depth of field' (1971), in Bill Nichols (ed.), *Movies and Methods Volume II*, Berkeley: University of California Press, 40–57.

Conrad, Joseph (1995), *Heart of Darkness* (1902), London, New York, Camberwell, Toronto, New Delhi, Albany and Rosebank: Penguin.

Crary, Jonathan (1988), 'Techniques of the Observer', *October*, 45, 3–35.

Creed, Barbara (1993), *The Monstrous-Feminine: Film, Feminism, Psychoanalysis*, London and New York: Routledge.

Cubitt, Sean (1999a), 'Le réel, c'est l'impossible: the sublime time of special effects', *Screen*, 40.2, 123–31.

— (1999b), 'Phalke, Méliès, and Special Effects Today', *Wide Angle* 21.1, 114–30.

— (2004), *The Cinema Effect*, Cambridge, MA and London: The MIT Press.

Darley, Andrew (2000), *Visual Digital Culture: Surface Play and Spectacle in New Media Genres*, London and New York: Routledge.

Dean, Tacita (2011a), 'Save celluloid, for art's sake', *The Guardian* (22 February), last accessed 1 January 2012 at http://www.guardian.co.uk/artanddesign/2011/feb/22/tacita-dean-16mm-film.

— (2011b), 'Film', in Nicholas Cullinan (ed.), *Tacita Dean: Film*, London: Tate Publishing, 15–17.

de Certeau, Michel (1984), *The Practice of Everyday Life* (1980), trans. Steven Rendell, Berkeley: University of California Press.

Dick, Philip K (1956), 'The Minority Report' (short story), in Leo Margulies (ed.), *Fantastic Universe: Science Fiction*, 4, 6 (magazine digest), New York: King-Size Publications.

Dimendberg, Edward (2004), *Film Noir and the Spaces of Modernity*, Cambridge, MA and London: Harvard University Press.

Dixon, Wheeler Winston (2007), 'Vanishing Point: The Last Days of Film', *Senses of Cinema* 43 (12 May), last accessed 1 January 2012 at http://sensesofcinema.com/2007/feature-articles/last-days-film/.

Douglas, Mary (1970), *Purity and Danger*, Harmondsworth: Pelican Books.

Dyer, Richard (1997), *White*, London and New York: Routledge.

Eagan, Daniel (2007), *300* film review, *Film Journal International* (2 July), last accessed 5 June 2008 at http://www.filmjournal.com/filmjournal/esearch/article_display.jsp?vnu_content_id=1003555969.

Ebert, Roger (2002), *Spider-Man* film review, *Chicago Sun Times*, 3 May, last accessed 6 April 2012 at http://rogerebert.suntimes.com/apps/pbcs.dll/article?AID=/20020503/REVIEWS/205030303/1023.

— (2005), *Spider-Man* film review, *Chicago Sun Times* (3 May), last accessed 28 March 2005 at http://rogerebert.suntimes.com/apps/pbcs.dll/article?AID=/20020503/REVIEWS/205030303/1023.

— (2008a), *300* film review, *Chicago Sun Times* (4 August), last accessed 5 June 2008 at http://rogerebert.suntimes.com/apps/pbcs.dll/article?AID=/20080804/REVIEWS/506949713/1023.

— (2008b), 'D-minus for 3-D', *Roger Ebert's Journal, Chicago Sun Times* (16 August), last accessed 23 August 2011 at http://blogs.suntimes.com/ebert/2008/08/dminus_for_3d.html.

— (2010), 'Why I Hate 3-D (And You Should Too)', *The Daily Beast* blog, *NewsWeek* (9 May), last accessed 23 August 2011 at http://www.thedailybeast.com/newsweek/2010/04/30/why-i-hate-3-d-and-you-should-too.html.

Elley, Derek (1984), *The Epic Film: Myth and History*, London and Boston: Routledge and Kegan Paul.

Elsaesser, Thomas (1972), 'Tales of Sound and Fury: Observations on the Family Melodrama', *Monogram*, 4, 2–15.

— (2000), 'The New New Hollywood: Cinema Beyond Distance and Proximity', in Ib Bondebjerg (ed.), *Moving Images, Culture and the Mind*, Luton: University of Luton Press, 187–204.

— (2010), 'The dimension of depth and objects rushing towards us *or* The tail that wags the dog. A discourse on digital 3-D cinema', *EDIT Filmmaker's Magazin*, 1, last accessed 1 November 2011 at http://www.filmmakersfestival.com/en/magazine/ausgabe-12010/the-dimension-of-depth/the-dimesion-of-depth-and-objects-rushing-towards-us.html.

— (2011), 'The Return of 3-D: Logics and Genealogies of the Image in the 21st Century', keynote address to the Postgraduate Research Conference, Department of Media Arts, Royal Holloway, University of London, 9 June 2011.

— (ed.) (1990), *Early Cinema: Space Frame Narrative*, London: BFI Publishing.

Elsaesser, Thomas and Malte Hagener (2010), *Film Theory: An Introduction Through The Senses*, London and New York: Routledge.

Erb, Cynthia (1998), *Tracking King Kong: A Hollywood Icon in World Culture*, Detroit: Wayne State University Press.

Everett, Anna (2003), 'Digitextuality and click theory: theses on convergence and media in the digital age', in Anna Everett and John Caldwell (eds), *New media: theories and practices of digitextuality*, London and New York: Routledge, 3–28.

Fabian, Johannes (1983), *Time and the Other: How Anthropology Makes Its Subject*, New York and Chichester: Columbia University Press.

Fell, John L. (ed.) (1983), *Film Before Griffith*, Berkeley: University of California Press.

Felperin, Leslie (2002), *Minority Report* film review, *Sight and Sound*, 12.8 (ns), 44–5.

— (2011), '*Pina*' (Berlinale International Film Festival review), *Variety* (13 February), last accessed 2 February 2012 at www.variety.com/review/VE1117944599?refcatid=31.

Flückiger, Barbara (2010), 'Digital Bodies', extract from Barbara Flückiger (2008): *Visual Effects: Filmbilder aus dem Computer*, trans. Mark Kyburz, revised by Barbara Flückiger 2010, Marburg: Schueren.

— (2011), 'Computer generated Characters in *Avatar* and *Benjamin Button*' ('Zur digitalen Animation von Körpern in *Benjamin Button* und *Avatar*'), in Harro Segeberg (ed.), *Film im Zeitalter Neuer Medien II: Digitalität und Kino*, trans. Benjamin Letzler, Munich: Fink (2012).

Fordham, Joe (2007), 'A Beautiful Death', *Cinefex*, 109, 64–70, 73–8, 81–6, 118.

Foucault, Michel (1991), *Discipline and Punish: The Birth of the Prison* (1975), London: Penguin Books, trans. Alan Sheridan (1977).

Friedberg, Anne (2006), *The Virtual Window: From Alberti to Microsoft*, Cambridge, MA and London: MIT Press.

Friedman, Lester D. (2006), *Citizen Spielberg*, Urbana and Chicago: University of Illinois Press.

Gaudreault, André and Tom Gunning (1989), 'Le cinéma des premiers temps: un défi a l'histoire du cinéma?' in Jacques Aumont, André Gaudreault and Michel Marie (eds), *Histoire du cinéma. Nouvelles approches*, Paris: Sorbonne, 49–63.

Giardina, Carolyn (2011), 'Deluxe, Technicolor Begin Orderly Retreat From Film Services', *The Hollywood Reporter* (18 July), last accessed at 1 January 2012 at http://www.hollywoodreporter.com/news/deluxe-technicolor-begin-orderly-retreat-212459.

Giardina, Carolyn, Pamela McClintock and Chris Godley (2011), '*Rise of the Planet of the Apes* First Look: The Many Faces of Andy Serkis', *The Hollywood Reporter* (4 August), last accessed 11 April 2012 at http://www.hollywoodreporter.com/gallery/rise-planet-apes-first-look-218818#5.

Gibbs, John (2002), *Mise-en-scène: Film Style and Interpretation*, London: Wallflower Press.

Goldman, Jonathan E (2006), *King Kong* (1933) and *King Kong* (2005) film review, *Scope: An Online Journal of Film and Television Studies*, 5 (June), last accessed 5 November 2007 at http://www.scope.nottingham.ac.uk/filmreview.php?issue=5&id=154.

Goldner, Orville and Turner, George E. (1975), *The Making of King Kong: The Story Behind a Film Classic*, New York: Ballantyne Books.

Gray, Simon (2005) 'Beauty and the Beast', *American Cinematographer* (December), last accessed 5 November 2007 at http://www.theasc.com/magazine/dec05/kingkong/page1.html.

Grodal, Torben (2009), *Embodied Visions: Evolution, Emotion, Culture, and Film*, Oxford: Oxford University Press.

Gunning, Tom (1986), 'The Cinema of Attraction: Early Film, Its Spectator and the Avant-Garde', *Wide Angle* 8.3–4 (Fall): 63–71, reprinted as 'The Cinema of Attractions: Early Film, Its Spectator and the Avant-Garde,' in Thomas Elsaesser (ed.), *Early Cinema: Space Frame Narrative*, 56–62.

— (1993), '"Now You See It, Now You Don't": The Temporality of the Cinema of Attractions', *Velvet Light Trap*, 32, 3–12.

— (2003), 'Re-Newing Old Technologies: Astonishment, Second Nature, and the Uncanny in Technology from the Previous Turn-of-the-Century', in David Thorburn and Henry Jenkins (eds), *Rethinking Media Change: The Aesthetics of Transition*, Cambridge, MA and London: MIT Press, 39–60.

Hale, Grace Elizabeth (1999), *Making Whiteness: The Culture of Segregation in the South, 1890–1940*, New York: Vintage.

Hanley, Lawrence F (1996), 'Popular Culture and Crisis: King Kong Meets Edmund Wilson', in Bill Mullen and Sherry Lee Linkton (eds), *Radical Revisions: Re-reading 1930s Culture*, Urbana and Chicago: University of Illinois Press, 242–63.

Hansen, Miriam (1991), *Babel and Babylon: Spectatorship in American Silent Film*, Cambridge, MA: Harvard University Press.

Haraway, Donna (1989), *Primate Visions: Gender, Race, and Nature in the World of Modern Science*, New York and London: Routledge.

Hark, Ina Rae (1993), 'Animals or Romans: Looking at Masculinity in *Spartacus*', in Steve Cohan and Ina Rae Hark (eds), *Screening the Male: Exploring Masculinities in Hollywood Cinema*, London and New York: Routledge.

Harpole, Charles H (1980), 'Ideological and Technological Determinism in Deep-Space Cinema Images', *Film Quarterly*, 23.3, 11–22.

Hayes, R. M. (1989), *3-D Movies: A History and Filmography of Stereoscopic Cinema*, Chicago and London: St James Press.

Hellenbrand, Harold (1983), 'Bigger Thomas Reconsidered: *Native Son*, Film, and *King Kong*', *Journal of American Culture*, 6.1: 84–95.

Heumann, Joe (1980–1), 'Controversy and Correspondence: Sharpening Deep Focus', *Film Quarterly*, 24.2, 62–4.

Higgins, Scott (2003), 'A New Colour Consciousness: Colour in the Digital Age', *Convergence: The International Journal of Research into New Media Technologies*, 9.4, 60–76.

Holben, Jay (2002), 'Criminal intent', *American Cinematographer*, 83.7, 34–45.

Holmberg, Jan (2003), 'Ideals of Immersion in Early Cinema', *Cinémas: revue d'études cinématographiques / Cinémas: Journal of Film Studies*, 14.1: 129–47.

hooks, bell (1992), *Black Looks: Race and Representation*, Boston, MA: South End Press.

Hope-Jones, Mark (2011), 'Through A Child's Eyes', *American Cinematographer* (December), 54–67.

Hornaday, Ann (2011), 'Hidden wonders revealed from 30,000 years ago', *The Washington Times* (6 May), last accessed 2 February 2012 at www.washingtonpost.com/gog/movies/cave-of-forgotten-dreams,1180693/critic-review.html#reviewNum1.

Huffstutter, P. J. and Alex Pham (2002), 'Putting a Human Face on "It"', *Los Angeles Times* (17 December), last accessed 11 April 2012 at http://articles.latimes.com/2002/dec/17/business/fi-gollum17.

Jones, Mike (2007), 'Vanishing Point: Spatial Composition and the Virtual Camera', *Animation*, 2.3, 225–44.

Karagosian, Michael (2009), 'SMPTE Report: Digital Cinema in 2009', MKPE Consulting LLC / SMPTE (published in *SMPTE 2009 Progress Report*, September 2009), last accessed 10 January 2012 at mkpe.com/publications/d-cinema/reports/June2009_report.php.

— (2011), 'Digital Cinema Experiences Strong Growth in 2011 – a Mid-Year Report', MKPE Consulting LLC / SMPTE (published in the September 2011 *SMPTE Journal*), last accessed 10 January 2012 at mkpe.com/publications/d-cinema/reports/June2011_report.php.

Kermode, Mark (2004), *Spider-Man 2* film review, *The Observer* (18 July), last accessed 28 March at http://film.guardian.co.uk/News_Story/Critic_Review/Observer_Film_of_the_week/0,4267,1263615,00.html.

— (2010), 'No, your eyes aren't deceiving you – 3-D really is a con', *The Observer* (11 April), last accessed 24 January 2012 at http://www.guardian.co.uk/commentisfree/2010/apr/11/3d-avatar-hollywood.

King, Geoff (2000), *Spectacular Narratives: Hollywood in the Age of the Blockbuster*, London and New York: I.B. Taurus.

Klein, Norman M. (2004), *The Vatican to Vegas: A History of Special Effects*, New York and London: The New Press.

Kozachik, Pete (2009), '2 Worlds in 3 Dimensions', *American Cinematographer* (February), last accessed 23 August 2011 at http://www.theasc.com/ac_magazine/February2009/Coraline/page1.php.

Kracauer, Siegfried (1997), *Theory of Film: The Redemption of Physical Reality* (1960), Princeton: Princeton University Press.

Krauss, Rosalind E. (2010), *Perpetual Inventory*, Cambridge, MA and London: MIT Press.

Kristeva, Julia (1982), *Powers of Horror: An Essay on Abjection*, trans. Leon S. Roudiez, New York and Chichester: Columbia University Press.

Kuhn, Annette (1990), *Alien Zone: Cultural Theory and Contemporary Science Fiction Cinema*, London and New York: Verso.

Lefebvre, Henri (2007), *The Production of Space* (1974), trans. Donald Nicholson-Smith (1991), Malden, MA, Oxford and Carlton, Victoria: Blackwell Publishing

Mak, Monica (2003), 'Keeping Watch of Time: The Temporal Impact of the Digital in Cinema', *Convergence*, 9.4, 38.47.

Magid, Ron (2002), 'Exploring a New Universe', *American Cinematographer* (September), last accessed 14 June 2008 at http://www.theasc.com/magazine/sep02/exploring/index.html.

— (2005), 'Building a Believable Blockbuster', *American Cinematographer* (August), last accessed 28 March 2005 at http://www.theasc.com/magazine/aug03/sub/index.html.

Mamet, David (2007), *Bambi vs. Godzilla: On the Nature, Purpose and Practice of the Movie Business*, London: Simon and Schuster UK Ltd.

Manovich, Lev (1999), 'What Is Digital Cinema?' in Peter Lunenfeld (ed.), *The Digital Dialectic: New Essays on New Media*, Cambridge, MA: MIT Press, 172–92.

— (2001), *The Language of New Media*, London and Cambridge, MA: MIT Press.

McCarthy, Todd (2002), *The Lord of the Rings: The Two Towers* film review, *Variety* (5 December), last accessed 6 April 2012 at http://www.variety.com/review/VE1117919497?refcatid=31.

McDonald, Keith (2003), *Minority Report* film review, *Scope: An Online Journal of Film and Television Studies* (August), last accessed 15 April 2004 at http://www.nottingham.ac.uk/film/journal/filmrev/films-august-03.htm.

McGurl, Mark (1996), 'Making It Big: Picturing the Radio Age in *King Kong*', *Critical Inquiry*, 22, 415–45.

McQuire, Scott (2000), 'Impact Aesthetics: Back to the Future in Digital Cinema?: Millennial Fantasies', *Convergence*, 6.2, 41–61.

Mendiburu, Bernard (2009), *3D Movie Making: Stereoscopic Digital Cinema from Script to Screen*, London: Focal Press.

Metz, Christian (2000), 'The Imaginary Signifier' (1975), in Robert Stam and Toby Miller (eds), *Film and Theory: An Anthology*, Oxford and Malden, MA: Blackwell Publishers Ltd, 408–36.

Miller, Frank (1991), *Sin City* serialisation (Dark Horse Comics), in *Dark Horse Fifth Anniversary Special* (April 1991) and *Dark Horse Presents* 51 (May 1991) to 62 (June 1992), reprinted in Miller, Frank (1996), *Sin City Books 1–7*, Milwaukie: Dark Horse Books.

— (1998), *300* limited series (May 1998–September 1998) (Dark Horse Comics), reprinted in Miller, Frank (1999), *300*, Milwaukie: Dark Horse Books.

Mitchell, Rick (2004), 'The tragedy of 3-D cinema', *Film History*, 16.3, 208–15.

Morris, Nigel (2007), *The Cinema of Steven Spielberg: Empire of Light*, London and New York: Wallflower Press.

Muir, Kate (2011), '*Pina* and *Life in a Day* at the Berlin Film Festival', in *The Times* (14 February), last accessed 24 January 2012 at http://www.thetimes.co.uk/tto/arts/film/reviews/article2912277.ece.

Mulvey, Laura (1975), 'Visual Pleasure and Narrative Cinema', *Screen*, 16.3, 6–18.

— (1977/8), 'Notes on Sirk & Melodrama', *Movie*, 25, 53–6.

— (2006), *Death 24x a Second: Stillness and the Moving Image*, London: Reaktion Books.
— (2007), 'A Clumsy Sublime', *Film Quarterly*, 60.3 (Spring), 3.
Naremore, James (1998), *More Than Night: Film Noir in its Contexts*, Berkeley and Los Angeles: University of California Press.
Ndalianis, Angela (1999), 'Architectures of vision: neo-baroque optical regimes and contemporary entertainment media', *Media in Transition* conference at MIT on 8 October 1999, last accessed 23 August 2011 at http://web.mit.edu/comm-forum/papers/ndalianis.html.
— (2004), *Neo-Baroque Aesthetics and Contemporary Entertainment*, London and Cambridge, MA: MIT Press.
Neale, Steve (1983), 'Masculinity as Spectacle: Reflections on Men and Mainstream Cinema', *Screen*, 24.6, 2–16.
— (1985), *Cinema and Technology: Image, Sound, Colour*, London: BFI.
— (2000), *Genre and Hollywood*, London and New York: Routledge.
Neate, Ruper (2012), 'Kodak falls in the "creative destruction of the digital age"', *The Guardian* (19 January), last accessed 20 January 2012 at http://www.guardian.co.uk/business/2012/jan/19/kodak-bankruptcy-protection?intcmp=239.
Nichols, Bill (ed.) (1985), *Movies and Methods Volume II*, Berkeley and Los Angeles: University of California Press.
— (1991), *Representing Reality: Issues and Concepts in Documentary*, Bloomington and Indianapolis: Indiana University Press.
North, Dan (2008), *Performing Illusions: Cinema, Special Effects and the Virtual Actor*, London: Wallflower Press.
O'Brien, Geoffrey (2003), 'Something's Gotta Give', *Film Comment*, 39.4 (July/August), 28–30.
Ogle, Patrick (1972), 'Technological and Aesthetic Influences upon the Development of Deep Focus Cinematography in the United States', *Screen*, 13.1, 45–72.
Paar, Morgan (2008), 'Time Remapping', *Videomaker* (February), last accessed 31 October 2008 at http://www.videomaker.com/article/13504/.
Paul, William (1993), 'The aesthetics of emergence', *Film History*, 5, 321–55.
Pavlus, John (2006), 'Production Slate: A Doomed Flight and a Broken Romance', *American Cinematographer*, 87.6, last accessed 9 January 2009 at http://www.highbeam.com/doc/1P3-1059113041.html.
Perkins, Victor F. (1972), *Film as Film: Understanding and Judging Movies*, Harmondsworth: Penguin Books.
Pierson, Michele (1999a), 'No Longer State-of-the-Art: Crafting a Future for CGI', *Wide Angle* 21.1 (January): 28–47.
— (1999b), 'CGI Effects in Hollywood Science Fiction Cinema 1989–1995: The Wonder Years', *Screen* 40.2 (Summer): 158–76.
— (2002), *Special Effects: Still in Search of Wonder*, New York and Chichester: Columbia University Press.
Porfirio, Robert G. (1996), 'No Way Out: Existential Motifs in the *Film Noir*' (1976), in Alain Silver and James Ursini (eds), *Film Noir Reader*, New York: Limelight Editions, 77–93.
Porges, Seth (2008), 'Are 3-D Movies Finally Ready for Their High-Tech Close-up?' *Popular Mechanics* (21 July), last accessed 23 August 2011 at http://www.popularmechanics.com/technology/digital/3d/4274447.
Prince, Stephen (2002), 'True Lies: Perceptual realism, digital images and film theory', in Graeme Turner (ed.), *The Film Cultures Reader*, London and New York: Routledge, 115–28, first published in *Film Quarterly*, 49.3 (Spring 1996), 27–37.

— (2004), 'The Emergence of Filmic Artefacts: Cinema and Cinematography in the Digital Era', *Film Quarterly* 57.3, 24–33.
— (2006), 'The End of Digital Special Effects', Paul Messaris and Lee Humphreys (eds), *Digital Media: Transformations in Human Communication*, Oxford: Peter Lang, 29–37.
Purse, Lisa (2009), 'Gestures and postures of mastery: CGI and contemporary action cinema's expressive tendencies', in Scott Balcerzak and Jason Sperb (eds), *Cinephilia in the Age of Digital Reproduction: Film, Pleasure and Digital Culture: Vol. 1*, London and New York: Wallflower Press, 214–34.
— (2011), *Contemporary Action Cinema*, Edinburgh: Edinburgh University Press.
Rehak, Bob (2007), 'The Migration of Forms: Bullet Time as Microgenre', *Film Criticism*, 32.1, 26–49.
— (2012), 'We Have Never Been Digital: CGI as the New "Clumsy Sublime"', *Graphic Engine* (24 March), last accessed 13 April 2012 at http://graphic-engine.swarthmore.edu/?p=1734.
Robertson, Barbara (2008), 'Rethinking Moviemaking', *Computer Graphics World*, 31.11 (November), last accessed 23 August 2011 at http://www.cgw.com/Publications/CGW/2008/Volume-31-Issue-11-Nov-2008-/Rethinking-Moviemaking.aspx.
Rodowick, D.N. (2007), *The Virtual Life of Film*, Cambridge, MA and London: Harvard University Press.
Rogin, Michael (1996), *Blackface, White Noise: Jewish Immigrants in the Hollywood Melting Pot*, Berkeley: University of California Press.
Rombes, Nicholas (2009), *Cinema in the Digital Age*, London: Wallflower Press.
Rony, Fatimah Tobing (1996), *The Third Eye: Race, Cinema, and Ethnographic Spectacle*, Durham and London: Duke University Press.
Rosen, Philip (2001), *Change Mummified: Cinema, Historicity, Theory*, Minneapolis: University of Minnesota Press.
Ross, Miriam (2011), 'Spectacular Dimensions: 3-D Dance Films', in *Senses of Cinema*, 61 (19 December), last accessed 2 January 2012 at http://www.sensesofcinema.com/2011/feature-articles/spectacular-dimensions-3d-dance-films/#2.
Roth, Eric (2011a), 'An Open Letter To VFX Artists And The Entertainment Industry At Large: Visual Effects Society 2.0', *Visual Effect Society* website (24 May), last accessed 14 April 2012 at http://www.visualeffectssociety.com/node/2425.
— (2011b), 'The Real Wizards of Oz Deserve Better Treatment', *Huffington Post* (22 December), last accessed 14 April 2012 at http://www.huffingtonpost.com/eric-roth/the-real-wizards-of-oz-de_b_1166422.html.
Sarris, Andrew (2007), *300* film review, *New York Observer* (25 March), last accessed 5 July 2008 at http://www.observer.com/node/36966.
Schrader, Paul (1996), 'Notes on *Film Noir*' (1972), in Alain Silver and James Ursini (eds), *Film Noir Reader*, New York: Limelight Editions, 53–63.
Schubart, Rikke (2001), 'Passion and Acceleration', in J. David Slocum (ed.), *Violence and American Cinema*, London: Routledge, 192–207.
Scott, A. O. (2003), 'Tall and Green, But No "Ho, Ho, Ho"', *The New York Times* (20 June), last accessed 28 March 2005 at http://query.nytimes.com/gst/fullpage.html?res=9404E0DF1E38F933A15755C0A9659C8B63.
— (2011), '3-D Tribute to Artistic Impulse', *The New York Times* (22 December), last accessed 2 February 2012 at http://movies.nytimes.com/2011/12/23/movies/pina-a-documentary-by-wim-wenders-review.html.
Selznick, Brian (2007), *The Invention of Hugo Cabret*, London: Scholastic Press.
Seymour, Mike (2006), '*United 93*', *FX Guide LLC* (May 19), last accessed 7 January 2009 at http://www.fxguide.com/featured/United_93/.

— (2011), '*Hugo*: a study of modern inventive visual effects', *FXGuide* (1
    December), last accessed 10 January 2012 at http://www.fxguide.com/featured/
    hugo-a-study-of-modern-inventive-visual-effects/.
Shaviro, Steven (2010), *Post-Cinematic Affect*, Winchester and Washington: Zero Books.
Simmel, Georg (2002), 'The Metropolis and Mental Life' (1903), in Gary Bridge and Sophie
    Watson (eds), *The Blackwell City Reader*, Oxford and Malden, MA: Wiley-Blackwell,
    11–19.
Slotkin, Richard (1992), *Gunfighter Nation: The Myth of the Frontier in Twentieth-Century
    America*, New York: Athenaeum.
Smith, Gavin (2006), 'Mission Statement', *Film Comment*, 42.3, 24–8.
Smith, Murray (1995), *Engaging Characters: Fiction, Emotion, and the Cinema*, Oxford: Oxford
    University Press.
Sobchack, Vivian (1987), *Screening Space: The American Science Fiction Film* (2nd edition),
    New York: Ungar.
— (1995), '"Surge and Splendor": A Phenomenology of the Hollywood Historical Epic'
    (1990), in Barry Keith Grant (ed.), *Film Genre Reader 2*, Austin: University of Texas Press,
    280–307.
Somalya, Ravi (2008), 'The return of the real fake', *The Guardian* (23 May), last accessed 27
    March 2009 at http://www.guardian.co.uk/film/2008/may/23/actionandadventure.
Spielberg, Steven et al. (2011), 'Steven Spielberg & Martin Scorsese: the joy of celluloid',
    The Guardian (10 October), last accessed 1 January 2012 at http://www.guardian.co.uk/
    artanddesign/2011/oct/10/steven-spielberg-martin-scorsese-celluloid.
Spielmann, Yvonne (1999a), 'Aesthetic Features in Digital Imaging: Collage and Morph',
    Wide Angle, 21.1, 131–48.
— (1999b), 'Expanding Film Into Digital Media', *Screen*, 40.2, 131–45.
Staiger, Janet (1989), 'Securing the Fictional Narrative as a Tale of the Historical Real', *South
    Atlantic Quarterly*, 88.2, 393–413.
Stam, Robert and Shohat, Ella (1994), *Unthinking Eurocentrism*, London and New York:
    Routledge.
Stranahan, Lee (2010), 'Open Letter To James Cameron: Fairness For Visual Effects Artists',
    Huffington Post (5 February), last accessed 14 April 2012 at http://www.huffingtonpost.
    com/lee-stranahan/open-letter-to-james-came_b_451922.html.
Strauven, Wanda (2006), 'Introduction to an Attractive Concept', in Wanda Strauven (ed.),
    The Cinema of Attractions Reloaded, Amsterdam: Amsterdam University Press, 11–27.
Tasker, Yvonne (1993), *Spectacular Bodies: Gender, Genre and the Action Cinema*, London and
    New York: Routledge.
— (2004), 'Introduction: action and adventure cinema', in Yvonne Tasker (ed.), *Action and
    Adventure Cinema*, London and New York: Routledge, 1–13.
Taylor Charles (2002), *The Lord of the Rings: The Two Towers* film review, Salon.com (18
    December), last accessed 6 April 2012 at http://www.salon.com/2002/12/18/two_
    towers/.
Thompson, Kirstin (2007), *The Frodo Franchise: The Lord of the Rings and Modern Hollywood*,
    Berkeley and Los Angeles: University of California Press.
— (2009), 'Has 3-D Already Failed?', *Observations on film art* blog (28 August), last
    accessed 23 August 2011 at http://www.davidbordwell.net/blog/2009/08/28/
    has-3–d-already-failed/.
— (2010), 'Motion-capturing an Oscar', *Observations on film art* blog (23 February),
    last accessed 11 April 2012 at http://www.davidbordwell.net/blog/2010/02/23/
    motion-capturing-an-oscar.

— (2011a), 'Has 3-D Already Failed? The sequel, part one: RealDlighted', *Observations on film art* blog (20 January), last accessed 23 August 2011 at http://www.davidbordwell.net/blog/2011/01/20/has-3d-already-failed-the-sequel-part-one-realdlighted/.

— (2011b), 'Has 3-D Already Failed? The sequel, part two: RealDsgusted', *Observations on film art* blog (25 January), last accessed 23 August 2011 at http://www.davidbordwell.net/blog/2011/01/25/has-3d-already-failed-the-sequel-part-2-realdsgusted/.

Thompson, Kristin and Bordwell, David (2007), 'Bwana *Beowulf*', *Observations on film art* blog (7 December), last accessed 5 August 2008 at http://www.davidbordwell.net/blog/?p=1669.

Todorov, Tzvetan (1977), 'The Typology of Detective Fiction' (1966), in *The Poetics of Prose*, trans. Richard Howard (1971), Oxford: Basil Blackwell, 42–52.

Tsivian, Yuri (1994), *Early Cinema in Russia and its Cultural Reception*, London and New York: Routledge.

United 93 Production Notes (2006), California: Universal Pictures, Studio Canal, Sidney Kammel Entertainment and Working Title.

VFXWorld Newsdesk (2006), 'Double Negative Recreates *United 93* Flight', *VFXWorld* (28 April), last accessed 4 June 2008 at http://www.vfxworld.com/?sa=adv&code=363ia5a1&atype=news&id=16822.

Wake, Jenny (2005), *The Making of* King Kong*: The Official Guide to the Motion Picture*, New York, London, Toronto and Sydney: Pocket Books.

Warner, Kara (2011), '"Transformers: Dark of the Moon": Michael Bay Talks Reboots, Action, Egos and More', *MTV Movies* blog (18 November), last accessed 24 January 2012 at http://www.moviesblog.mtv.com/2011/04/18/transformers_dark_of_the_moon_michael_bay_interview/.

Warner, Marina (2002), *Fantastic Metamorphoses, Other Worlds: Ways of Telling the Self*, Oxford: Oxford University Press.

Whissel, Kristen (2006), 'Tales of Upward Mobility: The New Verticality and Digital Special Effects', *Film Quarterly*, 59.4, 23–33.

White, Rob (2003), 'The rage of innocence', *Sight and Sound*, 13.8 (NS), 34–5.

Willemen, Paul (1981), 'Anthony Mann: Looking at the Male', *Framework*, 15–17, 16.

— (2003), 'The Zoom in Popular Cinema: A Question of Performance', *Rouge*, 1, last accessed 7 July 2008 at http://www.rouge.com.au/1/zoom.html.

Williams, Christopher (1972), 'The Deep Focus Question: Some Comments on Patrick Ogle's Article', *Screen*, 13.1, 73.

Williams, David E. (2003), 'Temper, Temper', *American Cinematographer* (July), last accessed 28 March 2005 at http://www.theasc.com/magazine/july03/cover/index.html.

— (2007a), 'Cold Case File', *American Cinematographer* (April), last accessed 12 January 2009 at http://www.theasc.com/magazine_dynamic/April2007/Zodiac/page1.php.

Williams, David E. et al. (2007b), 'The Future Is Now', *American Cinematographer* (May), 14–18, 20–4.

Williams, Raymond (2001), 'Base and Superstructure in Marxist Cultural Theory' (1973), in John Higgins (ed.), *The Raymond Williams Reader*, Oxford: Blackwell, 158–78.

Wilson, Edmund (1996), 'An Appeal to Progressives' (1931), *New Republic* (14 January), 235–38.

Winters Keegan, Rebecca (2008), '3-D Movies: Coming Back at You', *Time* magazine (14 August), last accessed 23 August 2011 at http://www.time.com/time/magazine/article/0,9171,1832842,00.html.

Wolff, Ellen (2004), '*Spider-Man 2*: A Conversation with Visual Effects Guru John Dykstra', *Animation World Network* (14 July), last accessed 6 April 2012 at http://www.awn.com/articles/production/ispider-man-2i-conversation-visual-effects-guru-john-dykstra/page/1,1.

Wood, Aylish (2002), 'Timespaces in spectacular cinema: crossing the great divide of spectacle versus narrative', *Screen*, 43.4, 370–86.

— (2004), 'The Metaphysical Fabric that Binds Us': Proprioceptive Coherence and Performative Space in *Minority Report*', *New Review of Film and Television Studies*, 2.1, 1–18.

— (2007a), *Digital Encounters*, London and New York: Routledge.

— (2007b), 'Pixel Visions: Digital Intermediates and Micromanipulations of the Image', *Film Criticism*, 32.1, 72–94.

Wood, Robin (1986), 'The American Nightmare: Horror in the 1970s' (1978), *Hollywood From Vietnam to Reagan*, New York and Chichester: Columbia University Press, 63–84.

Woolf, Virginia (2003), *Mrs Dalloway* (1925), London: CRW Publishing Limited.

Wyatt, Justin (1994), *High Concept: Movies and Marketing in Hollywood*, Austin: University of Texas Press.

Wyatt, Roger B (1999), 'The Emergence of a Digital Cinema', *Computers and the Humanities*, 33, 365–81.

Zone, Ray (2005), *3-D filmmakers: Conversations with Creators of Stereoscopic Motion Pictures*, Lanham, MD: The Scarecrow Press, Inc.

Filmography

The Abyss (James Cameron, 1989)
The Age of Innocence (Martin Scorsese, 1993)
Alice in Wonderland (Tim Burton, 2010)
Arrivée d'un train à La Ciotat (*Arrival of a Train at La Ciotat*, Auguste and Louise Lumière,
    1895)
The Artist (Michel Hazanavicius, 2011)
Avatar (James Cameron, 2009)
The Aviator (Martin Scorsese, 2004)
Batman (Tim Burton, 1989)
Ben-Hur (William Wyler, 1959)
Beowulf (Robert Zemeckis, 2007)
The Birth of A Nation (D.W. Griffith, 1915)
The Black Pirate (Albert Parker, 1926)
Blade Runner (Ridley Scott, 1982)
Bounce (Don Roos, 2000)
The Bourne Supremacy (Paul Greengrass, 2004)
Bourne Ultimatum (Paul Greengrass, 2007)
Brazil (Terry Gilliam, 1985)
Bwana Devil (Arch Oboler, 1952)
Casino Royale (Martin Campbell, 2006)
Cave of Forgotten Dreams (Werner Herzog, 2010)
Charlie's Angels: Full Throttle (McG, 2003)
Children of Men (Alfonso Cuarón, 2006)
A Christmas Carol (Robert Zemeckis, 2009)
Close Encounters of the Third Kind (Steven Spielberg, 1977)
Cloudy With a Chance of Meatballs (Phil Lord and Chris Miller, 2009)
Comin' At Ya! (Ferdinando Baldi, 1981)
Coraline (Henry Selick, 2009)
The Curious Case of Benjamin Button (David Fincher, 2008)
The Day After Tomorrow (Roland Emmerich, 2004)
Death Proof (Quentin Tarantino, 2007)
Drive Angry (Patrick Lussier, 2011)
E.T.: The Extra-Terrestrial (Steven Spielberg, 1982)

Fahrenheit 451 (François Truffaut, 1966)
Flags of Our Fathers (Clint Eastwood, 2006)
Friday the 13th Part III (Steve Miner, 1982)
G-Force (Hoyt Yeatman, 2009)
G.I. Joe: The Rise of Cobra (Stephen Sommers, 2009)
Gamer (Mark Neveldine and Brian Taylor, 2009)
Gattaca (Andrew Niccol, 1997)
Ghost Rider (Mark Steven Johnson, 2007)
The Good German (Steven Soderbergh, 2006)
The Great Train Robbery (Edwin S. Porter, 1903)
Harry Potter and the Deathly Hallows: Part 2 (David Yates, 2011)
Hero (Yimou Zhang, 2002)
Hulk (Ang Lee, 2003)
Hugo (Martin Scorsese, 2011)
I, Robot (Alex Proyas, 2004)
I Spit on Your Grave (Steven R. Monroe, 2010)
The Incredibles (Brad Bird, 2004)
Iron Man (Jon Favreau, 2008)
Jaws 3-D (Joe Alves, 1983)
Johnny Mnemonic (Robert Longo, 1995)
King Kong (Merian C. Cooper and Ernest B. Schoedsack, 1933)
King Kong (Peter Jackson, 2005)
Knight and Day (James Mangold, 2010)
The Last House on the Left (Dennis Iliadis, 2009)
Live Free or Die Hard (*Die Hard 4.0*) (Len Wiseman, 2007)
The Lord of the Rings: The Fellowship of the Ring (Peter Jackson, 2001)
The Lord of the Rings: The Two Towers (Peter Jackson, 2002)
The Lord of the Rings: The Return of the King (Peter Jackson, 2003)
Machete (Ethan Maniquis and Robert Rodriguez, 2010)
The Matrix (Andy and Larry Wachowski, 1999)
The Matrix Reloaded (Andy and Lana Wachowski, 2003)
The Matrix Revolutions (Andy and Lana Wachowski, 2003)
Metropolis (Fritz Lang, 1927)
Minority Report (Steven Spielberg, 2002)
Monsters, Inc. (Pete Docter et al., 2001)
My Bloody Valentine 3D (Patrick Lussier, 2009)
Le Palais des Mille et une nuits (*The Palace of the One Thousand and One Nights*, Georges
   Méliès, 1905),
The Perfect Storm (Wolfgang Petersen, 2000)
Pina (Wim Wenders, 2011)
Piranha 3D (Alexandre Aja, 2010)
Planet Terror (Robert Rodriguez, 2007)
Pirates of the Caribbean: On Stranger Tides (Rob Marshall, 2011)
Resident Evil: Afterlife (Paul W. S. Anderson, 2010)
Rise of the Planet of the Apes (Rupert Wyatt, 2011)
Le Royaume des Feés (*Fairyland: A Kingdom of Fairies*, Georges Méliès, 1903)
Russian Ark (Alexandr Sokurov, 2002)
Saving Private Ryan (Steven Spielberg, 1998)
Silent Running (Douglas Trumbull, 1972)

Sin City (Frank Miller and Robert Rodriguez, 2005)
Sky Captain and the World of Tomorrow (Kerry Conran, 2004)
Snatch (Guy Ritchie, 2000)
Solaris (Andrei Tarkovsky, 1972)
Soylent Green (Richard Fleischer, 1973)
Spacehunter: Adventures of the Forbidden Zone (Lamont Johnson, 1983)
Spartacus (Stanley Kubrick, 1960)
Speed Racer (Andy and Lana Wachowski, 2008)
Spider-Man (Sam Raimi, 2002)
Spider-Man 2 (Sam Raimi, 2004)
Stagecoach (John Ford, 1939)
Star Trek (J. J. Abrams, 2009)
Star Wars (George Lucas, 1977)
Star Wars Episode I: The Phantom Menace (George Lucas, 1999)
Star Wars Episode II: Attack of the Clones (George Lucas, 2002)
Star Wars Episode III: Revenge of the Sith (George Lucas, 2005)
The Stewardesses (Al Silliman Jr., 1969)
Super 8 (J. J. Abrams, 2011)
Superman (Richard Donner, 1978)
Surrogates (Jonathan Mostow, 2009)
Sweeney Todd: The Demon Barber of Fleet Street (Tim Burton, 2007)
The Texas Chainsaw Massacre (Marcus Nispel, 2003)
300 (Zack Snyder, 2006)
Titan A.E. (Don Bluth et al., 2000)
Titanic (James Cameron, 1997)
Total Recall (Paul Verhoeven, 1990)
Toy Story (John Lasseter, 1995)
Transformers (Michael Bay, 2007)
Transformers: Dark of the Moon (Michael Bay, 2009)
Transformers: Revenge of the Fallen (Michael Bay, 2011)
Tron (Steven Lisberger, 1982)
Tron: Legacy (Joseph Kosinski, 2010)
Twister (Jan de Bont, 1996)
2001: A Space Odyssey (Stanley Kubrick, 1968)
United 93 (Paul Greengrass, 2007)
WALL-E (Andrew Stanton, 2008)
Waltz with Bashir (Ari Folman, 2008)
Watchmen (Zack Snyder, 2009)
X-Men (Bryan Singer, 2000)
X2 (Bryan Singer, 2003)
X-Men: The Last Stand (Brett Ratner, 2006)
Zodiac (David Fincher, 2007)

Index

Printed and bound by CPI Group (UK) Ltd, Croydon, CR0 4YY

01/04/2025

01839600-0006